Josh,

I bought this /
— a gift from o[ne]
another. I'm no[t]
those designations will [every]
suit our   mutual situations
again,   The but I trust the
prayers   of this book
the God   who meets
them, +   the lives
who intersect the two, will
benefit regardless.

Much love,

Scott.
29 August 2022.

The Pastor at Prayer

D1457602

The
Pastor
at Prayer

George Kraus

Edited and Revised
Scot A. Kinnaman

CONCORDIA PUBLISHING HOUSE · SAINT LOUIS

Library of Congress Cataloging-in-Publication Data

Kraus, George, 1924-1989.
The pastor at prayer : a pastor's daily prayer and study guide / George
    Kraus ; edited and revised, Scot A. Kinnaman.
        pages cm
    ISBN 978-0-7586-4910-2
    1. Lutheran Church—Prayers and devotions. 2. Clergy—Prayers
        and devotions. I. Title.
    BX8067.P7K7 2014
    242'.8041--dc23
                                                              2014021798

1 2 3 4 5 6 7 8 9 10   23 22 21 20 19 18 17 16 15 14

To my beloved daughter
Georgette Elizabeth Bragdon,
Beautiful in the image of her mother,
Redeemed by our common Lord,
A faithful servant of the Most High;
Wife and companion of Dennis,
A young Timothy in our beloved church.

Indeed, a woman who walks
In the tradition of Sarah, Ruth, Lydia,
And the mother of our Lord.

"Behold, children are a heritage from the Lord,
the fruit of the womb a reward." (Psalm 127:3)

Contents

INTRODUCTION

Why another pastoral prayer book? Are there not enough on the market? The question deserves some kind of answer, at least an apology of sorts from the compiler and writer of this one. With the daily weight of the ministry, can one do less than begin each day with Word and prayer? This daily beginning constitutes one half of the need; the other half is found in the lack of suitable materials.

This, then, is a Lutheran, pastoral, devotional prayer guide, centered in the Scriptures and the Lutheran Confessions. In most devotional books for pastors, reading of the Scriptures is not a major feature, and the use of the Lutheran Confessions is nonexistent. Many volumes do follow a set of liturgical readings; however, it seems to this pastor that any daily personal, pastoral prayer and study program ought to be based on an intensive reading of God's Word. The Scripture reading guide covers fifty-two weeks and is arranged according to the Daily Lectionary introduced on pp. 299–304 in *Lutheran Service Book* (2006). The Psalms are read daily for six days and the Proverbs selection is for Sundays.

The liturgical approach to God's Word is also included. There is a complete set of daily readings arranged for the Lutheran calendar, plus the feasts, festivals, and commemorations. Using both sets of readings each day serves as a content study of the Bible and growth in the liturgical life.

The appointed Sunday and festival lessons follow the Lutheran liturgical calendar featured in *Lutheran Service Book*. They include Series A, B, C, and One-Year. One simply follows the series appointed for that year. The collects are those found in *Lutheran Service Book*, with additional collects by Veit Dietrich in the One-Year Series.

The Book of Concord readings follow *Concordia: The Lutheran Confessions*, Second Edition (2006). The Confessions reading guide in this volume covers the Book of Concord in fifty-two weeks. No attempt has been made to connect or match Scripture and Confessions as regards content. One simply finishes reading Scripture and the Confessions at the same time. The average lesson in the Confessions is a little more than two pages a day.

In language, the style of this revised edition is contemporary. Uncredited work is that of the author or from the liturgical tradition of the Lutheran Church, both historic and contemporary.

The hymns match those often thought of as the Hymn of the Day. In this way, a core of hymnody becomes part of the pastor's devotional life and thereafter available for meditation and comfort.

Each morning begins with God and His Word. It is as much of life as eating, dressing, and the like. Holidays and vacations are no exceptions. Occasional days will be missed, but the endeavor is always made. The use of this devotional guide, or some other one, is of secondary matter. What is important is that the undershepherds set aside time each day for Word and prayer. Their personal faith life and professional calling demands it.

Adapted from the Introduction by George Kraus in
By Word and Prayer and *The Pastor at Prayer* (1st Edition)

1
Daily Devotions

SUNDAY

The Preparation
The Hymn of the Day
The Prayer of Commitment

1.

O Lord, heavenly Father, You have safely brought me to the beginning of this day. In the same way, defend me with Your mighty power and grant that this day I fall into no sin, neither run into any kind of danger, but that all my doings, being ordered by Your governance, may be righteous in Your sight; through Jesus Christ, Your Son, my Lord, who lives and reigns with You and the Holy Spirit, one God, now and forever. Amen.

—Adapted from Prayer No. 409 (*LSB*, p. 228)

2.

Open my heart, O Lord, to the joy and worship of Your house. Attend Your people as they rejoice in Your presence around Word and Sacrament. Hear me, O Lord and Savior, because of Your grace and in Your name. Amen.

3.

Blessed Father, on this sacred day I remember the glorious resurrection of Your Son, Jesus Christ, my Lord. By His death and rising to life I am counted a forgiven sinner and worthy to stand in Your presence. Now fill my heart with an extra measure of Your Spirit as I prepare to worship in Your house. In prayer, in Scripture, in Eucharist, in song, in sermon, in all acts of worship may I lead Your people in a closer walk with You this day; through Jesus Christ, who with You and the Holy Spirit is one Lord and one God now and forever. Amen.

4.

Blessed be the Father of all mercies and the God of all comfort! Blessed be the most holy Trinity: Father, Son, and Holy Spirit. I praise and bless Your holy name, now and forever. Amen.

5.

O Spirit of the living God, be with me, Your servant, as I seek to guide Your people in worship and the living Word. Touch my heart, my mind, my tongue with the fire and wisdom from on high, that I may be an instrument of Your love and peace. Hear my prayer in the name above all names, Jesus Christ, my blessed Lord. Amen.

The Act of Reconciliation
The Confession of Sin

1.

Almighty God, my heavenly Father, on this memorial day of the resurrection of Your Son, I make my confession before Your throne of grace.

I readily confess that my sins have earned Your eternal wrath and judgment. I am without excuse and stand convicted before Your perfect law. I can only plead with the penitent tax collector: Lord, be merciful to me, a sinner!

Grant me Your everlasting mercy in Jesus Christ, and by the shedding of His most merciful blood, cancel out the handwriting that stands against me. I lay claim to Your gracious promise of forgiveness won by Your only-begotten Son on Calvary's cross. Lord, have mercy. Christ, have mercy. Lord, have mercy. Amen.

2.

Lord of heaven and earth, I confess that I have sinned by thought, word, and deed, through my own fault and no other. I have not been faithful in my service as pastor of Your flock. I have not lived the disciplined, obedient, loving life of servanthood You require of me. I have placed myself first and Your people last. This I readily confess with shame and without excuse. But through Your Son, Jesus Christ, my Lord, I claim Your forgiveness and renewal for this day to come. Hear my prayer through Jesus Christ, Your Son and my Lord. Amen. Lord, have mercy. Christ, have mercy. Lord, have mercy.

3.

Eternal and most blessed Trinity, comfort me with Your mercy and Your grace, for I cannot and will not hide my sin or my guilt from You. I have not deserved Your compassion and have no claim by my own merit on Your great forgiveness. Yet, O most merciful Lord, hear my prayer and grant my request for rescue and remission; by virtue of the incarnation, life, death, and resurrection of Jesus Christ, the chosen Lamb, slain before the foundation of the world. On account of Jesus alone, cancel out all my transgressions, from the greatest to the least. Amen. Lord, have mercy. Christ, have mercy. Lord, have mercy.

The Profession of Faith and Praise of the Divine Trinity

1.

"Hear, O Israel: The Lord our God, the Lord is one. Before Me no god was formed, nor shall there be any after Me. I, I am the Lord, and besides Me there is no savior. I declared and saved and proclaimed, when there was no strange god among you; and you are My witnesses," declares the Lord, "and I am God. Also henceforth I am He; there is none who can deliver from My hand; I work, and who can turn it back? I am the Lord, your Holy One, the Creator of Israel, your King. I, I am He who blots out your transgressions for My own sake, and I will not remember your sins."

Praise the Lord, all nations! Extol Him, all peoples! For great is His steadfast love toward us, and the faithfulness of the Lord endures forever. Praise the Lord! Amen.

—Deuteronomy 6:4; Isaiah 43:10–13, 15, 25; Psalm 117

2.

Long ago, at many times and in many ways, God spoke to our fathers by the prophets, but in these last days He has spoken to us by His Son, whom He appointed the heir of all things, through whom also He created the world. He is the radiance of the glory of God and the exact imprint of His nature, and He upholds the universe by the word of His power. After making purification for sins, He sat down at the right hand of the Majesty on high.

Since then we have a great high priest who has passed through the heavens, Jesus, the Son of God, let us hold fast our confession. For we do not have a high priest who is unable to sympathize with our weaknesses, but one who in every respect has been tempted as we are, yet without sin.

Let us then with confidence draw near to the throne of grace, that we may receive mercy and find grace to help in time of need. We have this as a sure and steadfast anchor of the soul, a hope that enters into the inner place behind the curtain, where Jesus has gone as a forerunner on our behalf, having become a high priest forever after the order of Melchizedek. Amen.

—Hebrews 1:1–3; 4:14–16; 6:19–20

3.

I love the LORD, because He has heard my voice and my pleas for mercy. Because He inclined His ear to me, therefore I will call on Him as long as I live. Gracious is the LORD, and righteous; our God is merciful. The LORD preserves the simple; when I was brought low, He saved me. Return, O my soul, to your rest; for the LORD has dealt bountifully with you. For You have delivered my soul from death, my eyes from tears, my feet from stumbling.

What shall I render to the LORD for all His benefits to me? I will lift up the cup of salvation and call on the name of the LORD; I will pay my vows to the LORD in the presence of all His people. O LORD, I am Your servant; I am Your servant, the son of Your maidservant. You have loosed my bonds. I will offer to You the sacrifice of thanksgiving and call on the name of the LORD. I will pay my vows to the LORD in the presence of all His people, in the courts of the house of the LORD, in your midst, O Jerusalem. Praise the LORD! Amen.

—Psalm 116:1–2, 5–8, 12–14, 16–19

The Word and Doctrine
The Proverb for the Day
The Scripture Appointed for Sunday

The Prayers

1.
The Long Prayer of the Day

I give thanks to You, Lord and Father, for the rest and peace of the night and for the grace to share another day of worship with Your saints. On this memorial day of the resurrection of Jesus, my Savior, be present with Your people as they gather around Word and Sacrament.

Prepare my heart and mind for the privileged task of leading Your flock in worship. From my thoughts and attitudes remove indifference, arrogance, fear, and egotism. Make me ready and eager to share the bread of life with those who gather in Your house this day. Cover my human frailties and errors from the congregation during the sacred hour, so they may see You clearly through me in spite of my faults and sins. May my words, my actions, and my intentions reflect the love of the Lamb of God who has taken away the sins of the world.

Inspire me with wisdom for the preaching of the Gospel. Enable me to explain and apply the living Word to the hearts and lives of Your people. May the words be Yours, not mine; and accompany them with Your Holy Spirit. Accept the prayers, the hymns, and the acts of worship our congregation brings to You this day. For those who will kneel at Your altar, may the body and blood of Christ be received with all repentance, thanksgiving, and joy in Your forgiveness. May the encounter with Your Word and Sacrament strengthen and build this people in the holy faith.

Be present in our Sunday School and Bible classes. Grant to all our teachers a love for Your Word and a concern for their students, both children and adults. Touch the hearts of all our parents so they realize the importance of their support for our educational programs.

For all who cannot publicly hear Your Word and join in the worship of the church today, for the sick, the homebound, the lonely, the discouraged, and the prisoner, visit them with Your mercy and help.

For the delinquents of our congregation, the lapsed in faith, and the indifferent; for those who worship other gods while still carrying Your name; and for the avowed enemies of the Gospel, visit them with Your enlightenment, Your renewing power.

Continue to bless Your universal Church of every tradition, especially in those countries where your children suffer persecution. Guide the clergy and laity alike to conform their faith and life to Your sure Word alone. Heal the divisions and schisms among Your people. Keep human personalities and ambitions to a minimum and Your person and will at a maximum. Make the crucified and risen Christ the very center of all worship, faith, and life.

Be with the seminaries of our own church. Grant us capable and dedicated men to study for the holy ministry. Bless our Synod with humble and learned instructors in theology, men who are captive to the Word. Be present with the Synod and District officers. Guide them with Your Holy Spirit, so they may reflect Your wisdom and will in the performance of their duties. Go with all the clergy of our

Church this day as they step into their pulpits to speak the Word of truth and share the bread of life.

Encourage our missionaries wherever they serve, both at home and abroad. (Especially this day I bring to your throne of grace _____ *name of mission field, ministers, agencies, commissions, departments, boards, etc.*) Remind our people to pray for them and support them with generous gifts of money. Let no area of Your vineyard wither because we have failed in our congregation to do what is required.

I ask for Your zeal and wisdom on our elders and deacons. Never let them forget the importance of their responsibilities in the spiritual life of Your people. Bless my ministry in this place with committed people for these tasks. Keep them from discouragement and bitterness. May they prove to be pillars of strength and encouragement for all God's people in our congregation.

And keep our officers in the congregation alert and concerned with the administration and growth of the parish. May our people support them as they lead and direct the affairs of the Kingdom in our common community.

(Special Requests and Thanksgivings)

Finally, Lord, accept my thanks for the privilege of serving in the holy ministry here in _____ congregation. Help me to grow intellectually, emotionally, spiritually, so I can be a faithful shepherd of Your sheep. Hear my prayer through Jesus Christ, Your Son, my Lord, who lives and reigns with You and the Holy Spirit, eternally one God. Amen.

Alleluia! Christ is risen! He is risen indeed! Alleluia!

2.

The Shorter Prayer of the Day

O Lord, our God, You have commanded the light to shine out of the darkness in the person of Your only-begotten Son. Now shine with the power of Your Holy Spirit into my heart as I prepare for this day of worship. Fill me with joyous anticipation as I look forward to leading Your chosen people in the adoration of the divine Trinity. Reign in my heart that it may be responsive to Your thoughts, Your will, Your desires, and Your love.

Forgive my sins of sloth, indifference, and carelessness as I ready myself to lead Your people in the way of peace. Grant me a clear vision of those holy things I am to proclaim without fear or favor, in the name of Your Son, our Redeemer. Speak mightily through me to the hearts of the faithful this day, and shower great and many blessings upon them.

Assist the saints at worship this day; let not the evil one have power over them. Encourage all our members to gather around Your Word and Sacraments. May they grow in the grace and knowledge of our Lord and Savior Jesus Christ. Remove from their thoughts the sinful desires of this world, and instill in them the holy desire for those things that are from above. Meet all Your chosen in the appointed hour, and may it prove to be the high point of the week for all Your children.

Watch over the sick and homebound. Shelter them from pain and loneliness and preserve them from a sense of futility and despair. Through Your Word, reveal to them that none of Your children suffer in vain or without Your divine permission. Strengthen them with Your support and healing presence.

Be with all the ministers of our Church who stand in Your pulpits today. May they speak with the authority of the Holy Spirit, well grounded in the living Word. Grant them the presence of Your holy angels to keep them in all their ways. Crown with success the spoken Word, the Gospel of Christ, in all Your churches this day.

(Special Requests and Thanksgivings)

Finally, Father in heaven, accept my thanks for all Your mercies, though I have not deserved them. It is by Your grace alone I serve in the ministry of Your Church. Hear my prayer through Jesus Christ, Your Son, my Savior, who lives and reigns with You and the Holy Spirit, eternally one God. Amen.

Alleluia! The Lamb who was slain lives and rules eternally! Alleluia!

3.

The Liturgical Prayer of the Day

With thankful and grateful hearts for all the good and perfect gifts my Savior Jesus Christ has bestowed on His Church, especially the gift of Himself, the forgiveness of sins, the Means of Grace, and the many opportunities to serve in the Kingdom:

O most glorious Trinity, I praise You and consecrate myself to Your service this day.

With thanksgiving and praise for the free gift of grace in Jesus Christ, the only-begotten, and for the sacrifice of Calvary and the full remission of all sins which the precious blood of the Lamb without spot has won for me and all mankind:

O most glorious Trinity, I worship You and consecrate myself to Your service this day.

For the hour of worship and Your people assembled around the Word and Sacraments, for the revelation of the most high and holy Trinity in the Sacred Scriptures, and to the only true God and Lord, Father, Son, and Holy Spirit:

O most glorious Trinity, I adore You and consecrate myself to Your service this day.

For establishing the holy ministry in Your Church, for the men and women who pray and work to make our worship beautiful and meaningful, and for the congregation of saints who gather to worship and serve in Your vineyard:

O most glorious Trinity, I revere You and consecrate myself to Your service this day.

For the proclamation of the Gospel of the crucified and risen Savior in _____ congregation, for the right administration of the Sacraments, for the pure exposition of the divine Word, and for the upbuilding of the saints in their most holy faith and life:

O most glorious Trinity, I laud You and consecrate myself to Your service this day.

For those who serve the sick and the dying, for the brothers and sisters in the household of faith unable to attend public worship, for those who counsel the distraught and the erring with Your powerful Word of wisdom, and for all who share Your grace with those in need:

O most glorious Trinity, I glorify You and consecrate myself to Your service this day.

For all programs of Christian education, the instruction of the young and the spiritual growth of all Your followers; for the teachers committed to Your Word, and especially for all who work with youth and small children:

O most glorious Trinity, I exalt You and consecrate myself to Your service this day.

For the commitment of Your people to a life of service and stewardship, for the many talents You have granted our congregation, for the vision of Your people in the service of Your kingdom, and for the many blessings that have enabled us to be Your faithful servants:

O most glorious Trinity, I honor You and consecrate myself to Your service this day.

For the many missionaries who carry the light of the Gospel to the far corners of the earth, and for the seminaries, which train men to be bearers of the Word, the light of the world:

O most glorious Trinity, I thank You and consecrate myself to Your service this day.

(Special Requests and Thanksgivings)

For the privilege of serving in Your kingdom as a minister of the Gospel, for the many gifts and graces You have showered on me, for the many promises to help in time of need, for Your support in my daily rounds, and for the hope of glory You have given through the resurrection of Your Son:

O most glorious Trinity, I thank You and consecrate myself to Your service this day; in the name of Jesus Christ, my Lord and Savior. Amen.

The Festival Prayer
The Lord's Prayer

1.

Our Father, who art in heaven, hallowed be Thy name. Thy kingdom come, Thy will be done on earth as it is in heaven. Give us this day our daily bread; and forgive us our trespasses as we forgive those who trespass against us; and lead us not into temptation, but deliver us from evil. For Thine is the kingdom and the power and the glory forever and ever. Amen.

2.

Our Father who art in heaven, hallowed be Thy name. Yes, Lord God, dear Father, hallowed be Your name, both in us and throughout the whole world. Destroy and root out the abominations, idolatry, and heresy of those who war against the Church: all false teachers and the divisive spirits who wrongly use Your name and in shameful ways take it in vain. They horribly blaspheme and insistently boast that in Your name they teach Your Word, when in reality it is the devil's deceit and trickery in the guise of Your name by which they seduce many poor souls throughout the world, even killing and shedding much innocent blood, and in such persecution they believe that they render You a divine service.

Dear Lord God, convert and restrain them, that together we may hallow and praise Your name both with true and pure doctrine and with a good and holy life. Restrain those who are unwilling to be converted so that they are forced to cease from misusing, defiling, and dishonoring Your holy name and from misleading the poor people. Amen.

—Martin Luther

The Closing Doxology

1.

Hear, O Israel, the Lord our God, He is One! Father Eternal, Son Most Gracious, Spirit of Life: to You alone I give all praise and glory, now and forevermore. Amen.

2.

Praise be to the Lord Most High, the Bulwark of Israel, the Rock of Ages, the Redeemer of the world, the Light of the nations, the Judge of the peoples. Praise Him forever. Amen.

3.

The grace of the Lord Jesus Christ be with me each hour of the day. The love of the heavenly Father surround me each step of the way. The communion of the Holy Spirit be my comfort and stay. Amen.

4.

I step forward in quiet boldness, Father, for I go forth in Your promise with great expectations and with a triumphant joy. I praise

You, Lord, for I have this confidence that the day is already won in Your Son. I praise and glorify Your name now and forevermore. Amen.

5.

May the presence of the eternal God be with me, and His grace in my word during the hours before me—
>His light to guide me,
>His power to strengthen me,
>His Spirit to cheer me. Amen.

The Evening Prayer

1.

Be present, O merciful God, and protect us through the silent hours of this night, so that we who are wearied by the changes and chances of this fleeting world may rest on Your eternal changelessness; through Jesus Christ, our Lord. Amen.

2.

God and Father, I thank You for the gift of this day with all its gifts of Your love for Your children. I especially praise You for the time with Your Word and Sacraments. May this involvement with the Means of Grace strengthen me for the week ahead. For my family, our health, our joys together, for the presence of Your holy angels to watch over us, for the rest and refreshment of this night of sleep, and for all and every gift You have showered on me and mine, I praise and thank You. Keep us all as the apple of Your eye this night; through Jesus Christ, our Lord. Amen.

3.

Creator and Redeemer, Shelter, Hiding Place, Shield and Buckler, I commend my body and soul and all things into Your care and protection this night. Keep me safe until the morning when I rise to meet a new day in Your name. Amen.

4.

Shepherd of souls and bodies, who neither forgets His own nor sleeps during the hours of the night, surround us now with Your holy protection; shelter us under Your wings that no terror or danger of the night may trouble our sleep. Hear our prayer through Jesus Christ, Your Son, our Lord. Amen.

5.

Into Your hands this night, gracious Father, I place all that I am and all that I have. You alone have made me Your own for time and eternity. You called me into Your presence, crowned me with Your gifts, and have kept me in this one true faith. Now, during the hours of darkness, I ask for Your protection for body and soul. Grant my family and me a restful night, that we may arise in the morning to another day in Your kingdom; through Jesus Christ, my merciful Lord. Amen.

MONDAY

The Preparation
The Hymn of the Day
The Prayer of Commitment

1.

Blessed Lord, be with me in my pastorate this day. Guide my tongue, my heart, and my mind as I seek to proclaim Your Word of life. Hear me, O Lord, in the name of Your Son, who gave Himself for me to redeem me and make me Your servant and son. Amen.

2.

Father, thank You for the rest and refreshment of the past night and for Your presence during my sleeping hours. Be with me also this day in all the tasks I undertake in Your name. As I begin a new week of Kingdom work, be my Guide, my Comforter, and my Protector. Whatever You have planned for me in the coming days I accept with thanksgiving, and pledge myself as a willing instrument in Your hands; through Jesus Christ, Your Son, my Lord. Amen.

3.

Almighty God and Savior, Lord of the universe, King of the Church, with love and thanksgiving I acknowledge Your glory and worship You, Father, Son, and Holy Spirit, eternal Trinity. As I begin this week in Your holy name, pledge to me Your renewing grace for the days ahead, for I trust solely in Your promises. Hear me, Father, for the sake of Jesus Christ, Your only Son, my Lord. Amen.

<h2 style="text-align:center">4.</h2>

Loving Father, make me ready and willing to serve and obey Your will in the Kingdom this new week. I place myself in Your care and power, to become and remain Your faithful servant in the days ahead. Despite my weaknesses and failings, use me mightily in the tasks You have chosen for me; through Jesus Christ, Your Son, my Lord and my Savior. Amen.

<h2 style="text-align:center">5.</h2>

Lord, Defender of the faithful, Shepherd of the undershepherds, I begin this day in Your name. Wipe weariness and sloth from my eyes. Inspire my heart for the work ahead. Surround my efforts this day with Your love. Protect me from the pitfalls of the ministry. Imbue me with a fervent spirit. Lord Christ, be my never-failing Guide each hour of the day. Amen.

The Act of Reconciliation
The Confession of Sin

<h3 style="text-align:center">1.</h3>

O Lord God Almighty, hear the prayer of Your servant and spare me. I confess my sins with shame and sorrow, and indeed deserve Your eternal wrath and judgment. Yet, of Your great mercy, O Lord, and by the death of Your beloved Son, the Lamb without blemish, deliver me from eternal judgment and place in my heart the peace, the joy, the confidence of Your complete forgiveness; in the name of the Blessed One, the only-begotten Son and Savior of the world. Amen.

<h3 style="text-align:center">2.</h3>

Lord God, Judge and Ruler of all, I kneel in humble penitence before You this day. I have much to confess, for I have sinned against You by thought, word, and deed. I do not merit Your favor or Your forgiveness, but I appeal to Your great mercy and to the suffering and death of Your Son, Jesus Christ, my Lord and Savior. Forgive me all my sins and all my guilt. I ask it in the name of Jesus Christ, the Paschal Lamb. Amen.

I come before the most holy Trinity with shame and sorrow, for my life has not been shaped by obedience, trust, and love. I have often refused to let Your Word rule my life. I deserve nothing but Your eternal anger and Your fearful punishment. But I appeal to You on account of the wounds of Christ, the only-begotten Son, for cleansing, forgiveness, and healing. To Him alone I flee for refuge and redemption; in His beloved name I pray. Amen.

The Profession of Faith and Praise of the Divine Trinity

1.

Blessed be the Lord, the God of Israel; He has come to His people and redeemed them. He has raised up for us a mighty Savior, born of the house of His servant David. Through His holy prophets He promised of old that He would save us from our enemies, from the hands of all who hate us. He promised to show mercy to our fathers and to remember His holy covenant. This was the oath He swore to our father Abraham: to set us free from the hands of our enemies, free to worship Him without fear, holy and righteous in His sight all the days of our life.

You, my child, shall be called the prophet of the Most High, for you will go before the Lord to prepare His way, to give His people knowledge of salvation by the forgiveness of their sins. In the tender compassion of our God, the dawn from on high shall break upon us to shine on those who dwell in darkness and the shadow of death and to guide our feet into the way of peace.

Glory be to the Father and to the Son and to the Holy Spirit; as it was in the beginning, is now, and will be forever. Amen.

—The Benedictus, Luke 1:68–79 (*LSB*, pp. 238–40)

2.

I believe in God, the Father Almighty, maker of heaven and earth.

And in Jesus Christ, His only Son, our Lord, who was conceived by the Holy Spirit, born of the virgin Mary, suffered under Pontius Pilate, was crucified, died and was buried. He descended into hell. The third day He rose again from the dead. He ascended into heaven and sits at the right hand of God the Father Almighty. From thence He will come to judge the living and the dead.

I believe in the Holy Spirit, the holy Christian Church, the communion of saints, the forgiveness of sins, the resurrection of the body, and the life everlasting. Amen.

—The Apostles' Creed

3.

"I will sing to the LORD, for He has triumphed gloriously; the horse and his rider He has thrown into the sea. The LORD is my strength and my song, and He has become my salvation; this is my God, and I will praise Him, my father's God, and I will exalt Him. The LORD is a man of war; the LORD is His name.

"Pharaoh's chariots and his host He cast into the sea, and his chosen officers were sunk in the Red Sea. The floods covered them; they went down into the depths like a stone. Your right hand, O LORD, glorious in power, Your right hand, O LORD, shatters the enemy. In the greatness of Your majesty You overthrow Your adversaries; You send out Your fury; it consumes them like stubble. At the blast of Your nostrils the waters piled up; the floods stood up in a heap; the deeps congealed in the heart of the sea. The enemy said, 'I will pursue, I will overtake, I will divide the spoil, my desire shall have its fill of them. I will draw my sword; my hand shall destroy them.' You blew with Your wind; the sea covered them; they sank like lead in the mighty waters.

"Who is like You, O LORD, among the gods? Who is like You, majestic in holiness, awesome in glorious deeds, doing wonders? You stretched out Your right hand; the earth swallowed them.

"You have led in Your steadfast love the people whom You have redeemed; You have guided them by Your strength to Your holy abode. The peoples have heard; they tremble; pangs have seized the inhabitants of Philistia. Now are the chiefs of Edom dismayed; trembling seizes the leaders of Moab; all the inhabitants of Canaan have melted away. Terror and dread fall upon them; because of the greatness of Your arm, they are still as a stone, till Your people, O LORD, pass by, till the people pass by whom You have purchased. You will bring them in and plant them on Your own mountain, the place, O LORD, which You have made for Your abode, the sanctuary, O LORD, which Your hands have established. The LORD will reign forever and ever."

Glory be to the Father and to the Son and to the Holy Spirit; as it was in the beginning, is now, and will be forever. Amen.

I will sing to the Lord, for He has triumphed gloriously; the horse and his rider He has thrown into the sea.

—The Song of Moses, Exodus 15:1–18; *antiphon* 21

The Word and Doctrine
The Psalm of the Day
The Liturgical Lesson of the Day
The Scripture Reading for Monday of the Week
The Book of Concord for the Day

The Prayers
1.
The Long Prayer of the Day

God and Father of all, You have made all people that they might serve You and enjoy Your presence forevermore. You have sent Your Son to call them back from death to life, from darkness to light, from sin to righteousness. You have loved this world, Your world, with an everlasting love. Now hear me this day as I pray for Your mercy and guidance in the witness of Your Church to the world.

You have said, Lord: "As I live . . . I have no pleasure in the death of the wicked, but that the wicked turn from his way and live" (Ezekiel 33:11). And this desire, too, is the hope and confidence of Your people. I pray that this congregation and this pastor will give themselves to witnessing to the world. In this hour I ask Your blessings on all the missionaries of our church. For those who work in big cities in our own nation, for those who toil in foreign fields, far from home, for those who hold up Christ as Lord in the classrooms of our schools at home and abroad, for the doctors and nurses who serve our church around the world, for all the professional people who seek to guide Your ambassadors in their goals of bringing men to Christ; grant me wisdom and grace.

Inspire the people of our congregation to see their responsibilities in the support and expansion of this Kingdom task. Prevent us from losing our enthusiasm, our vision, or our sense of commitment in mission work. Root out indifference from the hearts of Your disciples. By

Word and Sacrament kindle in them a burning zeal for the souls of men. Never let our people flag in their financial support of missions, both at home and abroad. Demonstrate to us the straight, clear line between stewardship of money and effective mission work around the globe. Protect us from fear and selfishness that seeks to keep money at home for ourselves and passes responsibility for mission support to congregations and organizations in faraway places.

Lead our individual members to speak of Christ and His salvation to others in our community. Forgive us for the sin of silence when we ought to speak of the one thing needful. Awaken our hearts to the spiritual needs of millions of souls who live and die without Christ. Bless our evangelism chairman and his committee with an extra measure of Your Spirit. May they prove to be a leaven in our congregation for initiating, training, and developing witnessing disciples of Christ among us. For the unbeliver of our community I also pray. Open their hearts to the message of the Gospel. Grace the lives of our people with good works and piety, that their verbal witness may ring with sincerity and truth.

Be with me today in all my undertakings—evangelism, stewardship, education, calling, studying, and praying. When I am depressed, downcast, despairing of all things in the Kingdom, lift me up with Your promises. I know I am not the strong man of God that many think I am. Without Your grace, I count as nothing and will accomplish nothing.

Encourage me in my personal Bible study and prayer life. Keep me from the temptation to excuse myself from time with You and Your Word, for I know there is no excuse.

In my encounter with people today, may they see Your Son in my life and words, and to do this, cause Your Spirit to work through me. Do not let me act the part of Christ, but rather be a little Christ to all my brothers and sisters. Preserve me from sloth, indifference, boredom, and arrogance in the routine of my holy calling as a minister of Your Gospel.

Be with the staff of _____ congregation. May they see their service as a service to You and Your kingdom. Crown their work with success for the sake of Your people and the growth of the whole Church. I pray this day for secretary and sexton, for parish worker and assistant, for teachers and all helpers, for music director, and vicar/interns.

Be with our youth workers and the youth of the church. Lead our congregation to see the importance of giving time, talent, and money to the support of this work. Deliver us from parents and adults who have no concern for the young. Send us able leaders for our youth program, that it may succeed in building young Christians. Watch over our youth, not only in church, but day by day. Send Your Holy Spirit and Your holy angels to guard them in all their ways.

All those in our parish this day who will meet calamity and suffering, bless them with Your presence. We cannot know what each day has in store for us, but we also know there are no surprises to You. Therefore comfort all of us who must deal with sorrow or crises this day. Grant us Your hope, Your deliverance, Your victory.

Guide all the churches of the community—those, too, of a different tradition than ours. Lead them to a faithful adherence to Your Word. Where they are in error, correct them by the power of Your Holy Spirit. Where we can bear joint witness to the lordship of Your Son—without compromise—help us to do so.

Accept my thanks for the blessings of the night, for my loving and faithful wife, my children, my parents, brothers, sisters, and also my close friends. Continue to shower Your joys, blessings, and even discipline on my wife and myself. Keep our love for each other wondrous and fresh, and may this day find us stronger in faith and Christian love. I commend my children to Your care, body and soul, and all things. May they be obedient in home, work, and school, and so witness to their membership in Your family.

(Special Requests and Thanksgivings)

And now, Father, accept all my requests and thanksgivings through the merits of Jesus Christ, Your Son, my Lord, who lives and rules with You and the Holy Spirit, eternally one God. Amen.

2.

The Shorter Prayer of the Day

Savior of the nations, come and inspire Your people to be faithful witnesses to Your great salvation. The harvest is indeed plentiful and the laborers few, so begin with me, Lord, and hold before my eyes the challenges and the needs of a world without Christ. Never let me weary of proclaiming the crucified and risen Christ.

Open my eyes and those of this congregation, that all may see their responsibility for the mission of Your Church in a pagan world. Never let them fear to speak on the one thing needful. Grant them also the wisdom and the will to speak of the Savior. May we all be instrumental in leading many to Christ and His saving cross. Continue to guide our evangelism committee in its tasks, and grant them success in all they do.

Stretch out Your mighty arm over all the missions of our church around the globe. May we be known for our mission outreach and our passion for the souls of all mankind. Do not let the work in Your vineyard suffer due to lack of funds. Open the hearts and wallets of Your redeemed, that the riches of their faith may supply Your work around the world. Send us many young men and women to serve in our far-flung mission fields.

Remain with Your universal Church. Support it with the rich grace of Your Holy Spirit through the Word. May all churches, of every tradition, hold high the cross of the Redeemer. May justification by faith be the central message preached and proclaimed this day, in every land and every tongue. Fire our hearts with a consuming zeal for lost souls, that our lives will be dedicated to that goal, that purpose, that will of the risen Christ.

(Special Requests and Thanksgivings)

Finally, Savior of the nations, Lord of all history, Shepherd of all mankind, match my desire to Your will that I may serve as an example to Your people in word and deed. May all who hear me this day hear You, not me; see You, not me. I ask all this in Your most holy name, O Christ. Amen.

3.

The Liturgical Prayer of the Day

In the name of the Father and of the Son and of the
    Holy Spirit. Amen.

Lord, have mercy. Christ, have mercy. Lord, have
    mercy.

I cry to You, O Lord;
    in the morning my prayer come before You.

My mouth is filled with Your praise,
    and with Your glory all the day.

O Lord, hide Your face from my sins,
   and blot out all my iniquities.

Create in me a clean heart, O God,
   and renew a right spirit within me.

Restore to me the joy of Your salvation,
   and uphold me with a willing spirit.

Help me, O Lord,
   to live this day without sin.

O Lord, have mercy on me;
   have mercy on me, O Lord.

O Lord, let Your mercy remain on me,
   just as my trust is in You.

Hear my prayer, O Lord,
   and let my cry come before You.

(Special Requests and Thanksgivings)

I thank You, my heavenly Father, through Jesus Christ, Your dear Son, that You have kept me this night from all harm and danger; and I pray that You would keep me this day also from sin and every evil, that all my doings and life may please You. For into Your hands I commend myself, my body and soul, and all things. Let Your holy angel be with me, that the evil foe may have no power over me. Amen.

I bless Your name, O Lord;
   and I give my thanks to You, O God.

The grace of my Lord Jesus Christ and the love of God and the fellowship of the Holy Spirit be with me now and forever. Amen.
—Adapted from the Morning Suffrages (*TLH*, p. 115)

(For those who conduct their personal devotion in the evening,
the following liturgical prayer may be used.)

The Liturgical Prayer for Evening

In the name of the Father and of the Son and of the
   Holy Spirit. Amen.

Lord, have mercy. Christ, have mercy. Lord, have
   mercy.

Blessed are You, O Lord, God of our fathers,
>	and greatly to be praised and glorified forever.

I bless You, Father, Son, and Holy Spirit,
>	I praise and glorify You forever.

Blessed are You, O Lord, in heaven,
>	and greatly to be praised and glorified and highly
>	exalted forever.

Help me, O Lord,
>	to live this night without sin.

O Lord, have mercy on me;
>	have mercy on me, O Lord.

O Lord, let Your mercy remain on me,
>	just as my trust is in You.

Hear my prayer, O Lord,
>	and let my cry come before You.

(Special Requests and Thanksgivings)

I thank You, my heavenly Father, through Jesus Christ, Your dear Son, that You have graciously kept me this day; and I pray that You would forgive me all my sins where I have done wrong, and graciously keep me this night. For into Your hands I commend myself, my body and soul, and all things. Let Your holy angel be with me that the evil foe may have no power over me. Amen.

I bless Your name, O Lord;
>	and I give my thanks to You, O God.

May the almighty and merciful Lord, the Father, Son, and Holy Spirit, bless and preserve me this night. Amen.

>	—Adapted from the Evening Suffrages
>	(*TLH*, pp. 115–16)

The Festival Prayer
The Lord's Prayer

1.

Our Father, who art in heaven, hallowed be Thy name. Thy kingdom come, Thy will be done on earth as it is in heaven. Give us this day our daily bread; and forgive us our trespasses as we forgive those who trespass against us; and lead us not into temptation, but deliver us from evil. For Thine is the kingdom and the power and the glory forever and ever. Amen.

2.

Our Father who art in heaven, Thy kingdom come. O dear Lord, God and Father, You see how the wisdom and reason of the world not only profane Your name but also take the power, might, and wealth You have given for ruling the world and serving You and use them in opposition to Your kingdom. They trouble and hinder the tiny flock of Your kingdom that is weak, despised, and few in number. They will not tolerate Your flock on earth.

Dear Lord, God and Father, convert and restrain them. Convert those who are still to become children and members of Your kingdom, so that together we may serve You in Your kingdom in true faith and true love and that from our life here we may enter into Your eternal kingdom. Restrain those who will not turn away their might and power from the destruction of Your kingdom, so when they are cast down from their seats of power and are being humbled, they will cease their efforts. Amen.

—Martin Luther

The Closing Doxology

1.

Honor, glory, might, dominion to the Father and the Son, with the everlasting Spirit, while eternal ages run. Amen.
—Doxology 10, Order of Worship for the Reformed Church.
Reformed Church Publication Board,
Philadelphia, 1885

2.

May the God of peace who brought again from the dead our Lord Jesus, the great shepherd of the sheep, by the blood of the eternal covenant, equip you with everything good that you may do His will, working in us that which is pleasing in His sight, through Jesus Christ, to whom be glory forever and ever. Amen.
—Hebrews 13:20–21

3.

I praise You, God my Father, for You have made me. I laud You, God the Son, for You have redeemed me. I honor You, God the Spirit, for You have called me. Amen.

4.

Righteous are You, O LORD, and right are Your rules. You have appointed Your testimonies in righteousness and in all faithfulness. Your testimonies are righteous forever; give me understanding that I may live. Amen.

—Psalm 119:137–38, 144

5.

Oh, the depth of the riches and wisdom and knowledge of God! How unsearchable are His judgments and how inscrutable His ways! For from Him and through Him and to Him are all things. To Him be glory forever. Amen.

—Romans 11:33, 36

The Evening Prayer

1.

Be present, Father of all mercies, with me this night. I give thanks for another day filled with Your grace, encouraged by Your promises, guided by Your wisdom, crowned with Your victories. Grant me now a night of rest and recuperation that I may serve You yet another day; through Jesus Christ, Your Son, my Lord. Amen.

2.

It is time, gracious Father, to relinquish my day to Your judgment and Your mercy. Where I have done wrong, forgive. When I have spoken hastily, repair and calm with Your love. What I have ignored, supply the healing balm. I close my eyes with trust in Your Son and with the knowledge that Your holy angels remain with me during the night hours. Amen.

3.

Lord of hosts, Majesty eternal, watch over me and my family this very night with Your holy angels. Defeat the hatred of the evil one and bring to nothing his attempts to lead us from Your hand. He is too strong for us, but under Your wings we rest in peace and have no fear. In the name of Christ, my Lord. Amen.

4.

Blessed Lord, for the many mercies of the day now behind me, for the overshadowing of Your protecting hand, for the privilege of serving in Your vineyard, I close my eyes with deep thanksgiving. I trust in Your care for the night hours. Bring me safely to the morning light through Christ, my Lord. Amen.

5.

Lord of creation, Giver of every good and perfect gift: the sun has set and as this day comes to a close, grant me the light of Your grace. As the darkness covers the earth, shine around me the rays of Your presence. As I surrender my mind and body to sleep, shield me with Your holy protection. Hear my prayer through Christ, my everliving Lord and Savior. Amen.

TUESDAY

The Preparation
The Hymn of the Day
The Prayer of Commitment

1.

Show me Your way, O Lord, and guide me in Your paths. Your Word is light and truth. Enlighten my mind, deepen my love, and strengthen my resolve as I seek to do Your work this day. Bless also my devotion in this hour, and may these moments with Your Word make me a better and stronger man; through Your Son, in whose name I pray. Amen.

2.

Father of lights, from the very first hour of this day be with me as Guide and Stay. Lead me in the paths You have chosen. When I want to stray, call me with Your tender look. If I chance to stumble, hold me with Your steady hand. Though I often fail, cheer me with Your renewing power; through Jesus Christ, my Lord. Amen.

3.

Savior, I commit my head, my heart, my tongue, my hands, my feet, my strength, my love, my all to You this day. Make me Your instrument of grace. Empty me of self-esteem and fill me with Your Spirit. May all who meet me this day meet You, not me. Amen.

4.

This day, Lord Jesus, I begin in Your name and in Your strength. It is Your day, and I am Your man. The events and persons I will meet are unknown to me; but I know You and Your promises. I can and I will carry the day, Lord, for the welfare of Your kingdom. I know I can, for I hold with St. Paul: There is nothing I cannot master with the help of the One who gives me strength. It is Your day, Lord, and I am Your man. Amen.

5.

Father, Creator, Savior of all, the light of Your wisdom shines from the pages of Your Holy Word into my heart this hour. May my tongue speak Your words and my hands move with Your love in my designated rounds. Bless me, Father, that I walk and speak and work in Your name and by Your Son's command. Amen.

The Act of Reconciliation
The Confession of Sin

1.

God of all compassion, full of long-suffering and great patience, hear my confession this hour, for without Your mercy all is lost— the work, the day, and myself. I openly confess to You that I have deserved Your wrath, for my life has been one of self-service and godlessness. I have worshiped the creature instead of the Creator. I have served my worldly passions instead of Your people. I have sought to build my kingdom instead of Yours. I have depended upon my abilities instead of Your promises. I have made pride and arrogance my dress instead of the humility of Your Son. Indeed, merciful Father, I do deserve Your pitiless anger, Your eternal judgment; yet in Your mercy hear my plea for forgiveness. I flee to Christ's cross for grace and cleansing. His atoning sacrifice is my only hope. I rejoice in His promise of pardon; I am a forgiven sinner. Amen.

2.

O Lord, eternal Father, with sorrow and remorse I approach Your throne of grace. I have much to confess, for I have not been Your obedient son or servant.

For the sins of pride, sloth, greed, lust, anger, envy, and gluttony I confess my guilt and know full well I deserve to stand under Your eternal judgment.

I am repentant, O Lord. By the holy blood of Your Son, Jesus Christ, cancel out the handwriting against me and renew me with Your Holy Spirit. Hear my prayer through the same, Jesus Christ, my Savior. Amen.

3.

Remember not my sins of body and soul, O Lord. I have no excuse for my rebellion against Your will; I am ashamed of my motives and actions. Although I deserve Your fierce anger, rather look upon the merits of Your Son, the Paschal Lamb, slain for my redemption. I claim the blessed pardon for all my transgressions that He has earned by His death and resurrection. Hear me in His name and for His sake. Amen.

The Profession of Faith and Praise of the Divine Trinity
1.

My soul magnifies the Lord, and my spirit rejoices in God, my Savior; for He has regarded the lowliness of His handmaiden. For behold, from this day all generations will call me blessèd. For the Mighty One has done great things to me, and holy is His name; and His mercy is on those who fear Him from generation to generation.

He has shown strength with His arm; He has scattered the proud in the imagination of their hearts. He has cast down the mighty from their thrones and has exalted the lowly.

He has filled the hungry with good things, and the rich He has sent empty away. He has helped His servant Israel in remembrance of His mercy as He spoke to our fathers, to Abraham and to his seed forever.

Glory be to the Father and to the Son and to the Holy Spirit; as it was in the beginning, is now, and will be forever. Amen.

—The Magnificat, Luke 1:46–55 (*LSB*, pp. 248–49)

2.

Great and marvelous are Your deeds, Lord God Almighty. Just and true are Your ways, King of ages. Who will not fear You, O Lord, and bring glory to Your name?

For You alone are holy. All nations will come and worship before You, for Your righteous acts have been revealed. Yes, Lord, God Almighty, true and just are Your judgments.

Alleluia! Salvation and glory and power belong to our God, for true and just are His judgments. Praise our God, all His servants, you who fear Him, both small and great.

Alleluia! Our Lord God Almighty reigns; let us rejoice and be glad and give Him glory! The wedding of the Lamb has come, and His bride has made herself ready. Fine linen, bright and clean, was given her to wear. Alleluia! Amen.

3.

Most gracious and glorious Lord, Your great name is glorified and sanctified throughout the world that You created by Your will alone. Establish Your kingdom of grace to the ends of the earth. Plant Your banner of salvation among the nations and spread the kingdom of our Redeemer and Lord, Your Son, Jesus Christ.

Let His name, the name above all names, be worshiped and adored by every tongue in every place. Blessed, praised, exalted, extolled, glorified, worshiped, and honored be the name of the Holy One, the King reigning supreme over the seraphim and cherubim, whose glory is beyond our blessing and hymns and praises and songs.

Blessed be the most holy and divine Trinity, the Creator, the Redeemer, the Sanctifier of life, now and forever. Amen.

—A Prayer of Praise adapted from the Kaddish Prayer

The Word and Doctrine
The Psalm of the Day
The Liturgical Lesson of the Day
The Scripture Reading for Tuesday of the Week
The Book of Concord for the Day

The Prayers

1.

The Long Prayer of the Day

Teach me, O Lord, the way of Your statutes;
and I will keep it to the end.

Give me understanding, that I may keep Your law
and observe it with my whole heart.

Lead me in the path of Your commandments,
for I delight in it.

Incline my heart to Your testimonies,
and not to selfish gain!

Turn my eyes from looking at worthless things;
and give me life in Your ways.

Confirm to Your servant Your promise,
that You may be feared.

Turn away the reproach that I dread,
for Your rules are good.

Behold, I long for Your precepts;
in Your righteousness give me life!

—Psalm 119:33–40

O Holy Spirit, source of all wisdom and Lord of all knowledge in heaven and earth, descend on me and bless with Your presence all I undertake this day for the Kingdom. Give me the wisdom, the knowledge, the attitude, the sensitivity, the concern, even the sternness needed for this day's tasks.

As I study Your Word, not only this day but also each day this week, guide my thoughts, my strength, and my intellect. Teach me as

You instructed the prophets and apostles and evangelists before me. If You lead, I will follow. Make Your dynamic Word a wellspring of faith, hope, and love for Your people and myself. Enable me to subject my pride, my stubbornness, my doubts, and my laziness to the power of Your written Word. Speak to my heart through its pages and enrich my ministry among Your people.

I pray for all the teachers in our congregation: those who instruct in Sunday School, those who teach in our weekday classes, all those who work with Your Scriptures and seek to show the love of Christ. For our children in all our classes: Sunday School, weekday, confirmation, I pray this hour. May each encounter with the Word of life make them better disciples of Jesus, our Lord. May a love and zeal for Your Word be planted and nourished in all our hearts, both young and old.

Especially, give to all instructors in our parish a holy fire for the message of the Gospel, the center of Your living Word. Deliver our congregation from indifferent and careless teachers, and I include myself. Imprint on our minds the richness and the value of Your Word. Help us to prepare for each class with joy and thoroughness. Grant that our teaching be infectious with enthusiasm, understanding, and love.

I remember also our board of Christian education and all its members. Encourage our congregation to support them and their tasks with prayer, work, and a ready heart as well as the money necessary for effective work.

I also bring adult Bible classes and courses to Your throne of grace, O Lord, for without Your blessing we can accomplish nothing. Remind our people that the inordinate love of things in this world locks up our hearts against the love of Your Word, Your doctrines. Open indifferent hearts to the excitement, the need, and the joy of sharing Your revelation. Those who are engaged in studying Your Word lead to great discoveries of faith and life.

Guide our District and Synod boards of education, for all their staff and workers. May the materials and programs they develop lead all to a closer walk with Christ, our Lord.

Spirit of life, I rejoice for this day's happiness and opportunities, for the great excitement of living, for the sense of achievement that comes with a task well done, for the family You have given me, for the sights and sounds of beauty and truth amid the noise and confusion of a fallen world, for good friends and their rich company, for my brothers in the ministry who hear me in time of need and share their lives with me, even for those events and moments filled with conflict and despair, for the hours this day when I can rest and play; for all these gifts, Lord, accept my gratitude.

During those times when I enjoy the pleasant activities of life, the gifts of Your grace, let me not be insensitive to those who struggle through dark, grinding despair. May they find in me not the quick answer and hasty dismissal, but one who feels with them, who hurts with them, who struggles with them, who walks with them to the Rock that is higher than we. And if, by Your love, You decide that adversity is my lot this day, protect me, please, Lord, from self-pity, jealous murmurings, and ungodly complaining. Give me first the strength to carry my cross before You remove it. Let no weight of personal difficulties affect my service as pastor of Your sheep.

Fill my mind today with everything that is true, everything that is noble, everything that is good and pure, everything that I love and honor, and everything that can be thought virtuous and worthy of praise. Let me place Your interests before mine, others before myself, spiritual needs before physical comforts, the goals of the Kingdom before personal ambition, right before wrong.

(Special Requests and Thanksgivings)

Holy Spirit, fill my ministry with Your presence from this very hour, and at sunset forgive my failures—no matter what the cause— and accept my accomplishments as signs of my thankfulness and proof of Your power. Hear me through Jesus Christ, my Lord and Savior. Amen.

2.

The Shorter Prayer of the Day

Divine Wisdom from on high, Source of all that is, I ask for guidance for the hours that lie ahead. I desire to walk in the Word and in the way of life that Your mercy has granted to me and to all who love Your Chosen One. I need Your wisdom this day if I am to be effective as Your witness. Advise me so that I speak gracious words, living words, redeeming words, comforting words to those in the darkness of despair and desperation. Fail me not, O loving Lord and Comforter.

Be with those who instruct and learn in our seminaries, universities, and colleges. Inspire our instructors with the wisdom from on high that those who listen and learn may see the full glory of Christ our Lord. Bless those men who have committed themselves to studies at our seminaries that they may be well qualified to receive a call in Your Church. I pray that many young men and women will want to serve as teachers, deaconesses, and lay ministers. Many of our young people in higher education need Your call to serve as well; so touch their hearts with the desire to offer their lives to the building of Your kingdom. Attend our parochial schools as well; may we have faithful, committed, competent teachers for our children.

Bless especially all the Bible classes and study groups in our congregation. Let the Word be central to all our worship and spiritual growth. Grace our congregation with dedicated teachers for the task of sharing the Word of life.

I remember, too, the secular universities, colleges, and schools of our nation. Send them Your blessings that they become centers of profitable learning, assisting all citizens of our land to serve the common good. I remember in my petitions those schools and institutions that work in special education—the blind, the deaf, those suffering with mental, behavioral, or emotional issues, or whatever area of the human condition we are called to serve. Send success to all those efforts, especially those done in the name of the blessed Savior, the Healer of all diseases and handicaps.

(Special Requests and Thanksgivings)

Hear my prayer, heavenly Spirit, through Jesus Christ, my Lord and Savior, who lives and rules with You and the Father, one God, now and forever. Amen.

3.

The Liturgical Prayer of the Day

God the Father in heaven, who watches over all Your children by night and by day,

Have mercy upon me.

God the Son, Light and Redeemer of the world,

Have mercy upon me.

God the Holy Spirit, Teacher, Comforter, Helper, Guide, and Paraclete,

Have mercy upon me.

Holy, most blessed, most glorious Trinity, with angels and arch-angels, with all the company of heaven, with all the faithful of Your holy, universal, apostolic Church:

I adore You this day and in this hour.

Whatsoever things are true, whatsoever things are honest, what-soever things are just, whatsoever things are pure, whatsoever things are lovely, whatsoever things are of good report; if there be any vir-tue, and if there be any praise:

Assist me, most high and holy Trinity, to think on these things this very day.

Pardon and remission of all sins; chastity of heart and life; strength to serve and please You; speech filled with grace, seasoned with the salt of love and humility; diligence in my allotted tasks; love active in all things; to be a thankful and forgiven sinner, wholly com-mitted to Your kingdom:

Grant all this unto me, O Lord, this very day.

On all who travel to work, on all whose labor brings them into danger, on all who will meet temptation, on all who can find no employment, on all children at home or at school, on all who keep house, and on all Christian homes:

Send Your rich blessings, O Lord.

On all near and dear to us, on our country and its rulers, on the nations of the earth, on the whole Christian Church, on our parish and all its people, on all missionaries throughout the world, and on all who travel by land or sea or air:

Send Your blessings and Your holy angels, O Lord.

On all who are in extreme necessity or deep affliction, on all who are hungry, thirsty, naked, or sick, on all who are discouraged, down-hearted, or lonely, and on all who have fallen into the power of sin and Satan through error, worldly desire, betrayal, or foolishness:

Send Your Spirit, O Lord, with Your call to repentance and renewal by the crucified and risen One.
Defend this day, O Lord, against my evil; against the
evil of this day defend me.

Order my steps by Your Word, and support me in
Your paths.
Let Your mercies be upon me, O Lord, and bless the
work of my heart and hands.
Preserve my going out and my coming in, by Your
grace and peace.

(Special Requests and Thanksgivings)

Hear my prayer through Jesus Christ, Your Son, my Lord, who lives and reigns with You and the Holy Spirit, one God, now and forever. Amen.

(Those who conduct their personal devotion in the evening may use the following liturgical prayer.)

The Liturgical Prayer for Evening

O God, Father, Son, and Holy Spirit, be near me during the night that stretches before me. Set Your holy angels around me that the evil one may have no power over me or mine:

Have mercy upon me, O Lord, and hear my prayer.

During the night hours may my slumbers not be troubled by evil thoughts and dreams, and grant me a refreshing sleep that I might awake to new tasks and challenges in Your kingdom with zeal and strength:

Have mercy upon me, O Lord, and hear my prayer.

Be the Stay and Defender of all those who serve and work this night, the police, the firefighters, those who serve the sick, and all others who must labor this night for the welfare of the common good:

Have mercy upon me, O Lord, and hear my prayer.

Cast away all my sins of the day by the holy blood of Your beloved Son, given into death for the sins of all mankind. Put my conscience at ease by Your assurance of that perfect forgiveness in Christ, that I may sleep the sleep of the righteous:

Have mercy upon me, O Lord, and hear my prayer.

Keep our nation under Your divine protection this night, though we have not deserved Your mercy, and establish righteousness, justice, and tranquility in the land:

Have mercy upon me, O Lord, and hear my prayer.

On my brothers and sisters who serve Your Church in far places, in different lands, and among strange languages, place Your hand of blessing, grant Your support, and crown all their godly efforts with Your success:

Have mercy upon me, O Lord, and hear my prayer.

(Special Requests and Thanksgivings)

Hear my prayer, O Lord, heavenly Father, through Jesus Christ, Your dear Son, who lives and reigns with You and the Holy Spirit, ever one God, world without end. Amen.

The Festival Prayer
The Lord's Prayer

1.

Our Father, who art in heaven, hallowed be Thy name. Thy kingdom come, Thy will be done on earth as it is in heaven. Give us this day our daily bread; and forgive us our trespasses as we forgive those who trespass against us; and lead us not into temptation, but deliver us from evil. For Thine is the kingdom and the power and the glory forever and ever. Amen.

2.

Our Father who art in heaven, Thy will be done on earth as it is in heaven. O dear Lord, You know that if the world cannot destroy Your name or Your kingdom, there are those who work day and night with tricks, fraud, and many strange conspiracies to try to do so. They encourage and support every evil intention raging against Your name, Your Word, Your kingdom, and Your children, threatening to destroy them.

Therefore, dear Lord, God and Father, convert and restrain them. Convert those who have yet to acknowledge Your good will, that together with them we may obey Your will. Let us gladly and patiently bear every cross and adversity and thereby acknowledge, test, and experience Your good, gracious, and perfect will. Constrain those who seek to harm us, and turn against them their own tricks and devices, as we sing:

He makes a pit, digging it out, and falls into the hole that he has made. His mischief returns upon his own head, and on his own skull his violence descends. I will give to the Lord the thanks due to His righteousness, and I will sing praise to the name of the Lord, the Most High (Psalm 7:15–17). Amen.

—Martin Luther

The Closing Doxology

1.

Praise God, from whom all blessings flow;
Praise Him, all creatures here below;
Praise Him above, ye heav'nly host;
Praise Father, Son, and Holy Ghost. Amen.
    (*LSB* 805)

2.

With a freewill offering I will sacrifice to You; I will give thanks to Your name, O Lord, for it is good. For He has delivered me from every trouble, and my eye has looked in triumph on my enemies.

—Psalm 54:6–7

3.

From You, O Lord, comes every good and perfect gift; to You belongs the praise, the majesty, the might, the glory, now and through all eternity! I adore and glorify You, O gracious Lord, now and forevermore. Amen.

4.

Of old You laid the foundation of the earth, and the heavens are the work of Your hands. They will perish, but You will remain; they will all wear out like a garment. You will change them like a robe, and they will pass away, but You are the same, and Your years have no end. Amen.

—Psalm 102:25–27

5.

May the Lord Himself grant us peace for our time and in every place. May His Spirit abound in our hearts and lives. May His Holy

39

Church be a leaven in a cold and hostile world. May His righteous people hold high the cross of the Redeemer of all mankind. Amen.

The Evening Prayer

1.

O Lord, my Source of strength and salvation, into Your hands I commend my soul, for You have redeemed me, called me as Your son, sealed me with Your grace, and trained me by Your Spirit. Amen.

2.

O heavenly Father, grant to my family and me the blessing of a quiet night. May Your almighty power surround this house and keep it from all evil. Hear my prayer through Jesus Christ, Your Son, and my Lord. Amen.

3.

O God, from whom come all holy desires, all good counsels, and all just works, give to us, Your servants, that peace which the world cannot give, that our hearts may be set to obey Your commandments and also that we, being defended from the fear of our enemies, may live in peace and quietness; through Jesus Christ, Your Son, our Lord, who lives and reigns with You and the Holy Spirit, one God, now and forever. Amen.

—The Collect for Peace (*LSB*, p. 233)

4.

Heavenly Savior, as You quieted the stormy sea and gave assurance to Your disciples, so calm my heart this night and place Your powerful hand over this dwelling that all who rest within these walls may rest in peace and tranquility, secure with Your promise and presence; in Your most holy name. Amen.

5.

Lord God, King of the universe, Guardian of Your people, hold us in the hollow of Your hand during the sleeping hours. Do not let Satan or his evil ones touch our slumbers with their dreadful presence, but give us a righteous night through Jesus Christ, our Lord. Amen.

WEDNESDAY

The Preparation
The Hymn of the Day
The Prayer of Commitment

1.

Blessed Lord Christ, I commend myself to Your care and direction this day. May I speak with Your tongue, work with Your hands, walk with Your feet, feel with Your heart, and think with Your thoughts; for I desire to be like You and seek to serve Your people in Your image. Amen.

2.

Lord, enable me to know how glorious it is

To love You,
To bear all things with You,
To weep with You,
To serve You faithfully,
To rejoice with You forever. Amen.

—Unknown

3.

O God, You are my God; earnestly I seek You; my soul thirsts for You; my flesh faints for You, as in a dry and weary land where there is no water. So I have looked upon You in the sanctuary, beholding Your power and glory. Amen.

—Psalm 63:1–2

4.

O God, You know that I am not sufficient of myself to do the tasks Your kingdom requires. My sufficiency is always in You alone. Assist me this day with Your power in the work I am about to undertake in Your name. Touch my heart with the importance of the work I do in Your name. Hold before me the responsibility of Kingdom tasks. Supply me with the strength and commitment I need to be effective this day; in the name of Your Son, my Savior. Amen.

5.

Heavenly Father, grant me wisdom this hour, the wisdom to know what is right and to teach what is true. Prevent my life from saying one thing to the people of this world while my words speak a different message. Remind me to be what I say I am. Hear my prayer through Jesus Christ, Your Son, my Lord. Amen.

The Act of Reconciliation
The Confession of Sin

1.

Merciful and forgiving God, Judge and Savior of all mankind, hear my confession this hour and attend me with Your loving kindness. I readily confess all my transgressions:

> the sin of laziness and pride and apathy,
> the sin of self-indulgence and falsehood and self-
> deception,
> the sin of degrading others and lust and greed,
> the sin of compromise with evil and callousness.

I confess to You, my Judge and Savior, all other sins I can name in my heart, as well as those I can never recall. I claim no excuse for them and know full well Your judgment. But I am sorry for them and claim forgiveness through Your Son, Jesus Christ. Forgive me and renew me, for You alone are my hope and my salvation; in the name above all names, Jesus Christ, the Righteous. Amen.

2.

Forgive, pardon, and remit all my guilt and transgressions, O most holy, most merciful, most gracious, most loving God and Father. I have not walked in Your paths nor obeyed Your voice. I have willfully and unwittingly ignored Your will for my life. Indeed, I have deserved Your displeasure, and Your punishment. But I flee for refuge to the cross of Your Son. Wash me clean in the fountain of His blood and renew me as son and servant in Your Church. Hear me, Father, for the sake of Your Son, Jesus Christ, my Lord. Amen.

Merciful Savior, Lamb of God, Suffering Servant, hear and heed my prayer of confession in this hour, for You alone are my hope and my salvation. Look with compassion on me and grant me Your assurance of grace and forgiveness.

I confess I have failed to serve Your people; I have neglected to grow in the grace and knowledge of Your Word. I have earnestly and aggressively sought my own welfare, my own ease, my own honor, my satisfaction; I have passed by the desperate needs of others and turned from Your holy will.

I have no excuse and stand under Your relentless judgment. Most merciful Savior, You have given Yourself for me on the cross and have atoned for my sins and those of the whole world. Now cast into the depths of the sea all my guilt, all my transgressions, and remember them no more. Amen.

The Profession of Faith and Praise of the Divine Trinity

1.

I believe in one God, the Father Almighty, maker of heaven and earth and of all things visible and invisible.

And in one Lord Jesus Christ, the only-begotten Son of God, begotten of His Father before all worlds, God of God, Light of Light, very God of very God, begotten, not made, being of one substance with the Father, by whom all things were made; who for us men and for our salvation came down from heaven and was incarnate by the Holy Spirit of the virgin Mary and was made man; and was crucified also for us under Pontius Pilate. He suffered and was buried. And the third day he rose again according to the Scriptures and ascended into heaven and sits at the right hand of the Father. And He will come again with glory to judge both the living and the dead, whose kingdom will have no end.

And I believe in the Holy Spirit, the Lord and giver of life, who proceeds from the Father and the Son, who with the Father and the Son together is worshiped and glorified, who spoke by the prophets. And I believe in one holy Christian and apostolic Church, I acknowledge one Baptism for the remission of sins, and I look for the resurrection of the dead and the life of the world to come. Amen.

—The Nicene Creed (*LSB*, p. 206)

2.

You are most worthily to be praised, O Lord, our Creator, who by the simple act of Your will ordained the universe to be. We bow in humble awe at Your goodness evidenced in the works of Your hands. O Redeemer, Your Holy Church throughout the world sings her praise and alleluias to Your greatness and goodness. We rest on bended knee in thanksgiving for Your great salvation by which You have made us Your people.

> Blessed are You who by speaking created all things;
> Blessed are You, O Lord!
> Blessed are You who maintains all of creation;
> Blessed are You whose word is deed, whose decrees
>   are fulfillments;
> Blessed are You who has compassion on all men;
> Blessed are You who sent Your Only Begotten as
>   Savior and Lord;
> Blessed are You, O Christ!
> Blessed are You who richly blesses all who serve You;
> Blessed are You who lives forever and exists from all
>   eternity;
> Blessed are You, O Lord, our God; we Your people
>   glorify You and worship You in the mystery of the
>   most high and holy Trinity, now and forever.
> Blessed is God's holy name!
>   Amen.

—A Prayer of Praise, Adapted from the Baruch She'Amar

3.

The wilderness and the dry land shall be glad; the desert shall rejoice and blossom like the crocus; it shall blossom abundantly and rejoice with joy and singing. The glory of Lebanon shall be given to it, the majesty of Carmel and Sharon. They shall see the glory of the Lord, the majesty of our God.

Strengthen the weak hands, and make firm the feeble knees. Say to those who have an anxious heart, "Be strong; fear not! Behold, your God will come with vengeance, with the recompense of God. He will come and save you."

Then the eyes of the blind shall be opened, and the ears of the deaf unstopped; then shall the lame man leap like a deer, and the tongue of the mute sing for joy. For waters break forth in the wilderness, and streams in the desert; the burning sand shall become a pool, and the thirsty ground springs of water; in the haunt of jackals, where they lie down, the grass shall become reeds and rushes.

And a highway shall be there, and it shall be called the Way of Holiness; the unclean shall not pass over it. It shall belong to those who walk on the way; even if they are fools, they shall not go astray. No lion shall be there, nor shall any ravenous beast come up on it; they shall not be found there, but the redeemed shall walk there. And the ransomed of the LORD shall return and come to Zion with singing; everlasting joy shall be upon their heads; they shall obtain gladness and joy, and sorrow and sighing shall flee away. Amen.

—Isaiah 35

The Word and Doctrine
The Psalm of the Day
The Liturgical Lesson of the Day
The Scripture Reading for Wednesday of the Week
The Book of Concord for the Day

The Prayers
1.
The Long Prayer of the Day

Lord of all creation, at the beginning of this new day hear my prayers of praise and honor for Your goodness and glory. For all that exists, for all that has life, for all that is beautiful, for the deep mysteries of the universe, for family structure, for human communities, for the wealth and resources of the earth, for the inventing and discovering human mind, for medicine and health, for education and learning, for government and personal responsibility, for all arts and sciences, for industry and commerce, for all Your gifts my mind can recall this day, accept my praise and honor and thanksgiving.

Most of all, Father and Creator, I offer my thanks for the richest gift of all, Your Son, Jesus Christ, my Savior. For His sharing of our humanity, for His acceptance of our guilt, for His carrying our sins, for His ministry of healing, for His words of forgiveness, for His gift of hope, for His redemption of the whole world, for His guarantee of life in glory after death, for my personal faith in Him; I give my thanks and rededicate myself to Your service.

Show Your eternal compassion and bring Your healing grace and peace to the nations and peoples in our world who in any place suffer the horror of war in any form or degree, especially for those who must fight, who must kill and be killed. May Your chosen people, those called to a living faith in Christ, demonstrate our Savior's concern and forgiving love. For the civilians and bystanders, for children and women, for the aged and infirm, for all humanity who are wounded, killed, maimed, for those who suffer the indignities of pain, of looting, rape, imprisonment, enemy occupation, for those who have lost their sanity and ability to be human, even, Lord, for those who have lost their faith in You through their suffering; have mercy on them all and remind them that You can bind up all wounds and heal all the divisions and hurts of all mankind. Bring peace, both temporal and spiritual, O Lord.

Remember, Lord, King of the nations, my own country, the United States of America *(or the name of your country)*. We, too, are in need of Your compassion. In all areas of human relationships we are in desperate need of Your aid. I confess that we, as a nation, have not always been just and compassionate with all our citizens, and because of our self-interest, injustice, hatred, and indifference, we have merited Your anger on citizens and government alike. Yet spare us Your judgment and have mercy on our nation; rather give to our citizenry an honest insight into our country's failures and weaknesses. Let men and women of integrity be appointed and elected to administer the offices in our land. Make every citizen aware of his responsibility to serve his nation as well as himself.

Raise up in our communities across the land honest, righteous, even angry leaders above self-service and bribery, dedicated to rooting out dishonesty and corruption, committed to bringing to justice those who use and even destroy the innocent, the helpless, and the disinherited for their own evil gain.

Shower Your gracious care on all classes and races of people in our land. Defeat all who would divide our nation on the basis of class or race. Our nation has been blessed with great resources and wonderful principles on which to build a just society; but without Your help, it cannot be done. Support our efforts with Your wisdom and power. Use Your Church, the family of Christ, to demonstrate to the community around us the acceptance, the love, the cooperation we need for our time. Remind Your faithful people that You have no favorites in language, race, or nationality.

Be with the governor of our state. Grant him/her advisers who have the interest of all our people in their hearts as well as in their speeches. Lead those in political office to seek unity, harmony, and the common good.

Give our mayor/city administrator the will and wisdom to use his/her office for the upbuilding of our city and not for gain of party, person, or selfish interest groups. May all our citizens support our government on all levels so fairness, justice, equity, and harmony can flourish.

Provide and be a blessing for the many organizations of community service: hospitals, schools, social service agencies, courts, the police department, the fire department, the sanitation department, all organizations and agencies seeking to serve mankind. May they not lack dedicated and capable workers or the financial resources to perform their tasks adequately. For all professions, trades, and laborers I give thanks and request Your blessing on them; for without them and Your gift of reason and the social order You have ordained, we would live in chaos and despair.

For children who live without family support and parental love, hear my pleas for Your mercy. For broken families, for abandoned wives and mothers, for fathers and husbands who cannot cope with their daily difficulties, for the homeless, for the alcoholic, the drug addict, the mentally troubled, for those trapped in the vise of poverty, for those who live in pain, for those who contemplate suicide because life has crushed them, for those enslaved under immorality of any kind, for all who need our compassion; Lord, hear my pleas for Your mercy.

I remember those in prison. They, too, need compassion and renewal as well as punishment and imprisonment. You command us to visit them and work with them. Where we have failed in this grim area of life, forgive us and grant us new opportunities to bring Christ's love and hope to those who have no freedom.

Enable this congregation and me to share the crucified and risen One with all for whom I pray this day, for in Him alone are all the answers we so desperately need.

(Special Requests and Thanksgivings)

Accept my praise for the responsibility and privilege of citizenship and voting. Prevent me from seizing the privilege and abdicating the responsibility. Make me a pastor whose concerns mirror the concerns of Christ. Prevent me from denying the Christ by making social renewal the equivalent of the Gospel. Keep me a balanced, Christ-centered pastor, preacher, prophet, and comforter. Hear me through Jesus Christ, Your Son, my Lord and Savior. Amen.

2.

The Shorter Prayer of the Day

Almighty God, merciful Father, I begin this day, this very hour, in Your name. Through the mercies of Christ, I claim Your support and presence for the day ahead. Be near me as I walk and work in Your name. Without Your aid I am surely lost and will accomplish nothing good. But in Your strength I will be Your servant this day.

May the community in which I live thrive under Your blessings. May Your Church be a leaven to infect this people with righteousness and be a blessing to every nation under the sun. Grant us men and women of vision and integrity to govern the affairs of our state and community. Protect us from greed, corruption, and indifference. Encourage our citizens to share in the tasks of building a just and successful society.

I give thanks for all the services that make our community possible and enjoyable. Raise up for these noble tasks men and women who will serve with dedication and self-sacrifice. As for our Christian brothers and sisters who serve in all useful vocations, remind them that they serve You first, not their fellow men. Surround them with the divine shield of Your holy angels that the demonic powers may have no influence over them.

Watch over the men and women in our armed forces. May they continue to defend our nation with a commitment to freedom and righteousness. May our nation always use its armed might in a just cause.

Watch over our nation and our national leaders. Let them serve with honest hearts for the common good. Keep the light of freedom bright in our homeland. We confess our many faults as a nation and beg Your forgiveness through our one and only Savior. Enable us to raise high the banners of justice, liberty, and equality across the land, not in hypocrisy but in sincerity and truth.

(Special Requests and Thanksgivings)

Now go with me, Your chosen servant and minister, in my work this day, that all will be done to the glory of Your name and for the salvation of all whom I meet. Hear my prayer through Jesus Christ, Your Son, my Lord, who lives and rules with You and the Holy Spirit, eternally one God. Amen.

3.

The Liturgical Prayer of the Day

Lord, have mercy. Christ, have mercy. Lord, have mercy. O Christ, hear me. Amen.

God the Father in heaven, God the Son, Redeemer of the world, God the Holy Spirit:

Have mercy. Be gracious to me and spare me, good Lord.

From all sin, from all error, from all evil; from the crafts and assaults of the devil; from sudden and evil death; from pestilence and famine; from war and bloodshed; from sedition and rebellion; from lightning and tempest; from all calamity by fire and water; and from everlasting death:

Good Lord, deliver me.

By the mystery of Your holy incarnation; by Your holy nativity; by Your Baptism, fasting, and temptation; by Your agony and bloody sweat; by Your cross and passion; by Your precious death and burial; by Your glorious resurrection and ascension; and by the coming of the Holy Spirit, the Comforter:

Help me, good Lord.

In all time of tribulation; in all time of prosperity; in the hour of death; and in the day of judgment:

Help me, good Lord.

Though unworthy because of my many sins:

I implore You to hear me, O Lord.

To rule and govern Your Holy Christian Church; to preserve all pastors and ministers of Your Church in the true knowledge and understanding of Your wholesome Word and to sustain them in holy living; to put an end to all schisms and causes of offense; to bring into the way of truth all who have erred and are deceived; to beat down

Satan under our feet; to send faithful laborers into Your harvest; and to accompany Your Word with Your grace and Spirit:

I implore You to hear me, O Lord.

To raise those who fall and to strengthen those who stand; and to comfort and help the weakhearted and the distressed:

I implore You to hear me, O Lord.

To give to all peoples concord and peace; to preserve our land from discord and strife; to give our country Your protection in every time of need; to direct and defend our president/queen/king and all in authority; to bless and protect our magistrates and all our people; to watch over and help all who are in danger, necessity, and tribulation; to protect and guide all who travel; to grant all women with child, and all mothers with infant children, increasing happiness in their blessings; to defend all orphans and widows and provide for them; to strengthen and keep all sick persons and young children; to free those in bondage; and to have mercy on us all:

I implore You to hear me, O Lord.

To forgive our enemies, persecutors, and slanderers and to turn their hearts; to give and preserve for our use the kindly fruits of the earth; and graciously to hear our prayers:

I implore You to hear me, O Lord.

Lord Jesus Christ, Son of God:

I implore You to hear me.

Christ, the Lamb of God, who takes away the sin of the world:

Have mercy and grant me Your peace.

Amen.

(Special Requests and Thanksgivings)

Lord, have mercy. Christ, have mercy. Lord, have mercy, and do not deal with me according to my sins. Do not reward me according to my iniquities.

Almighty God, our heavenly Father, You desire not the death of a sinner, but rather that I turn from my evil ways and live. Graciously spare me those punishments which I by my sins have deserved, and grant me always to serve You in holiness and pureness of living;

through Jesus Christ, Your Son, our Lord, who lives and reigns with You and the Holy Spirit, one God, now and forever. (437)

The Festival Prayer
The Lord's Prayer

1.

Our Father, who art in heaven, hallowed be Thy name. Thy kingdom come, Thy will be done on earth as it is in heaven. Give us this day our daily bread; and forgive us our trespasses as we forgive those who trespass against us; and lead us not into temptation, but deliver us from evil. For Thine is the kingdom and the power and the glory forever and ever. Amen.

2.

Our Father who art in heaven, give us this day our daily bread. Dear Lord, God and Father, grant us Your blessing in our temporal and physical life. Graciously grant us blessed peace. Protect us against war and disorder. Grant to our president/king/queen success against our enemies. Grant him/her wisdom and understanding to administer his/her duties and office in peace and happiness. Grant to all elected and appointed leaders good counsel and the will and ability to preserve this land and this people in tranquility and justice. Especially aid and guide the governor of this state, under whose protection You have sheltered us, so being protected against all harm, the administration may be blessed and we can live free from evil and disloyal people. Grant grace to all the people to serve our leaders loyally and obediently. Grant to all of us diligence in our vocation and charity in our dealings with one another. Grant us favorable weather and good harvest. I commend to You my house and home, spouse and children. Help me to manage my household well and support and educate my children as a Christian should. Defend us from the destroyer and his wicked angels, who work against us, looking for every opportunity to harm us and cause mischief in this life. Amen.

—Martin Luther

The Closing Doxology

1.

Because Your steadfast love is better than life, my lips will praise You. So I will bless You as long as I live; in Your name I will lift up my hands. Amen.

—Psalm 63:3–4

2.

I will extol You, my God, my King and my Righteousness; and I will bless Your holy name forever and ever. Every day I will bless You, O Holy One of Israel, King of glory, Lord of the universe, Savior of the Church; I will praise and honor Your name forever. Amen.

3.

Ascribe power to God, whose majesty is over Israel, and whose power is in the skies. Awesome is God from His sanctuary; the God of Israel—He is the one who gives power and strength to His people. Blessed be God! Amen.

—Psalm 68:34–35

4.

From Him is every good and perfect gift; to Him is all the praise, all the majesty, all the might, and all the glory, now and throughout eternity. All adoration to the most high and blessed Trinity! Amen.

5.

Great indeed, we confess, is the mystery of godliness: He was manifested in the flesh, vindicated by the Spirit, seen by angels, proclaimed among the nations, believed on in the world, taken up in glory. Amen.

—1 Timothy 3:16

The Evening Prayer

1.

Into Your hands I place my soul, for You have redeemed me, called me as Your own, sealed me with Your grace, trained me for work in Your kingdom; now, O Lord, I rest this night beneath Your care and protection, O Lord, my Strength and my Redeemer. Amen.

2.

O heavenly Father, give to me and to my family the quiet rest of a tranquil night. May divine assistance remain with us all during the dark hours; defend us from the might of the demonic powers; through Jesus Christ, my Lord and Savior. Amen.

3.

Heavenly Savior, attend this house this night. Bless it with Your holy presence, Your love, and Your protection. Continue as our Shield and Defender. We settle ourselves for rest in the palm of Your hand and under the light of Your eyes. Amen.

4.

Lord of the Church, Guardian and Friend, as my eyelids close in sleep, let Your holy peace rest upon my mind and heart. Fill my sleeping hours with Your divine presence, and may the morning hours find me rested and willing for the day's toils; in Your name. Amen.

5.

Divine and blessed Trinity, grace my bedroom with Your light and presence. May fear and doubt and perplexity flee away from Your promises. You are the Lord of night and day, Ruler of all that is, Comforter and Defender of Your elect, whether waking or sleeping. Hear me, O Lord. Amen.

THURSDAY

The Preparation
The Hymn of the Day
The Prayer of Commitment

1.

Take my head, my heart, my life; they are already Yours. Keep them in Your care this day also. Forbid that I should think them mine. Use me as Your instrument of grace and Your ambassador. Amen.

2.

Satisfy me with Your mercy, O Lord, at the beginning, the middle, and the end of the day. Let my thankfulness, my joy, and my hope manifest itself in the life I lead. Use me as Your servant. May all the people I encounter this day meet You in my words and actions; in Your name, O Christ. Amen.

3.

At the dawn of this day, O Lord, have mercy on me and refresh my soul. At the noon-hour of this day, O Christ, have mercy on me and be my Stay. At the sunset of this day, O Savior, have mercy on me and grant me Your peace. Amen.

4.

May the prayers of my heart and the acts of my hands be acceptable in Your sight this day, O Lord. Forbid that sin have dominion over me, and protect me from Satan's evil plans; in the name of Jesus Christ, my Lord. Amen.

5.

Stand with me at the head of this day, O Christ. Walk with me each step of my waking hours, O Savior. Guide speech and act by the power of Your eternal Word, O Redeemer. Hear me, blessed and only-begotten of the Father, full of grace and truth. Amen.

The Act of Reconciliation
The Confession of Sin

1.

Almighty God, merciful Father, I, a poor, miserable sinner, confess unto You all my sins and iniquities with which I have ever offended You and justly deserved Your temporal and eternal punishment. But I am heartily sorry for them and sincerely repent of them, and I pray You of Your boundless mercy and for the sake of the holy, innocent, bitter sufferings and death of Your beloved Son, Jesus Christ, to be gracious and merciful to me, a poor sinful being, and forgive all my transgressions; through the same Jesus Christ, Your Son, my Lord and Redeemer. Amen.

2.

Lord God, Creator and Judge of all mankind, hear my confession this day and favor me with Your steadfast love and kindness. I shamefully confess all my wrongs with which I have offended Your goodness. With fear and guilt I admit to a life of sin and a heart filled with self-love. I have no excuse and know Your judgment.

Yet I cast myself on Your eternal mercy through Jesus Christ and claim the reconciliation He won for me on the cross. Take away my guilt and renew me as Your child in thought, word, and deed. Hear my prayer through the merits of Jesus Christ, Your Son, my Lord. Amen.

3.

Save Your servant who trusts in You, O Lord, gracious Father; with hope I cry to You all the day long. I have done much to deserve Your wrath, and my life has been governed by selfishness. Lord, You are good and ready to forgive and to cleanse me from all unrighteousness. You are abundant in loving kindness to all who call to You. Now hear my confession in the name and for the sake of the Redeemer of the whole world, Jesus Christ, the righteous Lamb and Savior. Amen.

The Profession of Faith and Praise of the Divine Trinity

1.

I believe that God has made me and all creatures; that He has given me my body and soul, eyes, ears, and all my members, my reason and all my senses, and still takes care of them.

He also gives me clothing and shoes, food and drink, house and home, wife and children, land, animals, and all I have. He richly and daily provides me with all that I need to support this body and life.

He defends me against all danger and guards and protects me from all evil.

All this He does only out of fatherly, divine goodness and mercy, without any merit or worthiness in me. For all this it is my duty to thank and praise, serve and obey Him.

This is most certainly true. Amen.

—Martin Luther's Explanation of the First Article of the Apostles' Creed

2.

Therefore, following the holy fathers, I—with them in one accord—believe and teach men to acknowledge one and the same Son, our Lord Jesus Christ, at once complete in Godhead and complete in manhood, truly God and truly man, consisting also of a reasonable soul and body; of one substance with the Father as regards His Godhead, and at the same time of the same in nature with us as regards His manhood; like us in all respects, yet without sin; who as regards His Godhead, was begotten of the Father before the ages, but yet as regards His manhood, for us men and for our salvation, was born of the Virgin Mary, the Mother of God; one and the same Christ, Son, Lord, only begotten, to be acknowledged in two natures, without confusion, unchangeable, indivisible, inseparable; the distinction of natures being in no way annulled by the union, but rather the characteristics of each nature being preserved and concurring in one Person and one Subsistence, not parted or separated into two persons, but one and the same Son and only-begotten God the Word, Lord Jesus Christ; even as the prophets from the beginning have declared Him, and our Lord Jesus Christ Himself taught us, and the Creed of the fathers has handed down to us. Amen.

—The Creed of Chalcedon, Fourth Ecumenical Council, held at Chalcedon AD 451

3.

The earth will be filled with the knowledge of the glory of the Lord, as the waters cover the sea. The Lord is in His holy temple; let all the earth keep silence before Him.

O Lord, I have heard the report of You, and Your work, O Lord, do I fear. In the midst of the years revive it; in the midst of the years make it known; in wrath remember mercy.

His splendor covered the heavens, and the earth was full of His praise. His brightness was like the light; rays flashed from His hand; and there He veiled His power. He stood and measured the earth; He looked and shook the nations.

You went out for the salvation of Your people, for the salvation of Your anointed. I will rejoice in the Lord; I will take joy in the God of my salvation. God, the Lord, is my strength; He makes my feet like the deer's; He makes me tread on my high places. The Lord is in His holy temple; let all the earth keep silence before Him.

All honor and praise and glory and might be to You, O blessed Trinity! Amen.

—Habakkuk 2:14, 20; 3:2–4, 6a, 13a, 18–19; 2:20

The Word and Doctrine
The Psalm of the Day
The Liturgical Lesson of the Day
The Scripture Reading for Thursday of the Week
The Book of Concord for the Day

The Prayers

1.

The Long Prayer of the Day

Lord of glory, You have called us into Your family for one purpose, to become Your people and witnesses to Your salvation. We are called to be Your stewards, managers of Your great gifts to all mankind. This day, Lord, I pray for my own stewardship of life and that of Your congregation in this place. All that I have is from You: my length of time in this world, the physical and psychological talents I possess, the money I receive, my intellectual attainments, and each new day. Deliver me from considering them as my own, but rather help me see them as gifts on loan to me, for which I must give account to You.

This same attitude is needed in our congregation. Many forget that what we have is by Your grace alone and not by our skill and abilities. It is a great evil, Father, to forget the Giver. Forgive us for doing so, and remind us each day of Your goodness.

Encourage all Your people to pledge their gifts to Your kingdom. We have not done all we can to spread the Gospel. We have thought too much of our own needs and not enough of Your commands. Increase the giving of money in our congregation to the mission of Your Church at home and abroad. Lead our members to give of their time as well. Remind us all that our personal talents are not the exclusive property of our own desires but need to be put in the service of Your Son.

Especially this day I ask Your blessing and aid for the stewardship committee in this congregation and its chairman. Make them enthusiastic for this important task in the Kingdom. Crown with success all their efforts to make people aware of their responsibilities and privileges as ambassadors of Christ.

Cover our nation with Your divine protection, all our citizens, rich and poor, learned and uneducated, of all races and cultures, for those who work the land and bring the produce to our tables, for those who labor in the great and small industries of our nation to fashion the tools and appliances of our daily life. Grant success to those who think and reach for God-pleasing new discoveries in medicine, physics, biology, chemistry, and all the disciplines of modern science. May they prove a help to mankind and not a curse.

Be with all the elected and appointed leaders of our country, region, and community. Place in my heart a respect for life and property and a willingness to serve wherever needed as a good citizen. May no segment of my community fail because I have failed in my duty to You and them. For all those areas of our nation that suffer from injustice and deprivation send us wise and compassionate leaders who bring integrity and healing to broken lives and degraded existences.

I give thanks for all the uniformed services that keep our city alive and livable—the police, firefighters, and the various city service departments. Enable all our citizens to understand their responsibility to serve the common good. Be with all our chaplains as they seek to serve in hospitals, prisons, or whatever area of human misery they are called to touch with healing hand and voice. Be with all doctors and nurses who serve the sick; endow them with wisdom and compassion for their service to humanity.

I ask Your aid and support for the educational system in our urban and rural areas. Grant us dedicated teachers in our public schools so that our children may learn and grow into useful citizens of the nation. Bless also our church's parochial school system. Be with our colleges, seminaries, high schools, and elementary schools; may they contribute well-Educated and consecrated men and women to the mission of the Church.

Remain with me in my daily rounds this day. As I study, counsel, visit, pray, and plan, be my leader and helper. Grant that the people I meet may see Your beloved Son in me and see His love in my words and actions. Empty me of arrogant self-esteem and fill me with Your Holy Spirit.

Give life and direction to all the organizations in our congregation: women's groups, men's groups, youth, and all gatherings of Your people. May they prove themselves as genuine assets to Your kingdom of grace, committed to spreading the fellowship of Christ and building the faith within.

Grace all my brothers in the office of the holy ministry with the wisdom of Your Holy Spirit. May we all be of one mind and one spirit as we seek to share the Gospel of our Lord. Protect them all in their daily tasks. Remember the president of our Synod and all the officers who seek to serve Your greater Church by dedicated service. Remind all that You will never forsake Your children, but will remain with them in the dark hours as well as the joyous days.

Lord, without You our labor is lost, but with You even the weakest and least in the Kingdom becomes mighty in word and deed. Be present in all the works of Your Church and touch the hearts of all who want to be Your disciples. Remind us that You will lose none whom You elect to be Your children in time and eternity.

(Special Requests and Thanksgivings)

Almighty Father, I place myself and all for whom I pray into Your hands. You, who see every sparrow and every grain of sand; You, who hold the stars in Your hand and encompass the vastness of space, surround me with Your love and care. Let Your angels always accompany me, that the evil one may have no power over my actions or me; through Jesus Christ, Your Son, my Lord. Amen.

2.

The Shorter Prayer of the Day

Almighty God and most merciful Lord and Father of mankind, King of the universe, Redeemer of Israel and Defender of the Holy Church, look with favor on Your sons and daughters and mercifully grant us forgiveness and new life in Christ. Let not our selfishness and fear and ignorance hinder our work in Your vineyard. Renew us each day and use us mightily as Your workers. By Your Word give us the will to remain faithful witnesses to Christ and servants and lovers of all mankind.

Encourage all our members to be willing disciples of the Savior. Root out from our hearts the inordinate love of self that refuses to consider the needs of others or the divine commands You have placed before us. Mold our lives in the pattern of Your Son that we may show to others the love He showed to us. Help us use our gifts, our talents, our strengths, and even our weaknesses, for the upbuilding of Your holy people.

Make our people concerned for the growth of the Church, the body of Christ. May the Holy Spirit fill their hearts that they volunteer to work joyfully and effectively in the kingdom of Your Son. Protect us from the sin of worshiping You with our lips and not with our lives.

Lead our Synod as well in its desire to do Your work in our world. Shower Your blessings upon all the work we undertake in Your name. Stir up our people that they move and act with passion on behalf of those suffering in this world. May Christ always be our Model and Pattern as we reach for the lost. Through all our acts of compassion may we always hold high the cross of the Crucified and Risen One, the Savior of all.

God, be with me in my vineyard tasks this day. Uphold me by the strength of Your Word and enable me to speak with Your thoughts and act with Your loving kindness. At the end of the day may I know that Your words, "Well done, good and faithful servant!" apply to my ministry and me.

(Special Requests and Thanksgivings)

Heavenly Father, hear my prayers through Jesus Christ, Your Son, my only Savior and Lord, who lives and rules with You and the Holy Spirit, eternally one God. Amen.

3.
The Liturgical Prayer of the Day

Omnipotent and most loving Trinity, most holy and eternal Unity, Father, Son, and Holy Spirit, Light above all light, in whom exists no shadow, no change, no evil; I pray this day for my holy ministry and that of my brothers in Christ. Attend to my prayers for the sake of the blessed and perfect High Priest, Author, Support, and Perfecter of my own ministry, Jesus Christ, my Lord and theirs.

Hear my prayer, O Lord, and let Your blessings rest upon me.

How can I repay you, O Lord, for all Your goodness to me? O Lord Almighty, I will lift up the cup of salvation and call on Your name. I will trust in Your promises and no others.

Hear my prayer, O Lord, and let Your blessings rest upon me.

I give heartfelt thanks for the most precious gift of the blood of Your only-begotten Son, the eternal Lamb, the Paschal Sacrifice, the Redeemer of the whole world. For His gift of complete and perfect forgiveness of all my iniquity, I give thanks to the blessed Trinity.

Hear my prayer, O Lord, and let Your blessings rest upon me.

I will sacrifice a thank offering to You and call on Your name, I will fulfill my vows to You, O Lord, in the presence of Your people, in the courts of Your house, in the midst of Your chosen ones.

Hear my prayer, O Lord, and let Your blessings rest upon me.

I will remember Your deeds, O Lord; I will remember Your miracles of long ago. I will meditate on all Your words and consider Your mighty deeds. I will recount Your works.

Hear my prayer, O Lord, and let Your blessings rest upon me.

Blessed be the most high and holy Trinity in Unity. I praise Your name, O Lord. Blessed are You, O Lord our God, sovereign King of the universe.

Hear my prayer, O Lord, and let Your blessings rest upon me.

I thank You for calling me into the holy ministry to proclaim Your saving Word to the nations, Your comforting, redeeming Gospel to all mankind. Keep gratitude within me.

Hear my prayer, O Lord, and let Your blessings rest upon me.

I thank You for calling me to administer the Holy Sacraments of Baptism and the Eucharist; for the privilege of bringing hope to the lost, peace to the troubled, expectation of life to the dying, comfort to the sick, strength to the weak, challenge to the strong, the fire of Your Word to the indifferent, a gracious invitation to those who seek and hunger for God. Keep me a faithful minister of Your flock.

Hear my prayer, O Lord, and let Your blessings rest upon me.

I thank You also for the frustrations, the failures, and the trials of my daily ministry; for they bring me to my knees before Your throne of grace. I thank You for the honor of bearing a cross in Your holy name. May I never bear Your name with shame.

Hear my prayer, O Lord, and let Your blessings rest upon me.

I beseech Your presence with me as I walk Your paths through this new day. Forsake me not, O merciful Lord, and work with and through my ministry this day. Be with me as You accompanied the prophets before me. Make me an instrument of Your peace.

Hear my prayer, O Lord, and let Your blessings rest upon me.

Father and King, may others continually see Your Son in me during my waking hours; and may Your rich Word bear much fruit in the hearts of all who hear Your gracious words of life.

(Special Requests and Thanksgivings)

All honor, glory, praise, adoration, and blessing be to You, O holy and everlasting Trinity, through Jesus Christ, my Lord. Amen.

The Festival Prayer
The Lord's Prayer

1.

Our Father, who art in heaven, hallowed be Thy name. Thy kingdom come, Thy will be done on earth as it is in heaven. Give us this day our daily bread; and forgive us our trespasses as we forgive those who trespass against us; and lead us not into temptation, but deliver us from evil. For Thine is the kingdom and the power and the glory forever and ever. Amen.

2.

Our Father who art in heaven, forgive us our trespasses, as we forgive those who trespass against us. O dear Lord, God and Father, do not enter into judgment against us, for in Your sight no one who lives is justified before You. Do not count it against us as sin that we are so unthankful for all Your indescribable spiritual and physical blessings. Do not judge us on account of our daily sin. We stumble and sin many more times than we even know or recognize, "For He who avenges blood is mindful of them; He does not forget the cry of the afflicted" (Psalm 9:12).

Look away from our accomplishments as well as our wickedness; in Your boundless compassion look instead upon Your dear Son, Jesus Christ. Forgive also those who are our enemies or who have wronged us, just as we forgive them from our hearts. By their actions against us, they arouse Your anger and hurt themselves, yet we are not helped by their ruin and would much rather that they be saved with us. Amen.
—Martin Luther

The Closing Doxology

1.

The peace and grace of my blessed Savior, Jesus Christ, remain with me this day and always. Blessed be Your most high and holy name, O Lord; eternal is Your power and glory, wisdom and might; now and forever You alone I worship and adore. Amen.

2.

Bless the Lord, O my soul! O Lord my God, You are very great! Your are clothed with splendor and majesty, covering Yourself with light as with a garment, stretching out the heavens like a tent (Psalm 104:1–2). I adore and praise the blessed Trinity. Amen.

3.

The peace of the Lord that passes all understanding keep my heart and mind in the knowledge, the grace, the power, the hope, and the sanctification of the Lord of lords and King of kings, now and always. Glory, laud, and honor be to You, O Lord, forever and ever. Amen.

4.

Oh, the depth of the riches and wisdom and knowledge of God! How unsearchable are His judgments and how inscrutable His ways! "For who has known the mind of the Lord, or who has been His counselor?" "Or who has given a gift to Him that he might be repaid?" For from Him and through Him and to Him are all things. To Him be glory forever. Amen.

—Romans 11:33–36

5.

But as for me, I will look to the Lord; I will wait for the God of my salvation; my God will hear me (Micah 7:7). May all His redeemed praise and laud His holy name! Amen.

The Evening Prayer

1.

Spread the wings of Your mercy over this house during the night hours, O Lord, and remain our Guardian and Watchman against all forms of evil and danger. May our sleep be free from restlessness and trouble; may we rise tomorrow ready for the tasks You have ordained for us, Your children; in the name of Jesus Christ, my Savior and Friend. Amen.

2.

O Lord, our heavenly Father, supply me with Your grace and support that I may have a steady heart and be ready to do Your will at the break of day. Where I have faltered or erred this day, forgive and renew in Your Son. May all with whom I have dealt these past hours remember me as one who bears Your name and is Your child. Now as I prepare for sleep, give my family and me the divine assistance of Your holy angels, for into Your loving care I place all that I am and have; hear me through Jesus Christ, Your Son, my Lord. Amen.

3.

Father of all mankind, into Your hands I lay myself and all whom I care for and love. Forgive us all where we have done wrong today and assure us of Your forgiveness and comforting presence. We rest in the faith by which we were sealed in Baptism, in the sure knowledge of Your loving presence; through Jesus Christ, Your Son, my Lord and Savior. Amen.

4.

O most gracious Lord, establish the boundaries of Your protection around this house and those who lie down here to sleep. Keep watch through the night while Your children sleep until the dawn of the new day. Hear me in the name of Jesus Christ, Your Son, my Lord. Amen.

5.

Almighty and merciful Lord, bless and preserve us through the hours that lie ahead, even as You watched over the tents of Abraham, Isaac, and Jacob, that all of us may dwell securely in Your care through the helpless hours of the night. Hear my prayer in the name that is above all names, Jesus Christ, the Righteous. Amen.

FRIDAY

The Preparation
The Hymn of the Day
The Prayer of Commitment

1.

You have made us for Yourself, and our hearts are restless until they rest in You. Amen.

—St. Augustine

2.

God, my Father, be with me today and walk with me as I make Your rounds. Remind me constantly to do Your will, not in word only but in fact and deed. Chasten me when I need Your guiding hand, and then be quick to touch me with Your renewing power. May I desire to please You alone this day, not myself or others of this world. Hear my prayer through Jesus Christ, the Lord of lords and King of kings. Amen.

3. God and Father, You have granted me another day of service in Your vineyard, another free gift of love from on high, another opportunity to reflect on Your tender care for all humanity. Forbid that I should lose this day to idleness, indifference, and callousness. Let me not stain this day by being a stumbling block to others and hiding the light of Christ. Use me fully as an instrument of Your redeeming love for all who I encounter this day. Hear my prayer in the name and for the sake of the Only Begotten, Your Son, my Savior. Amen.

4.

O Lord, my Savior, who dwells securely in light unapproachable, by Your mercy You have kept me through the past night. Now by Your name and grace lead me, guide me, and teach me this day. From all unholy desires, all unworthy actions, all unseemly words, deliver me. Make my ministry one of all things beautiful, all things truthful, all things helpful. Where I will cause harm and anguish, bring healing and forgiveness. Where I will ignore great need, supply what is needed and forgive me. When I seek to flee the cause, remain and grant forgiveness to Your servant and son. Lord God, all is already lost unless You are with me and I with You. Hear me, O most holy Trinity. Amen.

5.

Remember, O Lord God, Your covenant with me, Your child and servant. Inspire all I think or say or do in the hours that lie ahead. May Your Holy Spirit go with me in gracious measure during the work You have ordained for me. May I know His wisdom, strength, hope, and love. May the Kingdom grow because of my work this day, O Lord, or rather because of Your work through me. Hear me in the holy name of the eternal Son, Lord and Lamb, Sovereign and Servant, Jesus Christ, the Holy One. Amen.

The Act of Reconciliation
The Confession of Sin

1.

Almighty God, my heavenly Father, Maker of all things, Judge of all people, I admit and confess my sinfulness. I have turned away from the needs and despair of others in my thoughts, words, and deeds. I have done the evil You clearly forbid and have failed to perform the good You demand. I repent and am sorry for these sins. Have mercy on me, kind Father, because of my Brother, Your Son, Jesus Christ. Amen.

2.

Forgive me for everything in the past that was contrary to Your will, and by the power of Your Spirit move me to serve You more faithfully in the days and years ahead. I confess that I have not been the committed shepherd of Your sheep You have willed me to be. I have often neglected Kingdom duties and passed by Your children in need. I deserve nothing but Your judgment; but, O Lord, have mercy on me and forgive all my transgressions for the sake of Jesus Christ, my hope and my salvation. Amen.

3.

Blessed Savior, most holy Redeemer, You know I am unworthy of Your grace. My sins have forced me from Your presence; My guilt has made Your judgment hard and my punishment everlasting. But by Your holy wounds, Your sacred blood, Your perfect obedience to the Father, cancel my guilt and remit my sins, O faithful and loving Redeemer. Amen.

4.

I confess to You, almighty Lord and heavenly Father, and willingly to my absent brothers in Christ, the many sins I have committed against You and them. I have sinned by thought, word, and deed, through my own fault and no other's. Extend Your mercy to me and forgive all my transgressions by the merits of the Paschal Lamb, the Son of the Highest, the Suffering Servant, the Redeemer of the world; in Him alone, O Lord, I take refuge and claim remission of all my guilt. Amen.

5.

With contrite heart, eternal Father, I approach Your throne of grace and petition Your forgiveness, Your loving kindness. Despite my weaknesses and selfishness, continue to use me in Your vineyard this day also. I stand in the fountain of life, the sacred blood of the Rose of Sharon, the Seed of Abraham, the Messiah, my Lord and Savior, Jesus Christ. I claim His promise of grace now and always. Amen.

The Profession of Faith and Praise of the Divine Trinity

1.

I believe that Jesus Christ, true God, begotten of the Father from eternity, and also true man, born of the Virgin Mary, is my Lord, who has redeemed me, a lost and condemned person, purchased and won me from all sins, from death, and from the power of the devil; not with gold or silver, but with His holy, precious blood and with His innocent suffering and death, that I may be His own and live under Him in His kingdom, and serve Him in everlasting righteousness, innocence, and blessedness, just as He is risen from the dead, lives and reigns to all eternity. This is most certainly true. Amen.

—Martin Luther's Explanation of the Second Article of the Apostles' Creed

2.

We praise You, O God; we acknowledge You to be the Lord. All the earth now worships You, the Father everlasting. To You all angels cry aloud, the heavens and all the powers therein. To You cherubim and seraphim continually do cry: Holy, holy, holy, Lord God of Sabaoth; heaven and earth are full of the majesty of Your glory.

The glorious company of the apostles praise You. The goodly fellowship of the prophets praise You. The noble army of martyrs praise You. The holy Church throughout all the world does acknowledge You: the Father of an infinite majesty; Your adorable, true, and only Son; also the Holy Ghost, the Comforter.

You are the king of glory, O Christ; You are the everlasting Son of the Father. When You took upon Yourself to deliver man, You humbled Yourself to be born of a virgin. When You had overcome the sharpness of death, You opened the kingdom of heaven to all believers. You sit at the right hand of God in the glory of the Father. We believe that You will come to be our judge.

We therefore pray You to help Your servants, whom You have redeemed with Your precious blood. Make them to be numbered with Your saints in glory everlasting.

O Lord, save Your people and bless Your heritage. Govern them and lift them up forever. Day by day we magnify You. And we worship Your name forever and ever.

Grant, O Lord, to keep us this day without sin. O Lord, have mercy upon us, have mercy upon us. O Lord, let Your mercy be upon us, as our trust is in You. O Lord, in You have I trusted; let me never be confounded. Amen.

—The Te Deum, Matins (*LSB*, pp. 223–25)

3.

My heart exults in the Lord; my horn is exalted in the Lord. My mouth derides my enemies, because I rejoice in Your salvation.

There is none holy like the Lord: for there is none besides You; there is no rock like our God. Talk no more so very proudly, let not arrogance come from your mouth; for the Lord is a God of knowledge, and by Him actions are weighed. The bows of the mighty are broken, but the feeble bind on strength. Those who were full have hired themselves out for bread, but those who were hungry have ceased to hunger. The barren has borne seven, but she who has many children is forlorn. The Lord kills and brings to life; He brings down to Sheol and raises up. The Lord makes poor and makes rich; He brings low and He exalts. He raises up the poor from the dust; He lifts the needy from the ash heap to make them sit with princes and inherit a seat of honor. For the pillars of the earth are the Lord's, and on them He has set the world.

He will guard the feet of His faithful ones, but the wicked shall be cut off in darkness, for not by might shall a man prevail. The adversaries of the Lord shall be broken to pieces; against them He will thunder in heaven. The Lord will judge the ends of the earth; He will give strength to His king and exalt the power of His anointed.

Glory be to the Father and to the Son and to the Holy Spirit; as it was in the beginning, is now, and will be forever. Amen.

—Hannah's Prayer, 1 Samuel 2:1–10

The Word and Doctrine

The Psalm of the Day
The Liturgical Lesson of the Day
The Scripture Reading for Friday of the Week
The Book of Concord for the Day

The Prayers

1.

The Long Prayer of the Day

God and Father, You have created the family and shared with us the gift of creation. I give thanks this day for parents who cared. I give thanks this day for the love and joy of a Christian wife. I give thanks this day for the gift of children. For my family, Lord, may I ever praise You.

Be with the families of our congregation. Where there is disharmony and stress, grant peace and concord. Where there is trial and tribulation, give help and rescue. Where there is fear and anguish, offer courage and hope. Instill in all our families the conviction that You are our Rock and Shield, a very present Help in danger. May we learn to begin each day with You.

Make Your Son the Center of the families in our parish. Teach parents and children alike that we need to grow in the grace and knowledge of our Lord Jesus. Make each family and Christian home Your Church; let the individual members share in the love and concern and forgiveness that are hallmarks of Your children.

For those homes under discord, under the threat of divorce, for those husbands and wives who fight and fear and hate each other, for children and parents who are estranged and alienated; Lord, hear my pleas for them all. Use me and my ministry—as it is Your will—to bring reconciliation, forgiveness, and renewal. Grant that Your Son may be evident in my words and attitudes to all who need the balm of divine healing.

Bless all our church agencies that specialize in working with social ills. Our homes and agencies for serving children, youth, and adults I bring to Your throne of grace for help and support. There are so many in need of Your powerful Gospel, Lord; give to our members the desire, the will to support and expand those saving arms of the Church.

I remember the aged today, Father; comfort and remain with each one in our congregation. They have borne the heat of the day; now give them joy and hope in the evening of life. May we listen to their advice, learn from their experience, show them godly respect, and accept their complaints and lack of flexibility.

Watch over the youth of our church. In their zest for life and their eagerness to change and progress, keep them steady in faith. May they prove a leaven to our people with their energy and joy of life. Enable us to touch the hearts of some of them, that they offer their lives in full-time service to the Church.

I also pray for the culture of our day. Grant Your Church men and women who will reflect Your glory and beauty in their creative acts of art, music, theater, and writing. Suppress the abuse, the misuse of those disciplines that add so much enjoyment and meaning to our earthly lives.

With war ever on the horizon, establish worldly peace. Deliver our nation from the horror of modern war. From waste, from suffering, from the total uselessness of it all, good Lord, deliver us. For all who may suffer this day—in any corner of the world—from bombs and bullets, grant us Your peace-giving presence. Make fighting cease and harmony abound. May our nation be known for its compassion, its cooperation, and its willingness to build and to aid—not for its military potential.

With all the weaknesses and failures of the United Nations, encourage our nation to work for and through that organization, for lasting peace and progress in the world. And by this terrestrial peace enable Your Christian witness to flourish.

(Special Requests and Thanksgivings)

And now, Father, make me bold to run the race set before me, and enable me to stand calmly in Your presence so that, leading a life of confident, quiet commitment, I can bear witness to Your grace and carry Your power into my community. Let Your light shine through me that people can see my good works and praise You. Direct my life this day that at the setting of the sun my hours will have been spent in Your service and under Your guidance. Hear me through Jesus Christ, my Lord, Your only Son. Amen.

2.

The Shorter Prayer of the Day

Holy Father, mighty, immortal, ever faithful, show us Your mercy and everlasting kindness; bestow upon us, Your chosen ones, everlasting salvation. Clothe Your ministers with righteousness, and continually fill Your people with praise for You.

Pour down peace and tranquility into the world; for only in You, O Lord, can we truly live in safety. Lord God, almighty King, keep our nation under Your most gracious protection and guide us in the way of justice, truth, and compassion for all Your people. Heavenly Father, let Your saving way be made known upon earth, Your saving health among the nations.

Let not the needy be forsaken nor forgotten, O Lord, our almighty and merciful King, nor let the hope of the poor be taken from them. O God, Savior of the nations, overflowing with mercy and compassion, have mercy upon me and all mankind, especially upon those who are suffering for Your name's sake. I am indeed a poor, penitent sinner and kneel before You in trust, earnestly asking Your forgiving grace through my merciful Lord and Savior, Jesus Christ. Open the hearts of all our people that they, too, may find in You their help and salvation. Lead Your people to hold high the cross of Your beloved Son, that others in our community may also find in the Crucified One the hope of everlasting life.

Do not forsake the sick, the homebound in our parish this day, but support them by Your great power and promises. Pour understanding and wisdom into the hearts of our leaders that they may lead and govern our people in the way of righteousness. Surely we have earned Your wrath and eternal judgment by our failure to be just and equitable with all our fellow citizens. Instead of Your judgment, O Lord, shower the soft rain of Your mercy upon our land and guide us in the way of justice. Encourage Your people to lift up rather than crush those in need.

Establish peace in our world that Your called people may continue as lights in a dark, inhospitable world. Mold our congregation by Your Word that we become an instrument of Your love for those who dwell under the burden of sin, death, and the power of the devil.

(Special Requests and Thanksgivings)

I will bless, praise, honor, and adore You, O Trinity in Unity; I will glorify, laud, and revere You, who lives in the praises of the heavenly host. Hear my petitions and thanksgivings in the name and for the sake of the Only Begotten, full of grace and truth. Amen.

3.

The Liturgical Prayer of the Day

Lord, have mercy. Christ, have mercy. Lord, have mercy. O blessed and divine Trinity in Unity, have mercy on us.

Hear my prayer, O Lord.

O Lord God, You have promised to hear us when we speak in the name of Your Son; now hear my intercession for those in need in body and soul.

Good Lord, hear my prayer.

From all sin, from all error, from all evil, from the crafts and assaults of the devil, from sudden and evil death, from pestilence and famine, from war and bloodshed, from sedition and rebellion, from lightning and tempest, from all calamity by fire and water and wind, and from everlasting death:

Good Lord, hear my prayer and deliver Your people.

From the pull of the flesh, from the sins of pride, avarice, anger, lust, sloth, gluttony, and envy; from the power of Satan and the call of this world:

Good Lord, hear my prayer and save Your people.

From the sins of the soul, from indifference, from cold resistance to the cries of those in need, from carelessness with holy things, from stubbornness, egotism, fear, and failure to heed Your call to duty:

Good Lord, hear my prayer and defend Your people.

In times of trial and tribulation, in their hour of temptation, in their hour of death, and in the Day of Judgment:

Good Lord, hear my prayer and rescue Your people.

Give to Your Church the faithful men and women it needs to proclaim and spread the Word of the Savior of the whole world; may Your Church ever preach the power of the cross, hold high His powerful Word, administer the Sacraments according to Your commands, and have a burning love for the souls of the lost.

Good Lord, hear my prayer on behalf of Your people.

Remain with all who serve Jesus Christ, Your Son, at home and abroad; watch over all the workers whom You have sent to work in the vineyard of the Kingdom; forget not Your workers in the lonely hours and difficult days; and remind us that You will never forsake us, never forget us.

Good Lord, hear my prayer and bless Your chosen ones.

Touch the hearts of our enemies and enable them to walk in peace with all men; visit us all with the wisdom from on high that we may speak Your Word of life with sincerity and truth; open the hearts of those who hear our witness to the Christ that they may believe and be saved.

Good Lord, hear my prayer and grant my request.

For all who face danger this day of body or soul; all who are persecuted for Your name's sake; all those for whom life has become unbearable; all who are under the bondage of sin, of drugs, of alcohol; all who are unable to cope with the difficulties of life; all who begin to know not the Savior of all men; all in need of Your divine assistance:

Good Lord, hear my prayer and be their Comfort and Stay.

Preserve our nation and our president; be with our Congress and our judiciary; give us men and women who seek the good and welfare of our citizens; keep us free from the curse of racism and bigotry; may we seek justice, equity, and fairness for all our people.

Good Lord, hear my prayer and prosper our nation under God.

(Special Requests and Thanksgivings)

O Lord, my God, look down from above and visit, help, and sustain all Your children. Hear my prayer through Jesus Christ, my Lord, who lives and rules with You and the Holy Spirit, eternally one God. Amen.

The Festival Prayer
The Lord's Prayer

1.

Our Father, who art in heaven, hallowed be Thy name. Thy kingdom come, Thy will be done on earth as it is in heaven. Give us this day our daily bread; and forgive us our trespasses as we forgive those who trespass against us; and lead us not into temptation, but deliver us from evil. For Thine is the kingdom and the power and the glory forever and ever. Amen.

2.

Our Father who art in heaven, lead us not into temptation. O dear Lord, Father and God, keep us prepared and alert, eager and diligent in Your Word and service, so that we do not become complacent and careless as though we had already achieved everything. We implore You by Your mercy not to let the devil sneak in and take away from us Your precious Word or stir up strife and factions among us, or otherwise lead us into spiritual and physical sin and disgrace. Grant us wisdom and strength through Your Spirit that we may bravely resist the devil and gain the victory. Amen.

—Martin Luther

The Closing Doxology

1.

Give glory to the Father Almighty; to His Son, Jesus Christ, our Lord; to the Spirit, who dwells in our hearts now and forevermore. Amen.

2.

This is the day the Lord has made. I will rejoice and be glad in it. I will serve His name from the rising of the sun to its setting. All praise, honor, glory, majesty, and might be to His most wonderful name now and forever. Amen.

3.

Blessed be the name of the LORD from this time forth and forevermore! From the rising of the sun to its setting, the name of the LORD is to be praised! Amen.

—Psalm 113:2–3

4.

The Lord will rescue me from every evil deed and bring me safely into His heavenly kingdom. To Him be the glory forever and ever. Amen.

—2 Timothy 4:18

5.

Then my soul will rejoice in the Lord, exulting in His salvation. All my bones shall say, "O Lord, who is like You, delivering the poor from him who is too strong for him, the poor and needy from him who robs him?" Then my tongue shall tell of Your righteousness and of Your praise all the day long. Amen.

—Psalm 35:9–10, 28

The Evening Prayer

1.

I thank You, Father, for the night with its sleep, its rest from the labors and cares of the day. I thank You for Your assurance of forgiveness for the day now past, with all its failures and sins. I thank You for the joys You gave me and the peace from on high. I thank You for the moon and stars and the quiet hours of the darkness. May I sleep the sleep of the righteous; hear me in the holy name of Your Son, Jesus Christ, my Lord. Amen.

2.

Almighty Father, Lord of the far-flung galaxies and Commander of the angelic host, hold me in Your hand these resting hours and bless my sleep with Your renewing presence. Cover me with peace, quiet, and the hand of Your power that I may be Your willing hands and feet and heart and mind at break of day. Hear my prayer through Jesus Christ, my Lord and Savior. Amen.

3.

Merciful Savior, as now I fold my hands in rest and sleep, attend me throughout the night. Watch over my family and support us by Your almighty power. I place us all in Your care—body, soul, and all things. Hear me for the sake of Jesus Christ, my Lord. Amen.

4.

The day is over, Lord, and sleep is near. Remain close by me, for You never sleep, and no darkness can dim Your sight. In confidence and hope I let go of this day and offer it up to Your judgment and grace. Guard my unconscious hours; place before me tomorrow another day of service in Your kingdom; hear me in the name of Your only Son, Jesus Christ, the Righteous. Amen.

5.

I thank You, my heavenly Father, through Jesus Christ, Your dear Son, that You have graciously kept me this day; and I pray You that You would forgive me all my sins where I have done wrong, and graciously keep me this night. For into Your hands I commend myself, my body and soul, and all things. Let Your holy angel be with me, that the evil foe may have no power over me. Amen.

—Martin Luther

SATURDAY

The Preparation
The Hymn of the Day
The Prayer of Commitment

1.

O Morning Star, Sun of the dawn, mighty Savior, Prince of peace, Son of the Highest, grace my waking hours with Your presence and lend me Your zeal for the Father's work. Fill my day with Your rich Spirit that all may encounter the Father's love through me. Hear me, blessed Jesus, in Your most holy name. Amen.

2.

O Lord, heavenly Father, let Your Holy Spirit remain with me this day. May the tasks and hours that lie before me be profitable to Your kingdom and to me; in the name of Jesus Christ, Your chosen Lamb. Amen.

3.

Grant me, O merciful Lord, ardently to desire, prudently to study, rightly to understand, and perfectly to fulfill that which pleases You, to the praise and glory of Your name. Amen.

—Thomas Aquinas

4.

O Almighty God, gracious Father, Your Word is a lamp to my feet and a light to my way. Now shine most clearly in my heart that I may remain Your obedient son and disciple. Bless my devotion this morning and inspire me for the goals You have placed before me. Hear me, Father, because of the life and death of Your Son, Jesus Christ, my Lord. Amen.

5.

Jesus, Savior, Guide, and Friend, go before me in the coming hours and lighten my way, ease my path. Keep my feet from stumbling, my heart from trembling, and my hands from indecision. Crown these hours, O Savior, with Your blessings. Amen.

The Act of Reconciliation
The Confession of Sin

1.

O blessed and compassionate Savior, hear my confession and give me the assurance of Your gracious Word this hour.

I, indeed, have been worthy of none of Your gifts; I have lived as an island to myself:

> caring only for my welfare,
> seeking only my pleasure,
> placing my goals first,
> ignoring Your will,
> lusting for this world's rewards,
> passing by those in dire need,
> manipulating fellow human beings for my own
>   purposes;
> indifferent to Your worship,
> lazy in my prayers,
> forgetful of my Baptism,

perfunctory at the Holy Supper,
lacking in zeal for Your service.

For these and all other sins, O Lord, have mercy on me. For all those sins I remember or forget, for those that have scarred my conscience and filled me with a holy dread, for those that seem as nothing to me, yet are abhorrent in Your sight:

O Lord Jesus Christ, by Your death, have mercy on me and forgive me both guilt and sin alike. Amen.

2.

Almighty Father, God of the ages, with humility and sorrow I confess my sin, my guilt, my helplessness to You. Against You only have I sinned and done evil in Your sight. I am worthy of none of Your mercies and deserve Your everlasting anger and judgment. But I am sincerely repentant of my iniquity and ask You to cancel out my guilt, my error, my sin, and renew me for service in Your kingdom; through the merits and reconciliation of Your Son, Jesus Christ, my Lord. Amen.

3.

Lord God, merciful Father, I am not worthy of the mercies You have showered upon me, nor can I claim Your revelation of truth as my innate right. Your compassion alone has called me into Your presence and forgiven all my guilt. Your grace alone has made me Your son and servant.

I have much to confess and, if I am to be effective in Your service this day, need the renewing power of Your forgiveness. For my little faith and lack of concern for holy things, for my willingness to compromise Your truth and my sloth in the daily fight against evil, for my many sins against Your will in my life and my cold indifference to the cries of others, for my laziness in the study of Your Word and my lack of enthusiasm for a life of prayer, for my desire for comfort rather than zeal for Your house, for my cunning in avoiding responsibilities and the many rationalizations I use to make excuse, for my self-centeredness and my insistence on my own way, for the masked goals of self-glorification and the absence of praise for You in daily life, for the pride and prejudice of my sinful nature and the oft-practiced refusal to be a little Christ to my neighbor:

Lord, have mercy. Christ have mercy. Lord, have mercy.
Amen.

The Profession of Faith and Praise
of the Divine Trinity

1.

Whoever desires to be saved must, above all, hold the catholic faith.

Whoever does not keep it whole and undefiled will without doubt perish eternally.

And the catholic faith is this, that we worship one God in Trinity and Trinity in Unity, neither confusing the persons nor dividing the substance.

For the Father is one person, the Son is another, and the Holy Spirit is another.

But the Godhead of the Father and of the Son and of the Holy Spirit is one: the glory equal, the majesty coeternal.

Such as the Father is, such is the Son, and such is the Holy Spirit: the Father uncreated, the Son uncreated, the Holy Spirit uncreated; the Father infinite, the Son infinite, the Holy Spirit infinite; the Father eternal, the Son eternal, the Holy Spirit eternal.

And yet there are not three Eternals, but one Eternal, just as there are not three Uncreated or three Infinites, but one Uncreated and one Infinite.

In the same way, the Father is almighty, the Son almighty, the Holy Spirit almighty; and yet there are not three Almighties, but one Almighty.

So the Father is God, the Son is God, the Holy Spirit is God; and yet there are not three Gods, but one God.

So the Father is Lord, the Son is Lord, the Holy Spirit is Lord; and yet there are not three Lords, but one Lord.

Just as we are compelled by the Christian truth to acknowledge each distinct person as God and Lord, so also are we prohibited by the catholic religion to say that there are three Gods or Lords.

The Father is not made nor created nor begotten by anyone.

The Son is neither made nor created, but begotten of the Father alone.

The Holy Spirit is of the Father and of the Son, neither made nor created nor begotten, but proceeding.

Thus, there is one Father, not three Fathers; one Son, not three Sons; one Holy Spirit, not three Holy Spirits.

And in this Trinity none is before or after another; none is greater or less than another; but the whole three persons are coeternal with each other and coequal, so that in all things, as has been stated above, the Trinity in Unity and Unity in Trinity is to be worshiped.

Therefore, whoever desires to be saved must think thus about the Trinity.

But it is also necessary for everlasting salvation that one faithfully believe the incarnation of our Lord Jesus Christ.

Therefore, it is the right faith that we believe and confess that our Lord Jesus Christ, the Son of God, is at the same time both God and man.

He is God, begotten from the substance of the Father before all ages; and He is man, born from the substance of His mother in this age: perfect God and perfect man, composed of a rational soul and human flesh; equal to the Father with respect to His divinity, less than the Father with respect to His humanity.

Although He is God and man, He is not two, but one Christ: one, however, not by the conversion of the divinity into flesh, but by the assumption of the humanity into God; one altogether, not by confusion of substance, but by unity of person.

For as the rational soul and flesh is one man, so God and man is one Christ, who suffered for our salvation, descended into hell, rose again the third day from the dead, ascended into heaven, and is seated at the right hand of the Father, God Almighty, from whence He will come to judge the living and the dead.

At His coming all people will rise again with their
    bodies and give an account concerning their own
    deeds.
And those who have done good will enter into eternal
    life, and those who have done evil into eternal fire.
This is the catholic faith; whoever does not believe it
    faithfully and firmly cannot be saved.

—Athanasian Creed (*LSB*, pp. 319–20)

2.

I believe that I cannot by my own reason or strength believe in Jesus Christ, my Lord, or come to Him; but the Holy Spirit has called me by the Gospel, enlightened me with His gifts, sanctified and kept me in the true faith.

In the same way He calls, gathers, enlightens, and sanctifies the whole Christian Church on earth, and keeps it with Jesus Christ in the one true faith.

In this Christian Church He daily and richly forgives all my sins and the sins of all believers.

On the Last Day He will raise me and all the dead, and give eternal life to me and all believers in Christ.

This is most certainly true. Amen.

—Martin Luther's Explanation of the Third Article of the
Apostles' Creed

3.

"I will give thanks to You, O Lord, for though You were angry with me, Your anger turned away, that You might comfort me. Behold, God is my salvation; I will trust, and will not be afraid; for the Lord God is my strength and my song, and He has become my salvation" . . .

"Give thanks to the Lord, call upon His name, make known His deeds among the peoples, proclaim that His name is exalted. Sing praises to the Lord, for He has done gloriously; let this be made known in all the earth. Shout, and sing for joy, O inhabitant of Zion, for great in your midst is the Holy One of Israel" (Isaiah 12). All praise and honor and glory be to the blessed and divine and holy Trinity, Father, Son, and Holy Spirit. Amen.

The Word and Doctrine
The Psalm of the Day
The Liturgical Lesson of the Day
The Scripture Reading for Saturday of the Week
The Book of Concord for the Day

The Prayers

1.
The Long Prayer of the Day

O God, Father, Son, and Holy Spirit, Savior and Preserver of all, bestow on me Your grace, Your wisdom, Your power as I prepare to lead Your people in Your worship. Be not far from me this day as I bend my heart and mind to holy things. Keep all thoughts and temptations of the evil one far from me. I place myself in Your hands. For without Your aid I am nothing and will accomplish nothing with the time before me.

In my sermon preparation today, most wise Father, be with me and teach me. Let not the difficulties of the text or the subject, or thoughts of this world, hinder my preparation of Your preached Word. Let no trial I face in my ministry, no fears, no frustrations, no apparent failures affect my proclamation of Your message. May Your blessed and most wise Spirit speak through my tongue the wonderful truths of the Crucified and Risen One, slain before the foundation of the world for the sins of all mankind. Open the hearts of my hearers tomorrow that ready minds will receive Your lively Word. May it bear much fruit in the lives of the saints. And forbid, Lord, that I should preach to others and forget my own needs.

In the Holy Sacrament strengthen Your people in their holy faith, comfort them with the forgiveness they receive through the body and blood of the eternal Son. Move all our members to be faithful in their use of this blessed Sacrament. Keep their Baptism ever fresh in their hearts and lives. Remind all Your children of the inheritance of the saints that is theirs by water and the Word.

Prevent all who assemble in Your name tomorrow from participating in the liturgy with indifference and apathy. In hymn and chant and verse and prayer and reading move hearts to worship with sincerity and truth. Continue with all who assist me during the worship hour and guide us all with a fatherly hand.

(Special Requests and Thanksgivings)

Continue to watch over Your universal Church and bless all ministers of the Gospel who proclaim Your Word in faithfulness and sincerity. Hear my prayer through Jesus Christ, our Redeemer and Lord. Amen.

2.

The Shorter Prayer of the Day

Great and glorious Lord, You inhabit the praises of Your people. Now receive my honor and reverence for all Your greatness, Your goodness, Your love. I readily acknowledge my dependence upon You for all things in body and soul. Most of all I join with all the saints to honor the gift of Your Son, our Savior.

As I make ready for the high calling in Jesus Christ that I am to exercise tomorrow, attend me with Your spirit of wisdom that my thoughts and words and attitude will reflect Your love for all mankind. Help me in my studies, my prayers, my thoughts, that all I do will be pleasing in Your sight. Touch the hearts of Your people when they gather in Your house for the Divine Service to nourish their souls on the Word of life. I know I am unworthy to be in Your service, but with Your help, O Lord, approve me to be a blessing to Your Church.

May those who kneel at Your altar for the body and blood of Your Son receive His precious gift of forgiveness. Assist our teachers in Sunday School and Bible class as they prepare for their classes this day. Move our delinquents to enter Your house and kneel in repentance at Your altar. May it be evident to the community around us that Your Spirit moves among us.

(Special Requests and Thanksgiving)

Be our God and our children's God now and forever. Hear my prayer through Jesus Christ, the Lamb and Priest and King, the Son and Savior of all. Lord, have mercy. Christ, have mercy. Lord, have mercy. Amen.

3.
The Liturgical Prayer of the Day

O God, the Father of all, especially of those who believe, now hear the prayers of all Your children as they pray for Your Church.

Lord, have mercy.

O Christ, Son of the Highest, Savior of all, Lamb of God, Victor over sin, death, and the devil, ascended and ruling King, bend down and listen to our pleas.

Christ, have mercy.

O Holy Spirit, Giver of life and faith, Sanctifier of the believers, Teacher of the Church, daily Leader of Your chosen ones, hear our prayer.

Lord, have mercy.

O high and holy Trinity, Creator, Redeemer, and Sanctifier of the world, remember Your people and bless our worship.

Almighty God and Lord, have mercy on us.

Remove our sins and guilt far from us, cancel all our offenses and transgressions, drown our insincerity and hardness of heart in the depths of Your mercy, wash us clean from the stain of our evil lives, for You have rescued us from everlasting death by the most precious and holy blood of Jesus Christ, our Redeemer; we thank You.

Almighty God and Lord, have mercy on us.

Be with Your people as they gather for worship and spiritual growth. Strengthen their faith and deepen their joy as they encounter You in Word and Sacrament. Never let them forget their baptismal covenant, which You have sealed by water and the Word.

Lord, have mercy.

Sear the conscience of those outside of Christ that with hungry hearts they may seek the hope of salvation in the Savior. Support the mission program of our church. Never let our congregation fail to do what is necessary for the success of the Gospel message.

Christ, have mercy.

Deliver Your Church from internal fighting and dissension. Let the gentle dew of tranquility and concord cover Your people, and keep us ever faithful to the truth.

Lord, have mercy.

Let us not forsake our first love to You because of the temptations of the world. Let not evil triumph in this world. Encourage Your children to reveal Your burning love to all mankind.

O heavenly Father, have mercy and hear our prayer.

May all who meet Your people meet Christ and His Gospel. May Your people continue to support the ministry in this place. By the power of Your Spirit may our congregation and all its organizations and agencies grow in the grace and knowledge of our Savior, Jesus Christ.

O Lord, have mercy and hear our prayer.

(Special Requests and Thanksgivings)

Above all, O Lord, our God, fill our hearts with love of worship. Let us experience joy, peace, and hope in the worship of the saints. Let none kneel at Your altar to complain or feel sorrow's dread; rather raise hearts and voices in songs of triumph.

O Lord, hear us. Amen.

The Festival Prayer
The Lord's Prayer

1.

Our Father, who art in heaven, hallowed be Thy name. Thy kingdom come, Thy will be done on earth as it is in heaven. Give us this day our daily bread; and forgive us our trespasses as we forgive those who trespass against us; and lead us not into temptation, but deliver us from evil. For Thine is the kingdom and the power and the glory forever and ever. Amen.

2.

Our Father who art in heaven, deliver us from evil. O dear Lord, God and Father, Your Son defeated sin, death, and the devil so that I may enjoy the fruits of His labor. You are faithful to me as you keep me in Your grace. Grant me faithfulness in this life, especially when I experience the attacks of the devil through misery and misfortune, uncertainty and evil. Should I grow weary of life and long for death, give me strength and confidence in my dear Savior's victory over sin, death, and the devil. And, when my last hour comes, mercifully grant me a blessed departure from this valley of sorrow. Grant that in the face of death I do not lose heart or fear it, but, with certain trust and hope in You, remain confident that You will take my soul into Your hands; for the sake of my Savior, Jesus Christ. Amen.

—Martin Luther

The Closing Doxology

1.

The grace of our Lord Jesus Christ, the love of God the Father, and the fellowship of the Holy Spirit be with me now and always. Amen.

2.

Blessed be the Lord, my rock, who trains my hands for war, and my fingers for battle; He is my steadfast love and my fortress, my stronghold and my deliverer, my shield and He in whom I take refuge. Amen.

—Psalm 144:1–2

3.

Not to us, O Lord, not to us, but to Your name I give glory, for the sake of Your steadfast love and Your faithfulness! Amen.

—Adapted from Psalm 115:1

4.

Blessed by the Holy One of Israel,
Who was and is and is to come.
Praise be to the Blessed, the Divine One.
Praise the Holy Trinity now and forever. Amen.

5.

I will extol You, my God and King, and bless Your name forever and ever. Every day I will bless You and praise Your name forever and ever. Great is the Lord, and greatly to be praised, and His greatness is unsearchable. I will declare Your greatness. Amen.

—Psalm 145:1–3, 6b

The Evening Prayer

1.

In Your hands, O Lord, I rest this very night. As the darkness settles over the earth, I pray that You, who are never in darkness, will continue as my Light and Helper; through Jesus Christ, my Lord, Your Son and Only Begotten. Amen.

2.

God of time and peace, opportunities and seasons, hear my prayer for Your divine protection. Cover me this night with Your presence. Close my eyes in tranquility and trust; in the name of Jesus Christ, my Redeemer and Savior. Amen.

3.

Lord God, support me all the day long in this earthly life until the shadows lengthen and the evening falls and the rush and fever of the day is over. By Your great mercy, Lord God, quiet my conscience, still my fears, and fill my heart with the knowledge of Your eternal watch over the saints. In the name and for the sake of Jesus Christ I offer this prayer. Amen.

4.

Watch, dear Lord, with those who wake, or watch, or weep tonight, and give Your angels charge over those who sleep. Tend Your sick ones, O Lord Christ. Rest Your weary ones. Bless Your dying ones. Soothe Your suffering ones. Pity Your afflicted ones. Shield Your joyous ones. And all this for Your love's sake. Amen.

—St. Augustine

2
Seasonal Propers for Use with Matins and Vespers

The *Invitatory* (the antiphon associated with the Venite—Psalm 95) is the reveille or wake-up cry of Matins, calling the worshiper into the praise of the Lord in Psalm 95. Varying with the season, the Invitatory reflects on the God who holds the deep places in His hands and is the Rock of our salvation. When used by an individual, both parts are spoken or sung by the worshiper. If Matins is being said in a family or group setting, the first part of the Invitatory is the variable part sung by the leader, while the second part of the Invitatory is the response of faith and worship made by the assembly or worshiper. The Invitatory is repeated at the conclusion of the Venite to resound the cry to worship God with our whole being. Generally, invitatories are provided for the seasons and principal feasts of the Church Year. Festivals days and occasions would use the Common Invitatory or the one appointed for the season in which the feast or occasion is celebrated.

In the same pattern as the Invitatory with the Venite, an *antiphon* may precede and follow the reading or singing of the Psalm(s), the Magnificat, and the Benedictus. Like the setting for a gem, as a sentence that frames the Psalm or Canticle, an antiphon stresses a key thought that links the Psalm to the theme of the feast day or time in the Church Year. It opens the door of our heart for the praying of the Psalm or Canticle.

The *Responsory* is an echo or reflection upon the readings. Through the responsories, the readings, in relation to the feast day and Church Year, become the concerns of our hearts. They encourage careful listening to God's Word. They rephrase the words of the readings so that they can echo in our voices and souls, turning the readings into prayer and contemplation of the Word. Responsories are provided for all of the seasons, feasts, and festivals of the Church Year.

The Responsory is structured as a series of verses and a common congregational response or refrain. The first two verses of the Responsory proclaim the scriptural revelation of the Lord in relation to the season or feast. The third verse is uniformly, with the exception of Lent, the first half of the Gloria Patri, "Glory be to the Father and to the Son and to the Holy Spirit," glorifying the God whose Word has spoken to us and called us to trust in Him. An individual in private devotion would speak or sing both the leader and congregational parts.

Common

Invitatory

Blessed be God, the Father, the Son,
and the Holy Spirit.*
O come, let us worship Him.

Antiphons

1. Sanctify us in the truth;*
   Your word is truth.
   (John 17:17)

2. Make me to know Your ways,
   O Lord;* teach me Your paths.
   (Psalm 25:4)

3. Bless the Lord, O my soul*
   and all that is within me, bless
   His holy name! *(Psalm 103:1)*

4. O Lord, You hear the desire
   of the afflicted;* You will
   strengthen their heart; You will
   incline Your ear.
   (Psalm 10:17)

5. Oh give thanks to the Lord, for
   He is good;* for His steadfast
   love endures forever! *(Psalm
   107:1)*

Responsory

L: Forever, O Lord, Your Word is
   firmly set in the heavens.
   (Psalm 119:89)

   Blessed are those who hear the
   Word of God and keep it.
   (Luke 11:28)

   Glory be to the Father and to
   the Son and to the Holy Spirit.

C: Lord, I love the habitation of
   Your house and the place where
   Your glory dwells.
   (Psalm 26:8)

Advent

Invitatory

Behold, the Lord comes to save us.*
O come, let us worship Him.

Antiphons

1. Behold, the name of the Lord
   comes from afar;* may the whole
   earth be filled with His glory!
   *(Isaiah 30:27;
   Psalm 72:19)*

2. Come, O Lord, and do not
   delay.* Loosen the bonds of Your
   people Israel. *(Liturgical text)*

3. Rejoice greatly, O Jerusalem!*
   Behold, your king is coming to
   You. *(Liturgical text drawn from
   Zechariah 9:9)*

4. Behold, the Lord shall come and
   all His saints with Him;*
   and in that day the light shall be
   great. Alleluia!
   (Liturgical text)

Responsory

L: Behold, the days are coming,
   says the Lord, when I will raise
   up for David a righteous Branch.
   (Jeremiah 23:5)

   In His days Judah will be saved,
   and Israel will dwell securely.
   (Jeremiah 23:6)

   Glory be to the Father and to
   the Son and to the Holy Spirit.

C: This is the name by which He
   will be called: The Lord Is Our
   Righteousness. *(Jeremiah 23:6)*

The Nativity of Our Lord and Christmastide

Invitatory

Lo, to us the Christ is born.*
O come, let us worship Him.

Antiphons

1. The Lord said to me,* "You are My Son; today I have begotten you." *(Psalm 2:7)*

2. [The Lord] sent redemption to His people.* He has commanded His covenant forever. *(Psalm 111:9)*

3. One of the sons of your body* I will set on your throne. *(Psalm 132:11)*

4. Christ the Lord, our Savior, everlasting God and Mary's Son,* we praise You evermore. *(Liturgical text)*

Responsory

L: The Word became flesh and dwelt among us, full of grace and truth. *(John 1:14)*

In the beginning was the Word, and the Word was with God, and the Word was God. *(John 1:1)*

Glory be to the Father and to the Son and to the Holy Spirit.

C: We have seen His glory, glory as of the only Son from the Father. *(John 1:14)*

The Epiphany of Our Lord and Epiphanytide

Invitatory

The Christ has appeared to us.*
O come, let us worship Him.

Antiphons

1. Ascribe to the Lord glory and strength.* Worship the Lord in the splendor of holiness. *(Psalm 29:1–2)*

2. The Lord has made known His Word. Alleluia!* The Word of His salvation. Alleluia! Alleluia! *(Liturgical text)*

3. A light for revelation to the Gentiles,* and for glory to Your people Israel. *(Luke 2:32)*

4. We saw His star when it rose* and have come to worship Him. *(Matthew 2:2)*

Responsory

L: The Lord will arise upon you, and His glory will be seen upon you. *(Isaiah 60:2)*

Nations shall come to your light, and kings to the brightness of your rising. *(Isaiah 60:3)*

Glory be to the Father and to the Son and to the Holy Spirit.

C: Arise, shine, for your light has come, and the glory of the Lord has risen upon you. *(Isaiah 60:1)*

Lent

Invitatory for Lent

The Lord has redeemed His people.*
    O come, let us worship Him.

Antiphons

1. Man shall not live by bread alone,* but by every word that comes from the mouth of God. *(Matthew 4:4)*

2. Behold, now is the favorable time;* behold, now is the day of salvation. *(2 Corinthians 6:2)*

3. He was oppressed, and He was afflicted, yet He opened not His mouth* and the Lord has laid on Him the iniquity of us all. *(Isaiah 53:7, 6)*

Responsory for Lent

L: We have an advocate with the Father; Jesus is the propitiation for our sins. *(1 John 2:1–2)*

Blessed is he whose transgression is forgiven and whose sin is put away. *(Psalm 32:1)*

We have an advocate with the Father; Jesus is the propitiation for our sins. *(1 John 2:1–2)*

C: He was delivered up to death; He was delivered for the sins of the people. *(Mark 10:33)*

Holy (Maundy) Thursday

Invitatory for Holy Week

Christ became obedient to death, even death on a cross.*
    O come, let us worship Him.

Antiphon

Man shall not live by bread alone,* but by every word that comes from the mouth of God. *(Matthew 4:4)*

Responsory

L: But he would feed you with the finest of the wheat, and with honey from the rock I would satisfy you. *(Psalm 81:16)*

For as often as you eat this bread and drink the cup, you proclaim the Lord's death until He comes. *(1 Corinthians 11:26)*

Just as I have loved you, you also are to love one another. *(John 13:34)*

C: The blood of Jesus, God's Son, cleanses us from all sin. *(1 John 1:7, alt.)*

Good Friday

Invitatory for Holy Week

Christ became obedient to death,
even death on a cross.*
O come, let us worship Him.

Antiphon

He was oppressed, and He was
afflicted, yet He opened not His
mouth* and the Lord has laid on
Him the iniquity of us all.
(Isaiah 53:7, 6)

Responsory

L: He was despised and rejected
by men; a man of sorrows, and
acquainted with grief.
(Isaiah 53:3)

He was oppressed, and He was
afflicted, yet He opened not His
mouth. *(Isaiah 53:7)*

He poured out His soul to death
and was numbered with the
transgressors. *(Isaiah 53:12)*

C: He humbled Himself by
becoming obedient to the point
of death, even death on a cross.
(Philippians 2:8)

Holy Saturday

Invitatory for Holy Week

Christ became obedient to death,
even death on a cross.*
O come, let us worship Him.

Antiphon

Every day I call upon You, O Lord;*
I spread out my hands to You.
(Psalm 88:9)

Responsory

L: Our shepherd, the source of the
water of life, has died. The sun
was darkened when He passed
away. *(Liturgical text)*

He has destroyed the barricades
of hell and overthrown the
sovereignty of the devil.
(Liturgical text)

But in fact Christ has been
raised from the dead, the
firstfruits of those who have
fallen asleep.
(1 Corinthians 15:20)

C: Therefore God has highly
exalted Him and bestowed on
Him the name that is above
every name. *(Philippians 2:9)*

Easter and Eastertide

Invitatory

The Lord is risen indeed. Alleluia!*
O come, let us worship Him.

Antiphons

1. Alleluia!* Alleluia! Alleluia!
   (Liturgical text)

2. I lay down and slept; I woke
   again,* for the Lord sustained
   me. Alleluia! Alleluia! *(Psalm 3:5)*

3. Alleluia! The Lord has risen.
   Alleluia!* Just as He told you.
   Alleluia! Alleluia! *(Luke 24:34;
   Mark 16:7)*

4. Alleluia! Stay with us, for it is
   toward evening* and the day is
   now far spent. Alleluia! Alleluia!
   (Luke 24:29)

Responsory

L: Sing to the Lord and bless His
   name, proclaim His salvation
   from day to day. *(Psalm 96:2)*

   Now is Christ risen from
   the dead and become the
   firstfruits of them that sleep.
   (1 Corinthians 15:20)

   Glory be to the Father and to
   the Son and to the Holy Spirit.

C: Ascribe to the Lord glory and
   strength. Ascribe to the Lord
   the glory due His name. Alleluia,
   alleluia.
   (Psalm 29:1–2)

Ascension and Ascensiontide

Invitatory

The King ascends to heaven.
Alleluia!*
O come, let us worship Him.

Antiphons

1. If I do not go away, the Helper
   will not come to you.* But if
   I go, I will send Him to you.
   Alleluia! *(John 16:7)*

2. Alleluia! Christ has ascended
   on high. Alleluia!* And led
   a host of captives. Alleluia!
   Alleluia! *(Liturgical text based on
   Ephesians 4:8)*

3. I am ascending to My Father
   and your Father,* to My God
   and your God. Alleluia!
   (John 20:17)

Responsory

L: God has gone up with a shout,
   the Lord with the sound of a
   trumpet. *(Psalm 47:5)*

   Go therefore and make disciples
   of all nations, baptizing them in
   the name of the Father and of
   the Son and of the Holy Spirit.
   (Matthew 28:19)

   Glory be to the Father and to
   the Son and to the Holy Spirit.

C: Go into all the world and
   proclaim the gospel to the whole
   creation. Whoever believes
   and is baptized will be saved.
   Alleluia! Alleluia!
   (Mark 16:15–16)

Pentecost (and Its Octave)

Invitatory

The Spirit of the Lord fills the world. Alleluia!*
O come, let us worship Him.

Antiphons

1. When You send forth Your Spirit, they are created,* and You renew the face of the ground. Alleluia! Alleluia! *(Psalm 104:30)*

2. I will not leave you as orphans. Alleluia!* I will come to you, and your hearts will rejoice. Alleluia! *(John 14:18; 16:22)*

Responsory

L: Divided tongues as of fire appeared to them and the Holy Spirit rested on each one of them. *(Acts 2:3)*

They were all filled with the Holy Spirit and began to speak in other tongues as the Spirit gave them utterance. *(Acts 2:4)*

Glory be to the Father and to the Son and to the Holy Spirit.

C: Repent and be baptized every one of you in the name of Jesus Christ for the forgiveness of your sins, and you will receive the gift of the Holy Spirit. Alleluia! Alleluia! *(Acts 2:38)*

Holy Trinity

Invitatory

The Lord has called us by the Gospel.*
O come, let us worship Him.

Antiphons

1. To You do we call, You do we praise, You do we worship,* O blessed Trinity. *(Liturgical text)*

2. Glory be to You, coequal Trinity,* one God before all worlds began, and now and forevermore. *(Liturgical text)*

3. Holy, holy, holy, is the Lord God Almighty,* who was and is and is to come! *(Revelation 4:8)*

Responsory

L: We bless the Father and the Son and the Holy Spirit. *(Liturgical text)*

Blessed are You, O Lord, in the expanse of heaven, and above all to be praised and glorified forever. *(Liturgical text with reference to Genesis 1:8, Psalm 96:4)*

Glory be to the Father and to the Son and to the Holy Spirit.

C: Let us praise Him and magnify Him above all things forever. *(Liturgical text with reference to Psalm 96:4, 1 Chronicles 16:25)*

The Post-Pentecost/ Trinity Season

Proper 3–7

(May 24—June 25) • **Trinity 1–8**

Invitatory

The Lord has gathered us in the true
   faith.*
   O come, let us worship Him.

Antiphons

1. Sanctify us in the truth;*
   Your word is truth. *(John 17:17)*

2. Out of the depths* I cry to You,
   O Lord! *(Psalm 130:1)*

3. Out of Zion, the perfection
   of beauty,* God shines forth.
   (Psalm 50:2)

4. Commit your way to the Lord;*
   trust in Him, and He will act.
   (Psalm 37:5)

5. Preserve my life* from dread of
   the enemy. *(Psalm 64:1)*

6. Make me understand the way of
   Your precepts.* Strengthen me
   according to Your word!
   (Psalm 119:27–28)

Responsory

L: Yours, O Lord, is the power,
   Yours is the kingdom, and You
   are exalted as head above all.
   (Based on 1 Chronicles 29:11)
   Creator of all things, You
   are fearful and strong, You
   are righteous and merciful.
   (Liturgical text)
   Glory be to the Father and to
   the Son and to the Holy Spirit.

C: Give peace in our time, O Lord.
   The Lord be with us all. *(Based
   on 2 Thessalonians 3:16)*

Proper 8–13

(June 26—August 6) • **Trinity 9–13**

Invitatory

The Lord has enlightened us in the
   true faith.*
   O come, let us worship Him.

Antiphons

1. Make me to know Your ways,
   O Lord;* teach me Your paths.
   (Psalm 25:4)

2. It is good to sing praises*
   to our God. *(Psalm 147:1)*

3. Do not forsake* the work of
   Your hands. *(Psalm 138:8)*

4. The Lord* is the stronghold of
   my life. *(Psalm 27:1)*

5. The Lord says to my Lord:*
   "Sit at My right hand."
   (Psalm 110:1)

6. May the Lord give strength to
   His people!* May the Lord bless
   His people with peace!
   (Psalm 29:11)

Responsory

L: Bless the Lord, and ask of Him
   that He would order your ways.
   (Liturgical text)
   Now, my child, remember my
   commandments, and fear not
   that you are poor, for you have
   much wealth if you fear God.
   (Liturgical text)
   Glory be to the Father and to
   the Son and to the Holy Spirit.

C: Commit your work to the
   Lord, and in all seasons let your
   plans rest with Him. *(Based on
   Proverbs 16:3)*

Proper 14–20

(August 7—September 24)
• Trinity 14–19

Invitatory

The Lord has sanctified us in the true
    faith.*
    O come, let us worship Him.

Antiphons

1. Bless the Lord, O my soul,*
   and all that is within me, bless
   His holy name! *(Psalm 103:1)*

2. Blessed be the Lord,* the God of
   Israel. *(Psalm 72:18)*

3. Blessed be the Lord from Zion,*
   He who dwells in Jerusalem!
   (Psalm 135:21)

4. Blessed be* His glorious name
   forever. *(Psalm 72:19)*

5. I was glad when they said to me,*
   "Let us go to the house of the
   Lord!" *(Psalm 122:1)*

6. Lord, teach me to do Your will.*
   Let Your good Spirit lead me on
   level ground! *(Psalm 143:10)*

Responsory

L: We know no other God except
    the Lord, in whom we trust.
    (Liturgical text)

    Let us seek His mercy with tears,
    and humble ourselves before
    Him. *(Liturgical text)*

    Glory be to the Father and to
    the Son and to the Holy Spirit.

C: He does not despise us, nor does
    He take away His salvation from
    us. *(Liturgical text based on Psalm
    69:3)*

Proper 21–25

(September 25—October 29)
• Trinity 20–24

Invitatory

Glorious is God with His angels and
    saints.*
    O come, let us worship Him.

Antiphons

1. O Lord, You hear the desire
   of the afflicted;* You will
   strengthen their heart; You will
   incline Your ear. *(Psalm 10:17)*

2. In the day of my trouble I call
   upon You,* for You answer me.
   (Psalm 86:7)

3. [I will] praise Your name*
   forever and ever. *(Psalm 145:2)*

4. You make known to me*
   the path of life. *(Psalm 16:11)*

5. We praise the Lord* now,
   henceforth, and forever.
   (Liturgical text)

6. I have trusted in Your steadfast
   love;* my heart shall rejoice in
   Your salvation. *(Psalm 13:5)*

Responsory

L: Oh, fear the Lord, you His
    saints, for those who fear Him
    have no lack! *(Psalm 34:9)*
    Send out Your light and Your
    truth; let them lead me!
    (Psalm 43:3)

    Glory be to the Father and to
    the Son and to the Holy Spirit.

C: Fear God and keep His
    commandments, for this is the
    whole duty of man.
    (Ecclesiastes 12:13)

Proper 26–29
(October 30—November 26)
• Trinity 25–27

Invitatory

The Lord will come again in glory.*
> O come, let us worship Him.

Antiphon

1. Oh give thanks to the Lord, for He is good.* For His steadfast love endures forever! *(Psalm 107:1)*

2. Blessed is the man* who fears the Lord. *(Psalm 112:1)*

3. The Lord is merciful and gracious,* slow to anger and abounding in steadfast love. *(Psalm 103:8)*

4. It is good to give thanks to the Lord,* to sing praises to Your name, O Most High. *(Psalm 92:1)*

5. He will command His angels concerning you* to guard you in all your ways. *(Psalm 91:11)*

6. Oh, save Your people and bless Your heritage!* Be their shepherd and carry them forever. *(Psalm 28:9)*

Responsory

L: Look down, O Lord, from Your holy place and consider us; incline Your ear and hear us, O God. *(Liturgical text)*
> Give ear, O Shepherd of Israel, You who lead Joseph like a flock! *(Psalm 80:1)*
> Glory be to the Father and to the Son and to the Holy Spirit.

C: Open Your eyes, O Lord, and behold our desolation. *(Liturgical text)*

The Circumcision and Name of Jesus (January 1)

Invitatory

Lo, to us the Christ is born.*
> O come, let us worship Him.

Antiphon

She will bear a son, and you shall call His name Jesus,* for He will save His people from their sins. *(Matthew 1:21)*

Responsory

L: God has highly exalted Him and bestowed on Him the name that is above every name. *(Philippians 2:9)*
> At the name of Jesus every knee should bow, in heaven and on earth and under the earth. *(Philippians 2:10)*
> Glory be to the Father and to the Son and to the Holy Spirit.

C: Now in Christ Jesus you who once were far off have been brought near by the blood of Christ. *(Ephesians 2:13)*

The Baptism of Our Lord (First Sunday after the Epiphany)

Invitatory

The Christ has appeared to us.*
> O come, let us worship Him.

Antiphon

You are My beloved Son;* with You I am well pleased. *(Mark 1:11b)*

Responsory

L: In those days Jesus came from Nazareth of Galilee and was baptized by John in the Jordan. *(Mark 1:9)*

Tremble, O earth, at the presence of the Lord, at the presence of the God of Jacob. *(Psalm 114:7)*

Glory be to the Father and to the Son and to the Holy Spirit.

C: For as many of you as were baptized into Christ have put on Christ. *(Galatians 3:27)*

The Transfiguration of Our Lord (Last Sunday after the Epiphany)

Invitatory

The Christ has appeared to us.*
O come, let us worship Him.

Antiphon

You are the most handsome of the sons of men;* grace is poured upon Your lips. *(Psalm 45:2a)*

Responsory

L: As for me, I have set my King on Zion, my holy hill. *(Psalm 2:6)*

Out of Zion, the perfection of beauty, God shines forth. *(Psalm 50:2)*

Glory be to the Father and to the Son and to the Holy Spirit.

C: When He appears we shall be like Him, because we shall see Him as He is. *(1 John 3:2)*

The Nativity of St. John the Baptist (June 24)

Invitatory

The Lord has gathered us in the true faith.* O come, let us worship Him.

Antiphon

He will go before Him in the spirit and power of Elijah* to make ready for the Lord a people prepared. *(Luke 1:17a, d)*

Responsory

L: Before I formed you in the womb I knew you, and before you were born I consecrated you. *(Jeremiah 1:5)*

Behold, I have put My words in your mouth. See, I have set you this day over nations and over kingdoms. *(Jeremiah 1:9–10)*

Glory be to the Father and to the Son and to the Holy Spirit.

C: Prepare the way of the Lord; make His paths straight. *(Matthew 3:3)*

Holy Cross (September 14)

Invitatory

The Lord has sanctified us in the true faith.*
O come, let us worship Him.

Antiphon

"Behold, I will lift up My hand to the nations,* and raise My signal to the peoples," [says the Lord.] *(Isaiah 49:22)*

Responsory

L: For behold, by the wood of Your cross joy has come into all the world. *(Liturgical text)*

Look to Jesus, the founder and perfecter of our faith, who for the joy that was set before him endured the cross, despising its shame. *(Hebrews 12:2)*

Glory be to the Father and to the Son and to the Holy Spirit.

C: We adore You, O Lord, and we praise and glorify Your holy resurrection. *(Liturgical text)*

St. Michael and All Angels (September 29)

Invitatory

Glorious is God with His angels and saints.*
O come, let us worship Him.

Antiphon

He will command His angels concerning you* to guard you in all your ways. *(Psalm 91:11)*

Responsory

L: The Lord Jesus will be revealed from heaven with His mighty angels in flaming fire. *(2 Thessalonians 1:7–8)*

When the Lord Jesus comes on that day to be glorified in His saints, and to be marveled at among all who have believed. *(2 Thessalonians 1:10)*

Glory be to the Father and to the Son and to the Holy Spirit.

C: For He will command His angels concerning you to guard you in all your ways. *(Psalm 91:11)*

Reformation (October 31)

Invitatory

The Lord will come again in glory.*
O come, let us worship Him.

Antiphon

I will also speak of Your testimonies before kings* and shall not be put to shame. *(Psalm 119:46)*

Responsory

L: I find my delight in your commandments, which I love. *(Psalm 119:47)*

Now the righteousness of God has been manifested apart from the law, the righteousness of God through faith in Jesus Christ for all who believe. *(Romans 3:21–22)*

Glory be to the Father and to the Son and to the Holy Spirit.

C: I will also speak of Your testimonies before kings and shall not be put to shame. *(Psalm 119:46)*

All Saints' Day and the Common for All Saints (November 1)

Invitatory

The Lord will come again in glory.*
    O come, let us worship Him.

Antiphon

These are the ones coming out of the
    great tribulation.* They have
    washed their robes and made
    them white in the blood of the
    Lamb. *(Revelation 7:14)*

Responsory

L: Then the kingdom of heaven
    will be like ten virgins who took
    their lamps and went to meet
    the bridegroom. *(Matthew 25:1)*

    Trim your lamps, O you wise
    virgins! *(Based on Matthew 25:7)*

    Glory be to the Father and to
    the Son and to the Holy Spirit.

C: At midnight there was a cry,
    "Here is the bridegroom! Come
    out to meet him."
    (Matthew 25:6)

Common for Apostles and Evangelists

Antiphon

How beautiful are the feet of those
    who preach the good news,*
    who publish peace and bring
    good news of salvation.
    (Romans 10:15b; Isaiah 52:7b, alt.)

Responsory

L: When you stand before
    governors and kings for My sake,
    do not be anxious how you are
    to speak or what you are to say.
    (Mark 13:9; Matthew 10:19)

    For it is not you who speak,
    but the Spirit of your Father
    speaking through you.
    (Matthew 10:20)

    Glory be to the Father and to
    the Son and to the Holy Spirit.

C: What you are to say will be given
    to you in that hour.
    (Matthew 10:19)

Common for Martyrs

Antiphon

Fear the Lord, you His saints,*
    for those who fear Him lack
    nothing! *(Psalm 34:9)*

Responsory

L: The Lord keeps all their bones,
    so that not one of them is
    broken. *(Based on John 19:36)*

    When the righteous cry for
    help, the Lord hears and delivers
    them out of all their troubles.
    (Psalm 34:17)

    Glory be to the Father and to
    the Son and to the Holy Spirit.

C: Precious in the sight of the Lord
    is the death of His saints.
    (Psalm 116:15)

Common for Pastors and Teachers in the Church

Antiphon

The Lord has made known His salvation;* He has revealed His righteousness in the sight of the nations. *(Psalm 98:2)*

Responsory

L: On your walls, O Jerusalem, I have set watchmen; all the day and all the night they shall never be silent. *(Isaiah 62:6)*

The Lord filled him with the spirit of wisdom and understanding. *(Liturgical text)*

Glory be to the Father and to the Son and to the Holy Spirit.

C: This is how one should regard us, as servants of Christ and stewards of the mysteries of God. *(1 Corinthians 4:1)*

Common of St. Mary, Mother of Our Lord

Antiphon

My soul magnifies the Lord,* and my spirit rejoices in God my Savior. *(Luke 1:46b–47)*

Responsory

L: The Holy Spirit will come upon you, and the power of the Most High will overshadow you. *(Luke 1:35)*

She gave birth to a male child, one who is to rule all the nations. *(Revelation 12:5)*

Glory be to the Father and to the Son and to the Holy Spirit.

C: Behold, I am the servant of the Lord; let it be to me according to your word. *(Luke 1:38)*

3

The Daily Propers

The following pages contain the collects, the appointed readings, and the hymns according to the outline above.

During The Time of Christmas and The Time of Easter, the appointed collects are the same for both the Three-Year Lectionary and One-Year Lectionary. For the second half of the Church Year, the collects vary between lectionaries, and so each are included in their own section.

THE TIME OF CHRISTMAS

First Sunday in Advent

The Lection		*The Hymn*

A Isaiah 2:1–5   332
Psalm 122 (v. 6)
Romans 13:(8–10) 11–14
Matthew 21:1–11
or Matthew 24:36–44

B Isaiah 64:1–9   332
Psalm 80:1–7 (v. 7)
1 Corinthians 1:3–9
Mark 11:1–10
or Mark 13:24–37

C Jeremiah 33:14–16   332
Psalm 25:1–10 (v. 6)
1 Thessalonians 3:9–13
Luke 19:28–40
or Luke 21:25–36

1Yr. Jeremiah 23:5–8   332
Psalm 24 (v. 7)
Romans 13:(8–10) 11–14
Matthew 21:1–9

The Liturgical Lessons for the Week

M   Isaiah 57:14–21
T   Acts 17:22–34
W   Luke 1:5–7
Th   Isaiah 59:15b–21
F   Revelation 1:1–3
S   Luke 1:8–23

Prayer of the Week

Stir up Your power, O Lord, and come, that by Your protection we may be rescued from the threatening perils of our sins and saved by Your mighty deliverance; for You live and reign with the Father and the Holy Spirit, one God, now and forever. (L01)

or

Lord God, heavenly Father, we thank You, we bless and praise You forever, that You sent Your Son to rule over us poor sinners, who for our transgressions justly deserved to remain in the bondage of sin and Satan, and that in Him You gave us a meek and righteous King, who by His death became our Savior from sin and eternal death. Enlighten, govern, and direct us by Your Holy Spirit, that we may ever remain faithful to this righteous King and Savior, and not, after the manner of the world, be offended by His humble form and despised Word, but, firmly believing in Him, obtain eternal salvation; through Your beloved Son, Jesus Christ, our Lord, who lives and reigns with You and the Holy Spirit, one true God, now and forever. (VD)

Second Sunday in Advent

The Lection		*The Hymn*
A	Isaiah 11:1–10	344
	Psalm 72:1–7 (v. 18)	
	Romans 15:4–13	
	Matthew 3:1–12	
B	Isaiah 40:1–11	344
	Psalm 85 (v. 9)	
	2 Peter 3:8–14	
	Mark 1:1–8	
C	Malachi 3:1–7b	344
	Psalm 66:1–12 (v. 12b)	
	Philippians 1:2–11	
	Luke 3:1–14 (15–20)	
1Yr.	Malachi 4:1–6	336
	Psalm 50:1–15 (v. 15)	
	Romans 15:4–13	
	Luke 21:25–36	

The Liturgical Lessons for the Week

M	Daniel 4:28–37
T	Romans 1:18–25
W	Matthew 7:13–20
Th	Ezekiel 43:1–9
F	Acts 24:24–27
S	John 2:23–25

Prayer of the Week

Stir up our hearts, O Lord, to make ready the way of Your only-begotten Son, that by His coming we may be enabled to serve You with pure minds; through the same Jesus Christ, our Lord, who lives and reigns with You and the Holy Spirit, one God, now and forever. (L02)

or

Lord God, heavenly Father, by Your Son You have revealed to us that heaven and earth shall pass away, that our bodies shall rise again, and that we all shall appear before the judgment seat. Graciously keep us in Your Word by Your Holy Spirit. Establish us in the true faith, defend us from sin, and preserve us in all temptations, that our hearts may not be weighed down with carousing, drunkenness, and cares of this life, but that we may ever watch and pray and, trusting fully in Your grace, await with joy the glorious coming of Your Son, and at last obtain eternal salvation; through Your beloved Son, Jesus Christ, our Lord, who lives and reigns with You and the Holy Spirit, one true God, now and forever. (VD)

Third Sunday in Advent

The Lection		*The Hymn*
A	Isaiah 35:1–10	345
	Psalm 146 (v. 5)	
	James 5:7–11	
	Matthew 11:2–15	
B	Isaiah 61:1–4, 8–11	345
	Psalm 126 (v. 5)	
	1 Thessalonians 5:16–24	
	John 1:6–8, 19–28	
C	Zephaniah 3:14–20	345
	Psalm 85 (v. 2)	
	Philippians 4:4–7	
	Luke 7:18–28 (29–35)	
1Yr.	Isaiah 40:1–8 (9–11)	345
	Psalm 85 (v. 9)	
	1 Corinthians 4:1–5	
	Matthew 11:2–10 (11)	

The Liturgical Lessons for the Week

M	Genesis 8:20–22
T	Colossians 2:1–7
W	Matthew 11:11–15
Th	2 Kings 19:20–31
F	1 Timothy 2:5–7
S	Luke 7:18–27

Prayer of the Week

Lord Jesus Christ, we implore You to hear our prayers and to lighten the darkness of our hearts by Your gracious visitation; for You live and reign with the Father and the Holy Spirit, one God, now and forever. (L03)

Lord God, heavenly Father, You gave Your Son, our Lord Jesus Christ, to become Man and to come into the world that He might destroy the works of the devil, deliver us poor offenders from sin and death, and give us everlasting life. Rule and govern our hearts by Your Holy Spirit that we may seek no other refuge than His Word, and thus avoid the sin to which we are by nature inclined, in order that we may always be found among the faithful followers of Your Son, Jesus Christ, and by faith in Him obtain eternal salvation; through Your beloved Son, Jesus Christ, our Lord, who lives and reigns with You and the Holy Spirit, one true God, now and forever. (VD)

Fourth Sunday in Advent

The Lection		*The Hymn*
A	Isaiah 7:10–17	357
	Psalm 24 (v. 7)	
	Romans 1:1–7	
	Matthew 1:18–25	
B	2 Samuel 7:1–11, 16	357
	Psalm 89:1–5 (19–29) (v. 8)	
	Romans 16:25–27	
	Luke 1:26–38	
C	Micah 5:2–5a	357
	Psalm 80:1–7 (v. 7)	
	Hebrews 10:5–10	
	Luke 1:39–45 (46–56)	
1Yr.	Deuteronomy 18:15–19	357
	Psalm 111 (v. 9)	
	Philippians 4:4–7	
	John 1:19–28	
	or Luke 1:39–56	

The Liturgical Lessons for the Week

M	Zechariah 6:12–15
T	Romans 1:8–17
W	Luke 8:26–39
Th	Isaiah 51:1–8
F	Jude 24–25
S	John 3:22–30

Prayer of the Week

Stir up Your power, O Lord, and come and help us by Your might, that the sins which weigh us down may be quickly lifted by

Your grace and mercy; for You live and reign with the Father and the Holy Spirit, one God, now and forever. (L04)

or

Lord God, heavenly Father, it is good and right that we should give thanks to You, that You have given us a glorious Baptism like that of John the Baptist, and that therein You have promised us the forgiveness of sins, the Holy Spirit, and everlasting life through Your Son, Jesus Christ. By Your grace and mercy preserve us in such faith, that we never doubt Your promise, but be comforted by our Baptism in all temptations. Grant us Your Holy Spirit that we may renounce sin, and ever continue in the righteousness bestowed on us in Baptism, until, by Your grace, we obtain our eternal salvation; through Your beloved Son, Jesus Christ, our Lord, who lives and reigns with You and the Holy Spirit, one true God, now and forever. (VD)

The Nativity of Our Lord—Christmas

Christmas Eve—December 24

The Lection   *The Hymn*

ABC, 1Yr.   Isaiah 7:10–14   359
      Psalm 110:1–4 (v. 2a)
      1 John 4:7–16
      Matthew 1:18–25

Christmas Midnight—December 24

The Lection   *The Hymn*

ABC, 1Yr.   Isaiah 9:2–7   358
      Psalm 96 (v. 2)
      Titus 2:11–14
      Luke 2:1–14 (15–20)

Christmas Dawn—December 25

The Lection   *The Hymn*

ABC Isaiah 62:10–12   375
      Psalm 98 (v. 2)
      Titus 3:4–7
      Luke 2:(1–14) 15–20

1Yr. Micah 5:2–5a   375
      Psalm 80:1–7 (v. 7)
      Titus 3:4–7
      Luke 2:(1–14) 15–20

Christmas Day—December 25

Week after Christmas

Prayer of the Week

(Christmas Eve) O God, You make us glad with the yearly remembrance of the birth of Your only-begotten Son, Jesus Christ. Grant that as we joyfully receive Him as our Redeemer, we may with sure confidence behold Him when He comes to be our Judge; through the same Jesus Christ, our Lord, who lives and reigns with You and the Holy Spirit, one God, now and forever. (L05)

(Christmas Midnight) O God, You make this most holy night to shine with the brightness of the true Light. Grant that as we have known the mysteries of that Light on earth we may also come to the fullness of His joys in heaven; through the same Jesus Christ, Your Son, our Lord, who lives and reigns with You and the Holy Spirit, one God, now and forever. (L06)

(Christmas Dawn) Most merciful God, You gave Your eternal Word to become incarnate of the pure Virgin. Grant Your people grace to put away fleshly lusts, that they may be ready for Your

visitation; through Jesus Christ, our Lord, who lives and reigns with You and the Holy Spirit, one God, now and forever. (L07)

(Christmas Day) Almighty God, grant that the birth of Your only-begotten Son in the flesh may set us free from the bondage of sin; through Jesus Christ, Your Son, our Lord, who lives and reigns with You and the Holy Spirit, one God, now and forever. (L08)

or

Lord God, heavenly Father, we give thanks to You that of Your mercy and compassion You caused Your Son to become incarnate, and through Him redeemed us from sin and everlasting death. So enlighten our hearts by Your Holy Spirit, that we may ever be thankful for such grace, and comfort ourselves thereby in all tribulation and temptation, and at last obtain eternal salvation; through Your beloved Son, Jesus Christ, our Lord, who lives and reigns with You and the Holy Spirit, one true God, now and forever. (VD)

First Sunday after Christmas

	The Lection	*The Hymn*
A	Isaiah 63:7–14	389
	Psalm 111 (v. 9a, b)	
	Galatians 4:4–7	
	Matthew 2:13–23	
B	Isaiah 61:10—62:3	389
	Psalm 111 (v. 9a, b)	
	Galatians 4:4–7	
	Luke 2:22–40	
C	Exodus 13:1–3a, 11–15	389
	Psalm 111 (v. 9a, b)	
	Colossians 3:12–17	
	Luke 2:22–40	
1Yr.	Isaiah 11:1–5	389
	or 2 Samuel 7:1–16	
	Psalm 89:1–8 (v. 8)	
	Galatians 4:1–7	
	Luke 2:(22–32) 33–40	

The Liturgical Lessons for the Week

M*	Zechariah 2:10–13
T	Revelation 5:1–5
W	Luke 5:30–39
Th	1 Samuel 2:1–10

F   Hebrews 3:1–6
S   Luke 12:4–12

The days after Christmas vary with the calendar. These days may be observed as noted above under The Nativity: Week after Christmas

Prayer of the Week

O God, our Maker and Redeemer, You wonderfully created us and in the incarnation of Your Son yet more wondrously restored our human nature. Grant that we may ever be alive in Him who made Himself to be like us; through Jesus Christ, our Lord, who lives and reigns with You and the Holy Spirit, one God, now and forever. (L09)

or

Almighty and everlasting God, direct our actions according to Your gracious will, that in the name of Your beloved Son, we may be made to abound in good works; through the same, Jesus Christ, our Lord, who lives and reigns with You and the Holy Spirit, one true God, now and forever. (*TLH*, p. 57)

or

O almighty and everlasting God, mercifully direct our ways that we may walk in Your Law, and be made to abound in good works; through Your beloved Son, Jesus Christ, our Lord, who lives and reigns with You and the Holy Spirit, one true God, now and forever. (VD)

Second Sunday after Christmas

The Lection	*The Hymn*
ABC* 1 Kings 3:4–15	410
Psalm 119:97–104 (v. 99)	
Ephesians 1:3–14	
Luke 2:40–52	
1Yr. Genesis 46:1–7	385
Psalm 77:11–20 (v. 13)	
1 Peter 4:12–19	
Matthew 2:13–23	

The Liturgical Lessons for the Week

M   Song of Solomon 5:10–16
T   Hebrews 6:13–20
W   John 6:35–40
Th   Proverbs 8:1–21

F   1 John 5:13–21
S   Mark 8:11–21

* The weekly readings will be affected by the calendar. Epiphany, January 6th, takes precedence over any other reading. The readings following Epiphany will then be used.

Prayer of the Week

Almighty God, You have poured into our hearts the true Light of Your incarnate Word. Grant that this Light may shine forth in our lives; through the same Jesus Christ, Your Son, our Lord, who lives and reigns with You and the Holy Spirit, one God, now and forever. (L10)

or

O Lord God, heavenly Father, You allowed Your dear Son, Jesus Christ, to become a stranger and a sojourner in Egypt for our sakes, and led Him safely home to His fatherland. Mercifully grant that we poor sinners, who are strangers and sojourners in this perilous world, may soon be called home to our true fatherland, the kingdom of heaven, where we shall live in eternal joy and glory; through Your beloved Son, Jesus Christ, our Lord, who lives and reigns with You and the Holy Spirit, one true God, now and forever. (VD)

The Epiphany of Our Lord—January 6

The Lection   *The Hymn*

ABC Isaiah 60:1–6   395
        Psalm 72:1–11 (12–15) (v. 18)
        Ephesians 3:1–12
        Matthew 2:1–12

1Yr. Isaiah 60:1–6   395
        Psalm 24 (v. 7)
        Ephesians 3:1–12
        Matthew 2:1–12

The Liturgical Lessons for the Week

M   Zechariah 14:8–11
T   Ephesians 1:7–14
W   Matthew 13:10–17
Th   Genesis 8:1–14
F   Romans 15:14–21
S   Mark 7:24–30

Prayer of the Week

O God, by the leading of a star You made known Your only-begotten Son to the Gentiles. Lead us, who know You by faith, to enjoy in heaven the fullness of Your divine presence; through the same Jesus Christ, our Lord, who lives and reigns with You and the Holy Spirit, one God, now and forever. (L11)

or

Lord God, heavenly Father, You have given us the light of Your Holy Word, the guiding star that leads us to the Christ Child. Send Your Holy Spirit into our hearts, that we may receive this light and make use of it for our salvation, and that we, like the Wise Men, when they were seeking the star, may not be afraid because of any hardship or peril, but put all our trust in Your only-begotten Son as our only Savior, devote our earthly possessions to the advancement of Your kingdom, and in all things serve Him, Your only-begotten Son, Jesus Christ, our Lord, who lives and reigns with You and the Holy Spirit, one true God, now and forever. (VD)

The Baptism of Our Lord

The Lection		*The Hymn*
A	Isaiah 42:1–9	406/407
	Psalm 29 (v. 3)	
	Romans 6:1–11	
	Matthew 3:13–17	
B	Genesis 1:1–5	406/407
	Psalm 29 (v. 3)	
	Romans 6:1–11	
	Mark 1:4–11	
C	Isaiah 43:1–7	406/407
	Psalm 29 (v. 3)	
	Romans 6:1–11	
	Luke 3:15–22	
1Yr.	Joshua 3:1–3, 7–8, 13–17	406/407
	or Isaiah 42:1–7	
	Psalm 85 (v. 9)	
	1 Corinthians 1:26–31	
	Matthew 3:13–17	

The Liturgical Lessons for the Week
M   Genesis 14:17–24
T   Hebrews 7:1–10
W   Matthew 12:46–50

116

Th   Leviticus 8:1–36
F   Acts 10:1–23
S   Luke 9:1–11

Prayer of the Week

Father in heaven, at the Baptism of Jesus in the Jordan River You proclaimed Him Your beloved Son and anointed Him with the Holy Spirit. Make all who are baptized in His name faithful in their calling as Your children and inheritors with Him of everlasting life; through the same Jesus Christ, our Lord, who lives and reigns with You and the Holy Spirit, one God, now and forever. (L12)

or

Lord God, heavenly Father, You manifested Yourself, with the Holy Spirit, in the fullness of grace at the Baptism of Your dear Son, and with Your voice directed us to Him who has borne our sins, that we might receive grace and the remission of sins. Keep us in the true faith; and inasmuch as we have been baptized in accordance with Your command, and the example of Your dear Son, we pray You to strengthen our faith by Your Holy Spirit, and lead us to everlasting life and salvation; through Your beloved Son, Jesus Christ, our Lord, who lives and reigns with You and the Holy Spirit, one true God, now and forever. (VD)

First Sunday after the Epiphany (One-Year Lectionary)

The Lection   *The Hymn*

1Yr. 1 Kings 8:6–13   410
      Psalm 50:1–15 (v. 15)
      Romans 12:1–5
      Luke 2:41–52

The Liturgical Lessons for the Week

M   Genesis 14:17–24
T   Hebrews 7:1–10
W   Matthew 12:46–50
Th   Leviticus 8:1–36
F   Acts 10:1–23
S   Luke 9:1–11

Prayer of the Week

O Lord, mercifully receive the prayers of Your people who call upon You and grant that they both perceive and know what things they ought to do and also may have grace and power faithfully to fulfill the same; through Jesus Christ, Your Son, our Lord, who lives and reigns with You and the Holy Spirit, one God, now and forever. (L13)

or

Lord God, heavenly Father, in mercy You have established the Christian home among us. Rule and direct our hearts, that we may be good examples to children and those subject to us, and not offend them by word or deed, but faithfully teach them to love Your Church and hear Your blessed Word. Give them Your Spirit and grace, that this seed may bring forth good fruit, so that our home life may advance Your glory, honor, and praise, our own improvement and welfare, and give offense to no one; through Your beloved Son, Jesus Christ, our Lord, who lives and reigns with You and the Holy Spirit, one true God, now and forever. (VD)

Second Sunday after the Epiphany

The Lection		*The Hymn*
A	Isaiah 49:1–7	402
	Psalm 40:1–11 (v. 3)	
	1 Corinthians 1:1–9	
	John 1:29–42a	
B	1 Samuel 3:1–10 (11–20)	402
	Psalm 139:1–10 (v. 14)	
	1 Corinthians 6:12–20	
	John 1:43–51	
C	Isaiah 62:1–5	402
	Psalm 128 (v. 5)	
	1 Corinthians 12:1–11	
	John 2:1–11	
1Yr.	Exodus 33:12–23	402
	or Amos 9:11–15	
	Psalm 67 (v. 1)	
	or Psalm 111 (v. 9)	
	Ephesians 5:22–33	
	or Romans 12:6–16	
	John 2:1–11	

The Liturgical Lessons for the Week

M	Isaiah 1:18–20
T	Titus 1:1–4
W	Matthew 8:18–22
Th	Leviticus 10:1–11
F	Acts 26:1–20
S	Mark 8:1–10

Almighty and everlasting God, who governs all things in heaven and on earth, mercifully hear the prayers of Your people and grant us Your peace through all our days; through Jesus Christ, Your Son, our Lord, who lives and reigns with You and the Holy Spirit, one God, now and forever. (L14)

or

Lord God, heavenly Father, we thank You, that by Your grace You have instituted holy matrimony, in which You keep us from unchastity, and other offenses. Graciously send Your blessing upon every husband and wife, that they may not provoke each other to anger and strife, but live peaceably together in love and godliness, receive Your gracious help in all temptations, and raise their children in accordance with Your will. Grant that we all might walk before You in purity and holiness, put our trust in You, and lead such lives on earth, that in the world to come we may have everlasting life, through Your beloved Son, Jesus Christ, our Lord, who lives and reigns with You and the Holy Spirit, one true God, now and forever. (VD)

Third Sunday after the Epiphany

The Lection		*The Hymn*
A	Isaiah 9:1–4	839
	Psalm 27:1–9 (10–14) (v. 1)	
	1 Corinthians 1:10–18	
	Matthew 4:12–25	
B	Jonah 3:1–5, 10	839
	Psalm 62 (v. 8)	
	1 Corinthians 7:29–31 (32–35)	
	Mark 1:14–20	
C	Nehemiah 8:1–3, 5–6, 8–10	839
	Psalm 19:(1–6) 7–14 (v. 14)	
	1 Corinthians 12:12–31a	
	Luke 4:16–30	
1 Yr.	2 Kings 5:1–15a	401
	Psalm 110:1–4 (v. 2a)	
	Romans 1:8–17	
	or Romans 12:16–21	
	Matthew 8:1–13	

The Liturgical Lessons for the Week

M   Jeremiah 33:1–11

119

T	1 Peter 5:1–5
W	Matthew 9:5–15
Th	Numbers 24:10–18
F	1 Timothy 4:12–16
S	John 4:27–38

Prayer of the Week

Almighty and everlasting God, mercifully look upon our infirmities and stretch forth the hand of Your majesty to heal and defend us; through Jesus Christ, Your Son, our Lord, who lives and reigns with You and the Holy Spirit, one God, now and forever. (L15)

or

O almighty and everlasting God, mercifully look upon our infirmities, and in all dangers and necessities stretch forth Your mighty hand to defend us against our enemies; through Jesus Christ, Your Son, who lives and reigns with You and the Holy Spirit, one true God, now and forever. (VD)

Fourth Sunday after the Epiphany

The Lection		*The Hymn*
A	Micah 6:1–8	842
	Psalm 15 (Ps. 16:1)	
	1 Corinthians 1:18–31	
	Matthew 5:1–12	
B	Deuteronomy 18:15–20	842
	Psalm 111 (v. 3)	
	1 Corinthians 8:1–13	
	Mark 1:21–28	
C	Jeremiah 1:4–10 (17–19)	842
	Psalm 71:1–6 (7–11) (v. 12)	
	1 Corinthians 12:31b—13:13	
	Luke 4:31–44	
1Yr.	Jonah 1:1–17	557
	Psalm 96 (v. 2)	
	Romans 8:18–23	
	or Romans 13:8–10	
	Matthew 8:23–27	

The Liturgical Lessons for the Week

M	Haggai 2:1–9
T	1 Corinthians 4:14–21
W	John 4:39–45
Th	Daniel 6:16–24

F   1 Timothy 5:17–25
S   Luke 18:18–30

Prayer of the Week

Almighty God, You know we live in the midst of so many dangers that in our frailty we cannot stand upright. Grant strength and protection to support us in all dangers and carry us through all temptations; through Jesus Christ, Your Son, our Lord, who lives and reigns with You and the Holy Spirit, one God, now and forever. (L16)

or

Lord God, heavenly Father, in Your divine wisdom and fatherly goodness You cause Your children to bear the cross, and send many afflictions upon us to subdue our sinful flesh, and to enliven our hearts to faith, hope, and unceasing prayer. Have mercy upon us, and graciously deliver us out of our trials and afflictions, so that we may perceive Your grace and fatherly help, and with all the saints forever praise and worship You; through Your dear Son, Jesus Christ, our Lord, who lives and reigns with You and the Holy Spirit, one true God, now and forever. (VD)

Fifth Sunday after the Epiphany

The Lection		*The Hymn*
A	Isaiah 58:3–9a	578
	Psalm 112:1–9 (v. 4)	
	1 Corinthians 2:1–12 (13–16)	
	Matthew 5:13–20	
B	Isaiah 40:21–31	398
	Psalm 147:1–11 (v. 5)	
	1 Corinthians 9:16–27	
	Mark 1:29–39	
C	Isaiah 6:1–8 (9–13)	398
	Psalm 138 (v. 5)	
	1 Corinthians 14:12b–20	
	Luke 5:1–11	
1Yr.	Genesis 18:20–33	578
	Psalm 80:1–7 (v. 7)	
	Colossians 3:12–17	
	Matthew 13:24–30 (36–43)	

The Liturgical Lessons for the Week

M   Ezekiel 33:1–6
T   Acts 20:17–27

W	Luke 19:41–48
Th	1 Kings 2:1–4
F	Acts 20:28–38
S	John 5:10–18

Prayer of the Week

O Lord, keep Your family the Church continually in the true faith that, relying on the hope of Your heavenly grace, we may ever be defended by Your mighty power; through Jesus Christ, Your Son, our Lord, who lives and reigns with You and the Holy Spirit, one God, now and forever. (L17)

or

Lord God, heavenly Father, we thank You that You have sown the good seed, Your Holy Word, in our hearts. We pray that by Your Holy Spirit You will cause this seed to grow and bring forth fruit, and defend us from the enemy, that he may not sow tares. Keep us from carnal security, help us in all temptations, and give us at last eternal salvation; through Your beloved Son, who lives and reigns with You and the Holy Spirit, one true God, now and forever. (VD)

Sixth Sunday after the Epiphany (Three-Year Lectionary)

The Lection		*The Hymn*
A	Deuteronomy 30:15–20	394
	Psalm 119:1–8 (v. 1)	
	1 Corinthians 3:1–9	
	Matthew 5:21–37	
B	2 Kings 5:1–14	394
	Psalm 30 (v. 2)	
	1 Corinthians 10:(19–30) 31—11:1	
	Mark 1:40–45	
C	Jeremiah 17:5–8	394
	Psalm 1 (v. 2)	
	1 Corinthians 15:(1–11) 12–20	
	Luke 6:17–26	

The Liturgical Lessons for the Week

M	Joshua 24:19–28
T	1 Timothy 1:18–20
W	Luke 4:40–44
Th	1 Samuel 15:16–23
F	2 Timothy 2:1–7
S	Matthew 15:1–9

Prayer of the Week

O Lord, graciously hear the prayers of Your people that we who justly suffer the consequence of our sin may be mercifully delivered by Your goodness to the glory of Your name; through Jesus Christ, Your Son, our Lord, who lives and reigns with You and the Holy Spirit, one God, now and forever. (L18)

Seventh Sunday after the Epiphany
(Three-Year Lectionary)

The Lection		*The Hymn*
A	Leviticus 19:1–2, 9–18	820 or 834
	Psalm 119:33–40 (v. 35)	
	1 Corinthians 3:10–23	
	Matthew 5:38–48	
B	Isaiah 43:18–25	820 or 834
	Psalm 41 (v. 4)	
	2 Corinthians 1:18–22	
	Mark 2:1–12	
C	Genesis 45:3–15	820 or 834
	Psalm 103:1–13 (v. 8)	
	1 Corinthians 15:21–26, 30–42	
	Luke 6:27–38	

The Liturgical Lessons for the Week

M	Jeremiah 38:1–6
T	1 Timothy 3:1–7
W	Luke 6:1–5
Th	1 Kings 19:1–8
F	2 Timothy 3:10–16
S	Matthew 13:53–58

Prayer of the Week

O God, the strength of all who put their trust in You, mercifully grant that by Your power we may be defended against all adversity; through Jesus Christ, Your Son, our Lord, who lives and reigns with You and the Holy Spirit, one God, now and forever. (L19)

Eighth Sunday after the Epiphany
(Three-Year Lectionary)

The Lection		*The Hymn*
A	Isaiah 49:8–16a	819
	Psalm 115:(1–8) 9–18 (v. 1)	
	1 Corinthians 4:1–13	
	Matthew 6:24–34	
B	Hosea 2:14–20	819
	Psalm 103:1–13 (v. 22)	
	2 Corinthians 2:12—3:6	
	Mark 2:(13–17) 18–22	
C	Jeremiah 7:1–7 (8–15)	819
	Psalm 92 (v. 4)	
	1 Corinthians 15:42–52 (53–58)	
	Luke 6:39–49	

The Liturgical Lessons for the Week

M	Jonah 4:6–11
T	1 Corinthians 14:1–12
W	John 5:19–24
Th	Joshua 1:1–9
F	Titus 3:8–15
S	Luke 6:6–11

Prayer of the Week

O Lord, mercifully hear our prayers and having set us free from the bonds of our sins deliver us from every evil; through Jesus Christ, Your Son, our Lord, who lives and reigns with You and the Holy Spirit, one God, now and forever. (L20)

The Transfiguration of Our Lord—
The Last Sunday after Epiphany

The Lection		*The Hymn*
A	Exodus 24:8–18	413
	Psalm 2:6–12 (v. 6)	
	2 Peter 1:16–21	
	Matthew 17:1–9	
B	2 Kings 2:1–12	413
	or Exodus 34:29–35	
	Psalm 50:1–6 (v. 2)	
	2 Corinthians 3:12–13 (14–18); 4:1–6	
	Mark 9:2–9	
C	Deuteronomy 34:1–12	413
	Psalm 99 (v. 9)	

Hebrews 3:1–6
Luke 9:28–36

1Yr.   Exodus 34:29–35   413
     or Exodus 3:1–14
     Psalm 2 (v. 7)
     2 Peter 1:16–21
     Matthew 17:1–9

The Liturgical Lessons for the Week

M   Psalm 21
T   Acts 15:12–21

Prayer of the Week

O God, in the glorious transfiguration of Your beloved Son You confirmed the mysteries of the faith by the testimony of Moses and Elijah. In the voice that came from the bright cloud You wonderfully foreshowed our adoption by grace. Mercifully make us co-heirs with the King in His glory and bring us to the fullness of our inheritance in heaven; through the same Jesus Christ, our Lord, who lives and reigns with You and the Holy Spirit, one God, now and forever. (L21)

or

O merciful and everlasting God, heavenly Father, we thank You that You have revealed to us the glory of Your Son, and let the light of Your Gospel shine upon us. Guide us by this light that we may walk diligently as Christians in all good works, ever be strengthened by Your grace, and conduct our lives in all godliness; through Your beloved Son, Jesus Christ, our Lord, who lives and reigns with You and the Holy Spirit, one true God, now and forever. (VD)

THE TIME OF EASTER

Septuagesima (One-Year Lectionary)

The Lection   *The Hymn*

1Yr.   Exodus 17:1–7   555
      Psalm 95:1–9 (v. 6)
      1 Corinthians 9:24—10:5
      Matthew 20:1–16

The Liturgical Lessons for the Week

M   Joshua 24:19–28

T	1 Timothy 1:18–20
W	Luke 4:40–44
Th	1 Samuel 15:16–23
F	2 Timothy 2:1–7
S	Matthew 15:1–9

Prayer of the Week

O Lord, favorably hear the prayers of Your people, that we, who are justly punished for our offenses, may be mercifully delivered by Your gracious goodness, for the glory of Your name; through Jesus Christ, Your Son, our Savior, who lives and reigns with You and the Holy Spirit, one true God, now and forever. (*TLH*, p. 61)

or

Lord God, heavenly Father, through Your Holy Word You have called us into Your vineyard. Send Your Holy Spirit into our hearts, that we may labor faithfully in Your vineyard, shun sin and all offense, obediently keep Your Word and do Your will, and put our whole and only trust in Your grace, which You have bestowed upon us so abundantly; through Your Son Jesus Christ, that we might obtain eternal salvation through Him; who lives and reigns with You and the Holy Spirit, one true God, now and forever. (VD)

Sexagesima (One-Year Lectionary)

The Lection	*The Hymn*
1Yr. Isaiah 55:10–13	823/824
Psalm 84 (v. 4)	
2 Corinthians 11:19—12:9	
or Hebrews 4:9–13	
Luke 8:4–15	

The Liturgical Lessons for the Week

M	Jeremiah 38:1–6
T	1 Timothy 3:1–7
W	Luke 6:1–5
Th	1 Kings 19:1–8
F	2 Timothy 3:10–16
S	Matthew 13:53–58

Prayer of the Week

O God, You see that we do not put our trust in anything we do. Mercifully grant that by Your power we may be defended against all adversity; through Jesus Christ, Your Son, our Lord, who lives and reigns with You and the Holy Spirit, one true God, now and forever. (*TLH*, p. 61)

or

Lord God, heavenly Father, we thank You that through Your Son Jesus Christ You have sown Your Holy Word among us. Prepare our hearts by Your Holy Spirit, that we may diligently and reverently hear Your Word, keep it in good hearts, and bring forth fruit with patience; and that we may not incline to sin, but subdue it by Your power, and in all persecutions comfort ourselves with Your grace and continual help; through Your beloved Son, Jesus Christ, our Lord, who lives and reigns with You and the Holy Spirit, one true God, now and forever. (VD)

Quinquagesima (One-Year Lectionary)

The Lection	*The Hymn*
1Yr. 1 Samuel 16:1–13	849
or Isaiah 35:3–7	
Psalm 89:18–29 (v. 20)	
or Psalm 146 (v. 2)	
1 Corinthians 13:1–13	
Luke 18:31–43	

The Liturgical Lessons for the Week

M   Jonah 4:6–11
T   1 Corinthians 14:1–12

Prayer of the Week

O Lord, mercifully hear our prayers, and having set us free from the bonds of sin, defend us from all evil; through Jesus Christ, Your Son, our Lord, who lives and reigns with You and the Holy Spirit, one true God, now and forever.

Ash Wednesday

The Lection	*The Hymn*
ABC Joel 2:12–19	607
Psalm 51:1–13 (14–19) (v. 17)	
2 Corinthians 5:20b—6:10	
Matthew 6:1–6, 16–21	
1Yr. Joel 2:12–19	607
or Jonah 3:1–10	
Psalm 51:1–13 (14–19) (v. 17)	

2 Peter 1:2–11
Matthew 6:(1–6) 16–21

The Liturgical Lessons for the Week
Th   Deuteronomy 7:6–11
F   2 Corinthians 5:1–5
S   Luke 6:46–49

Prayer of the Week

Almighty and everlasting God, You despise nothing You have made and forgive the sins of all who are penitent. Create in us new and contrite hearts that lamenting our sins and acknowledging our wretchedness we may receive from You full pardon and forgiveness; through Jesus Christ, Your Son, our Lord, who lives and reigns with You and the Holy Spirit, one God, now and forever. (L22)

First Sunday in Lent

(*Invocavit* One-Year Lectionary)

The Lection		*The Hymn*
A	Genesis 3:1–21	656/657
	Psalm 32:1–7 (v. 7a)	
	Romans 5:12–19	
	Matthew 4:1–11	
B	Genesis 22:1–18	656/657
	Psalm 25:1–10 (v. 14)	
	James 1:12–18	
	Mark 1:9–15	
C	Deuteronomy 26:1–11	656/657
	Psalm 91:1–13 (v. 1)	
	Romans 10:8b–13	
	Luke 4:1–13	
1Yr.	Genesis 3:1–21	656/657
	or 1 Samuel 17:40–51	
	Psalm 32 (v. 7)	
	or Psalm 118:1–13 (v. 5)	
	2 Corinthians 6:1–10	
	or Hebrews 4:14–16	
	Matthew 4:1–11	

The Liturgical Lessons for the Week
M   Ezekiel 25:1–7
T   2 Corinthians 6:1–10
W   Matthew 19:16–22
Th   Psalm 137:1–9

F   Galatians 2:1–10
S   Matthew 19:23–30

Prayer of the Week

O Lord God, You led Your ancient people through the wilderness and brought them to the promised land. Guide the people of Your Church that following our Savior we may walk through the wilderness of this world toward the glory of the world to come; through Jesus Christ, Your Son, our Lord, who lives and reigns with You and the Holy Spirit, one God, now and forever. (L23)

(Invocavit) O Lord, mercifully hear our prayer, and stretch forth the right hand of Your majesty to defend us from all that rise up against us; through Jesus Christ, Your Son, our Lord, who lives and reigns with You and the Holy Spirit, one true God, now and forever. (*TLH*, p. 62)

or

Lord God, heavenly Father, inasmuch as the adversary does continually afflict us, and as a roaring lion walks about, seeking to devour us: For the sake of the suffering and death of Your Son, Jesus Christ, help us by the grace of the Holy Spirit, and strengthen our hearts by Your Word, that our enemy may not prevail over us, but that we may evermore abide in Your grace, and be preserved unto everlasting life; through Your beloved Son, Jesus Christ, our Lord, who lives and reigns with You and the Holy Spirit, one true God, now and forever. (VD)

Second Sunday in Lent

(*Reminiscere* One-Year Lectionary)

The Lection		*The Hymn*
A	Genesis 12:1–9	708
	Psalm 121 (v. 8)	
	Romans 4:1–8, 13–17	
	John 3:1–17	
B	Genesis 17:1–7, 15–16	708
	Psalm 22:23–31 (v. 22)	
	Romans 5:1–11	
	Mark 8:27–38	
C	Jeremiah 26:8–15	708

Psalm 4 (v. 8)
Philippians 3:17—4:1
Luke 13:31–35

1Yr.   Genesis 32:22–32   615
      Psalm 121 (vv. 1–2)
      1 Thessalonians 4:1–7
        or Romans 5:1–5
      Matthew 15:21–28

The Liturgical Lessons for the Week

M   Leviticus 16:3–14
T   Hebrews 1:10–14
W   Matthew 15:29–31
Th   Genesis 22:15–19
F   Revelation 19:1–8
S   Luke 8:1–3

Prayer of the Week

O God, You see that of ourselves we have no strength. By Your mighty power defend us from all adversities that may happen to the body and from all evil thoughts that may assault and hurt the soul; through Jesus Christ, Your Son, our Lord, who lives and reigns with You and the Holy Spirit, one God, now and forever. (L24)

or

Lord God, heavenly Father, grant us Your Holy Spirit, that He may strengthen our hearts and confirm our faith and hope in Your grace and mercy, so that, although we have reason to fear because of our conscience, our sin, and our unworthiness, we may nevertheless, with the woman of Canaan, hold fast to Your grace, and in every trial and temptation find You a present help and refuge; through Your beloved Son, Jesus Christ, our Lord, who lives and reigns with You and the Holy Spirit, one true God, now and forever. (VD)

Third Sunday in Lent

(*Oculi* One-Year Lectionary)

The Lection   *The Hymn*

A   Exodus 17:1–7   823/824
      Psalm 95:1–9 (v. 6)
      Romans 5:1–8
      John 4:5–26 (27–30, 39–42)

B   Exodus 20:1–17   823/824

Psalm 19 (v. 8)
1 Corinthians 1:18–31
John 2:13–22 (23–25)

C   Ezekiel 33:7–20   823/824
    Psalm 85 (v. 8)
    1 Corinthians 10:1–13
    Luke 13:1–9

1Yr.   Exodus 8:16–24   659
     or Jeremiah 26:1–15
    Psalm 136:1–16 (v. 26)
     or Psalm 4 (v. 8)
    Ephesians 5:1–9
    Luke 11:14–28

The Liturgical Lessons for the Week

M   Job 22:21–30
T   Acts 22:6–16
W   Luke 8:16–18
Th   1 Kings 11:34–39
F   Acts 26:19–23
S   John 7:14–24

Prayer of the Week

O God, whose glory it is always to have mercy, be gracious to all who have gone astray from Your ways and bring them again with penitent hearts and steadfast faith to embrace and hold fast the unchangeable truth of Your Word; through Jesus Christ, Your Son, our Lord, who lives and reigns with You and the Holy Spirit, one God, now and forever. (L25)

(Oculi) Almighty God, look upon the hearty desires of Your humble servants, and stretch forth the right hand of Your majesty to be our defense against all our enemies; through Jesus Christ, Your Son, our Lord, who lives and reigns with You and the Holy Spirit, one true God, now and forever. (*TLH*, p. 63)

or

Lord God, heavenly Father, You have sent Your Son, our Lord Jesus Christ, to take upon Himself our flesh, that He might overcome the devil, and defend us poor sinners against the adversary: We give thanks to You for Your merciful help. Attend us with Your grace in all temptations, preserve us from carnal security, and by Your Holy Spirit keep us in Your Word in Your fear, that we may be delivered from the enemy and obtain eternal salvation; through Your beloved Son, Jesus Christ, our Lord, who lives and reigns with You and the Holy Spirit, one true God, now and forever. (VD)

Fourth Sunday in Lent

(*Laetare* One-Year Lectionary)

The Lection	*The Hymn*
A Isaiah 42:14–21	571 or 972
Psalm 142 (v. 5)	
Ephesians 5:8–14	
John 9:1–41	
or John 9:1–7, 13–17, 34–39	
B Numbers 21:4–9	571 or 972
Psalm 107:1–9 (v. 19)	
Ephesians 2:1–10	
John 3:14–21	
C Isaiah 12:1–6	571 or 972
Psalm 32 (v. 11)	
2 Corinthians 5:16–21	
Luke 15:1–3, 11–32	
1Yr. Exodus 16:2–21	743
or Isaiah 49:8–13	
Psalm 132:8–18 (v. 13)	
Galatians 4:21–31	
or Acts 2:41–47	
John 6:1–15	

The Liturgical Lessons for the Week

M	Leviticus 16:15–24
T	Hebrews 8:1–7
W	Mark 9:30–32
Th	Leviticus 8:5–13
F	Hebrews 8:8–13
S	Luke 23:44–49

Prayer of the Week

Almighty God, our heavenly Father, Your mercies are new every morning; and though we deserve only punishment, You receive us as Your children and provide for all our needs of body and soul. Grant that we may heartily acknowledge Your merciful goodness, give thanks for all Your benefits, and serve You in willing obedience; through Jesus Christ, Your Son, our Lord, who lives and reigns with You and the Holy Spirit, one God, now and forever. (L26)

(Laetare) Almighty God, grant that we, who deserve to be punished for our evil deeds, may mercifully be relieved by the comfort of Your grace; through Jesus Christ, Your Son, our Lord, who lives and reigns with You and the Holy Spirit, one true God, now and forever. (*TLH*, p. 64)

or

Lord God, heavenly Father, by Your Son You fed five thousand men in the wilderness with five loaves and two fish. Graciously abide also with us in the fullness of Your blessing. Preserve us from greed and the cares of this life, that we may seek first Your kingdom and Your righteousness, and in all things perceive Your fatherly goodness; through Jesus Christ, who lives and reigns with You and the Holy Spirit, one true God, now and forever. (VD)

Fifth Sunday in Lent

(*Judica* One-Year Lectionary)

The Lection		*The Hymn*
A	Ezekiel 37:1–14	430
	Psalm 130 (v. 7)	
	Romans 8:1–11	
	John 11:1–45 (46–53)	
	or John 11:17–27, 38–53	
B	Jeremiah 31:31–34	430
	Psalm 119:9–16 (v. 10)	
	Hebrews 5:1–10	
	Mark 10:(32–34) 35–45	
C	Isaiah 43:16–21	430
	Psalm 126 (v. 3)	
	Philippians 3:(4b–7) 8–14	
	Luke 20:9–20	
1Yr.	Genesis 22:1–14	430
	Psalm 43 (v. 5)	
	Hebrews 9:11–15	
	John 8:(42–45) 46–59	

The Liturgical Lessons for the Week

M	Job 25:1–6
T	Hebrews 7:11–19
W	Luke 23:1–5
Th	Leviticus 16:1–5
F	Revelation 15:1–8
S	John 7:25–31

Almighty God, by Your great goodness mercifully look upon Your people that we may be governed and preserved evermore in body and soul; through Jesus Christ, Your Son, our Lord, who lives and reigns with You and the Holy Spirit, one God, now and forever. (L27)

Palm Sunday/Sunday of the Passion

The Lection	*The Hymn*
A John 12:12–19 (Procession)	442
Isaiah 50:4–9a	438
Psalm 118:19–29 (v. 26)	
or Psalm 31:9–16 (v. 5)	
Philippians 2:5–11	
Matthew 26:1—27:66	
or Matthew 27:11–66	
or John 12:20–43	
B John 12:12–19 (Procession)	442
Zechariah 9:9–12	438
Psalm 118:19–29 (v. 26)	
or Psalm 31:9–16 (v. 5)	
Philippians 2:5–11	
Mark 14:1—15:47	
or Mark 15:1–47	
or John 12:20–43	
C John 12:12–19 (Procession)	442
Deuteronomy 32:36–39	438
Psalm 118:19–29 (v. 26)	
or Psalm 31:9–16 (v. 5)	
Philippians 2:5–11	
Luke 22:1—23:56	
or Luke 23:1–56	
or John 12:20–43	
1Yr. Matthew 21:1–9 (Procession)	442
or John 12:12–19 (Procession)	
Zechariah 9:9–12	438
Psalm 118:19–29 (v. 26)	
or Psalm 31:9–16 (v. 5)	
Philippians 2:5–11	
Matthew 26:1—27:66	
or Matthew 27:11–54	

Prayer of the Day

Almighty and everlasting God, You sent Your Son, our Savior Jesus Christ, to take upon Himself our flesh and to suffer death upon the cross. Mercifully grant that we may follow the example of His great humility and patience and be made partakers of His resurrection; through the same Jesus Christ, our Lord, who lives and reigns with You and the Holy Spirit, one God, now and forever. (L28)

or

Almighty and everlasting God, You have caused Your beloved Son to take our nature upon Himself, that He might give us the example of humility and suffer death upon the cross for our sins. Mercifully grant us a believing knowledge of this, that we may follow the example of His patience and be made partakers of the benefits of His sacred Passion and death; through Your beloved Son, Jesus Christ, our Lord, who lives and reigns with You and the Holy Spirit, one true God, now and forever. (VD)

Monday in Holy Week

The Lection	*The Hymn*
ABC Isaiah 50:5–10	434
Psalm 36:5–10 (v. 9)	
Hebrews 9:11–15	
Matthew 26:1—27:66	
or John 12:1–23	
1Yr. Isaiah 50:5–10	434
Psalm 36:5–10 (v. 9)	
1 Peter 2:21–24	
John 12:1–36 (37–43)	

Prayer of the Day

Almighty God, grant that in the midst of our failures and weaknesses we may be restored through the Passion and intercession of Your only-begotten Son, who lives and reigns with You and the Holy Spirit, one God, now and forever. (L29)

Tuesday in Holy Week

The Lection	*The Hymn*
ABC Isaiah 49:1–7	453
Psalm 71:1–14 (v. 12)	
1 Corinthians 1:18–25 (26–31)	
Mark 14:1—15:47	
or John 12:23–50	
1Yr. Jeremiah 11:18–20	453

Psalm 54 (v. 4)
1 Timothy 6:12–14
Mark 14:1—15:47

Prayer of the Day

Almighty and everlasting God, grant us by Your grace so to pass through this holy time of our Lord's Passion that we may obtain the forgiveness of our sins; through Jesus Christ, Your Son, our Lord, who lives and reigns with You and the Holy Spirit, one God, now and forever. (L30)

Wednesday in Holy Week

The Lection		*The Hymn*
ABC	Isaiah 62:11—63:7	425/426
	Psalm 70 (v. 5)	
	Romans 5:6–11	
	Luke 22:1—23:56	
	or John 13:16–38	
1Yr.	Isaiah 62:11—63:7	425/426
	Psalm 60 (v. 5)	
	Revelation 1:5b–7	
	Luke 22:1—23:56	

Prayer of the Day

Merciful and everlasting God, You did not spare Your only Son but delivered Him up for us all to bear our sins on the cross. Grant that our hearts may be so fixed with steadfast faith in Him that we fear not the power of sin, death, and the devil; through the same Jesus Christ, our Lord, who lives and reigns with You and the Holy Spirit, one God, now and forever. (L31)

Holy (Maundy) Thursday

The Lection		*The Hymn*
A	Exodus 24:3–11	617
	Psalm 116:12–19 (v. 17)	
	Hebrews 9:11–22	
	Matthew 26:17–30	
B	Exodus 24:3–11	617
	Psalm 116:12–19 (v. 17)	
	1 Corinthians 10:16–17	
	Mark 14:12–26	
C	Jeremiah 31:31–34	617

Psalm 116:12–19 (v. 17)
Hebrews 10:15–25
Luke 22:7–20

ABC (alt.)Exodus 12:1–14   617
       Psalm 116:12–19 (v. 17)
       1 Corinthians 11:23–32
       John 13:1–17, 31b–35

1Yr.   Exodus 12:1–14   617
         or Exodus 24:3–11
       Psalm 116:12–19 (v. 17)
       1 Corinthians 11:23–32
       John 13:1–15 (34–35)

Prayer of the Day

O Lord, in this wondrous Sacrament You have left us a remembrance of Your passion. Grant that we may so receive the sacred mystery of Your body and blood that the fruits of Your redemption may continually be manifest in us; for You live and reign with the Father and the Holy Spirit, one God, now and forever. (L32)

or

O Lord Jesus Christ, we thank You, that of Your infinite mercy You have instituted this Your Sacrament, in which we eat Your body and drink Your blood. Mercifully grant us, that by Your Holy Spirit we may not receive this gift unworthily, but that we may confess our sins, remember Your agony and death, believe the forgiveness of sin, and day by day grow in faith and love, until we obtain eternal salvation; through You, who live and reign with the Father and the Holy Spirit, one true God, now and forever. (VD)

Good Friday

The Lection	*The Hymn*
ABC Isaiah 52:13—53:12	454
Psalm 22 (v. 1)	
or Psalm 31 (v. 1)	
Hebrews 4:14–16; 5:7–9	
John 18:1—19:42	
or John 19:17–30	
1Yr. Isaiah 52:13—53:12	454
Psalm 22 (v. 1)	
or Psalm 31 (v. 1)	
2 Corinthians 5:14–21	
John 18:1—19:42	

Prayer of the Day

Almighty God, graciously behold this Your family for whom our Lord Jesus Christ was willing to be betrayed and delivered into the hands of sinful men to suffer death upon the cross; through the same Jesus Christ, Your Son, our Lord, who lives and reigns with You and the Holy Spirit, one God, now and forever. (L33)

or

Almighty and everlasting God, You willed that Your Son should bear for us the pains of the cross, that You might remove from us the power of the adversary. Help us to remember and give thanks for our Lord's Passion that we may obtain remission of sin and redemption from everlasting death; through our Lord Jesus Christ. (VD)

Holy Saturday

The Lection		*The Hymn*
ABC	Daniel 6:1–24	448
	Psalm 16 (v. 10)	
	1 Peter 4:1–8	
	Matthew 27:57–66	
1Yr.	Daniel 6:1–24	448
	Psalm 16 (v. 10)	
	1 Peter 3:17–22	
	Matthew 27:57–66	

Prayer of the Day

O God, creator of heaven and earth, grant that as the crucified body of Your dear Son was laid in the tomb and rested on this holy Sabbath, so we may await with Him the coming of the third day, and rise with Him to newness of life, who lives and reigns with You and the Holy Spirit, one God, now and forever. (L34)

The Resurrection of Our Lord

Vigil of Easter

See the readings appointed in the *LSB Altar Book*, pp. 537–541 and p. 549.

Prayer of the Day

O God, You made this most holy night to shine with the glory of the Lord's resurrection. Preserve in us the spirit of adoption which

You have given so that, made alive in body and soul, we may serve You purely; through Jesus Christ, Your Son, our Lord, who lives and reigns with You and the Holy Spirit, one God, now and forever. (466)

The Resurrection of Our Lord
Easter Sunrise

The Lection		*The Hymn*
A	Exodus 14:10—15:1	467
	Psalm 118:15–29 (v. 1)	
	or The Song of Moses and Israel	
	1 Corinthians 15:1–11	
	John 20:1–18	
B	Exodus 15:1–11	467
	Psalm 118:15–29 (v. 1)	
	1 Corinthians 5:6b–8	
	John 20:1–18	
C	Job 19:23–27	467
	Psalm 118:15–29 (v. 1)	
	1 Corinthians 15:51–57	
	John 20:1–18	
1Yr.	Isaiah 25:6–9	467
	or Exodus 14:10—15:1	
	Psalm 16 (v. 11)	
	or The Song of Moses and Israel	
	1 Corinthians 15:1–11	
	or 1 Corinthians 15:12–25	
	John 20:1–18	

Prayer of the Day

Almighty God, through Your only-begotten Son, Jesus Christ, You overcame death and opened to us the gate of everlasting life. We humbly pray that we may live before You in righteousness and purity forever; through the same Jesus Christ, our Lord, who lives and reigns with You and the Holy Spirit, one God, now and forever. (L35)

The Resurrection of Our Lord
Easter Day

The Lection		*The Hymn*
A	Acts 10:34–43	458
	or Jeremiah 31:1–6	
	Psalm 16 (v. 10)	
	Colossians 3:1–4	

Matthew 28:1–10

B   Isaiah 25:6–9   458
       Psalm 16 (v. 10)
       1 Corinthians 15:1–11
       Mark 16:1–8

C   Isaiah 65:17–25   458
       Psalm 16 (v. 10)
       1 Corinthians 15:19–26
       Luke 24:1–12

1Yr.   Job 19:23–27   458
       Psalm 118:15–29 (v. 1)
       1 Corinthians 5:6–8
        or 1 Corinthians 15:51–57
       Mark 16:1–8

Prayer of the Day

Almighty God the Father, through Your only-begotten Son, Jesus Christ, You have overcome death and opened the gate of everlasting life to us. Grant that we, who celebrate with joy the day of our Lord's resurrection, may be raised from the death of sin by Your life-giving Spirit; through Jesus Christ, our Lord, who lives and reigns with You and the Holy Spirit, one God, now and forever. (L36)

or

O God, for our redemption You gave Your only-begotten Son to the death of the cross and by His glorious resurrection delivered us from the power of the enemy. Grant that all our sin may be drowned through daily repentance and that day by day we may arise to live before You in righteousness and purity forever; through Jesus Christ, our Lord, who lives and reigns with You and the Holy Spirit, one God, now and forever. (L37)

or

O almighty God, grant that we who celebrate the solemnities of the Lord's resurrection may by the renewal of Your Holy Spirit rise again from the death of the soul and walk in newness of life; through Jesus Christ, Your Son, our Lord, who lives and reigns with You and the Holy Spirit, one true God, now and forever. (*TLH*, p. 68)

or

Lord God, heavenly Father, You delivered Your Son for our offenses, and raised Him again for our justification. Grant us Your Holy Spirit, that He may rule and govern us according to Your will. Graciously keep us in the true faith, defend us from all sins, and after this life raise us to eternal life; through Your beloved Son, who lives and reigns with You and the Holy Spirit, one true God, now and forever. (VD)

The Resurrection of Our Lord
Easter Monday

The Lection		*The Hymn*
ABC	Exodus 15:1–18	463
	or Daniel 12:1c–3	
	Psalm 100 (v. 5)	
	Acts 10:34–43	
	or 1 Corinthians 5:6b–8	
	Luke 24:13–35 (36–49)	
1Yr.	Exodus 15:1–18	463
	Psalm 100 (v. 5)	
	Acts 10:34–43	
	Luke 24:13–35	

Prayer of the Day

O God, in the paschal feast You restore all creation. Continue to send Your heavenly gifts upon Your people that they may walk in perfect freedom and receive eternal life; through Jesus Christ, Your Son, our Lord, who lives and reigns with You and the Holy Spirit, one God, now and forever. (L38)

The Resurrection of Our Lord
Easter Tuesday

The Lection		*The Hymn*
ABC	Daniel 3:8–28	490
	Psalm 2 (v. 7)	
	Acts 13:26–33	
	Luke 24:36–49	
1Yr.	Daniel 3:8–28	490
	Psalm 2 (v. 7)	
	Acts 13:26–33	
	Luke 24:36–48 (49)	

Prayer of the Day

Prayer of the Day

Almighty God, through the resurrection of Your Son You have secured peace for our troubled consciences. Grant us this peace evermore that trusting in the merit of Your Son we may come at last to the perfect peace of heaven; through the same Jesus Christ, Your Son, our Lord, who lives and reigns with You and the Holy Spirit, one God, now and forever. (L39)

The Resurrection of Our Lord
Easter Wednesday

The Lection		*The Hymn*
ABC, 1Yr.	Acts 3:13–15, 17–19	485
	Psalm 61 (vv. 6–7)	
	Colossians 3:1–7	
	or 1 Corinthians 11:23–26	
	John 21:1–14	

The Liturgical Lessons for the Week

Th	Matthew 28:11–15
F	Revelation 18:1–10
S	Mark 16:9–20

Prayer of the Day

Almighty God, by the glorious resurrection of Your Son, Jesus Christ, You destroyed death and brought life and immortality to light. Grant that we who have been raised with Him may abide in His presence and rejoice in the hope of eternal glory; through the same Jesus Christ, our Lord, who lives and reigns with You and the Holy Spirit, one God, now and forever. (L40)

Second Sunday of Easter
(*Quasimodogeniti* One-Year Lectionary)

The Lection		*The Hymn*
A	Acts 5:29–42	470/471
	Palm 148 (v. 13)	
	1 Peter 1:3–9	
	John 20:19–31	
B	Acts 4:32–35	470/471
	Psalm 148 (v. 13)	
	1 John 1:1—2:2	
	John 20:19–31	

C	Acts 5:12–20 (21–32)	470/471
	Psalm 148 (v. 13)	
	Revelation 1:4–18	
	John 20:19–31	
1Yr.	Ezekiel 37:1–14	470/471
	Psalm 33 (v. 6)	
	1 John 5:4–10	
	John 20:19–31	

The Liturgical Lessons for the Week

M	Isaiah 10:20–27
T	Revelation 19:11–16
W	Matthew 9:18–26
Th	Hosea 14:1–7
F	Revelation 20:11–15
S	Matthew 20:29–34

Prayer of the Week

Almighty God, grant that we who have celebrated the Lord's resurrection may by Your grace confess in our life and conversation that Jesus is Lord and God; through the same Jesus Christ, Your Son, who lives and reigns with You and the Holy Spirit, one God, now and forever. (L41)

or

Lord God, heavenly Father, we thank You, that of Your indescribable grace, for the sake of Your Son, You have given us the holy Gospel, and have instituted the Holy Sacraments, that through these we may have comfort and forgiveness of sin. Mercifully grant us Your Holy Spirit, that we may heartily believe Your Word; and through the Holy Sacraments day by day establish our faith, until we at last obtain eternal salvation; through Jesus Christ our Lord, who lives and reigns with You and the Holy Spirit, one true God, now and forever. (VD)

Third Sunday of Easter
(*Misericordias Domini* One-Year Lectionary)

The Lection		*The Hymn*
A	Acts 2:14a, 36–41	483
	Psalm 116:1–14 (v. 5)	
	1 Peter 1:17–25	
	Luke 24:13–35	
B	Acts 3:11–21	483
	Psalm 4 (v. 7)	

                1 John 3:1–7
                Luke 24:36–49
C   Acts 9:1–22   483
                Psalm 30 (vv. 11a, 12b)
                Revelation 5:(1–7) 8–14
                John 21:1–14 (15–19)
1Yr.   Ezekiel 34:11–16   709
                Psalm 23 (v. 6)
                1 Peter 2:21–25
                John 10:11–16

The Liturgical Lessons for the Week
M   Isaiah 25:1–5
T   Acts 18:1–11
W   John 16:16–24
Th   Exodus 14:1–18
F   2 Timothy 4:9–18
S   Mark 3:7–12

Prayer of the Week

O God, through the humiliation of Your Son You raised up the fallen world. Grant to Your faithful people, rescued from the peril of everlasting death, perpetual gladness and eternal joys; through Jesus Christ, our Lord, who lives and reigns with You and the Holy Spirit, one God, now and forever. (L42)

or

Lord God, heavenly Father, out of Your fatherly goodness You have been mindful of us poor, miserable sinners, and have given Your beloved Son to be our Shepherd, not only to nourish us by His Word, but also to defend us from sin, death, and the devil. Mercifully grant us Your Holy Spirit, that, even as this Shepherd knows us and helps us in every affliction, we also may know Him, and, trusting in Him, seek help and comfort in Him, from our hearts obey His voice, and obtain eternal salvation; through Your beloved Son, Jesus Christ, our Lord, who lives and reigns with You and the Holy Spirit, one true God, now and forever. (VD)

Fourth Sunday of Easter
(*Jubilate* One-Year Lectionary)

The Lection   *The Hymn*
A   Acts 2:42–47   709

Psalm 23 (v. 1)
1 Peter 2:19–25
John 10:1–10

B   Acts 4:1–12   709
    Psalm 23 (v. 6)
    1 John 3:16–24
    John 10:11–18

C   Acts 20:17–35   709
    Psalm 23 (v. 4)
    Revelation 7:9–17
    John 10:22–30

1Yr. Isaiah 40:25–31   483
        or Lamentations 3:22–33
      Psalm 147:1–11 (v. 5)
      1 Peter 2:11–20
        or 1 John 3:1–3
      John 16:16–22

The Liturgical Lessons for the Week

M   Exodus 14:19–25
T   1 John 2:18–25
W   John 21:15–19
Th   2 Kings 20:1–11
F   Philippians 4:21–23
S   Mark 3:7–12

Prayer of the Week

Almighty God, merciful Father, since You have wakened from death the Shepherd of Your sheep, grant us Your Holy Spirit that when we hear the voice of our Shepherd we may know Him who calls us each by name and follow where He leads; through the same Jesus Christ, Your Son, our Lord, who lives and reigns with You and the Holy Spirit, one God, now and forever. (L43)

(Jubilate) Almighty God, You show those in error the light of Your truth so that they may return to the way of righteousness. Grant faithfulness to all who are admitted into the fellowship of Christ's Church that they may avoid whatever is contrary to their confession and follow all such things as are pleasing to You; through Jesus Christ, Your Son, our Lord, who lives and reigns with You and the Holy Spirit, one God, now and forever. (L44)

or

Lord God, heavenly Father, of Your fatherly goodness You allow Your children to come under Your chastening rod here on earth, that we might be like Your only-begotten Son in suffering and hereafter in glory. Comfort us by Your Holy Spirit in all temptations and afflictions, that we may not fall into despair, but that we may continually trust in Your Son's promise, that our trials will endure but a little while, and will then be followed by eternal joy, in order that, in patient hope, we may overcome all evil, and at last obtain eternal salvation; through Your Son, Jesus Christ our Lord, who lives and reigns with You and the Holy Spirit, one true God, now and forever. (VD)

Fifth Sunday of Easter
(*Cantate* One-Year Lectionary)

The Lection		*The Hymn*
A	Acts 6:1–9; 7:2a, 51–60	633
	Psalm 146 (v. 2)	
	1 Peter 2:2–10	
	John 14:1–14	
B	Acts 8:26–40	633
	Psalm 150 (v. 6)	
	1 John 4:1–11 (12–21)	
	John 15:1–8	
C	Acts 11:1–18	633
	Psalm 148 (v. 13)	
	Revelation 21:1–7	
	John 16:12–22	
	or John 13:31–35	
1Yr.	Isaiah 12:1–6	556
	Psalm 66:1–8 (v. 5)	
	James 1:16–21	
	John 16:5–15	

The Liturgical Lessons for the Week

M	Isaiah 40:25–31
T	Jude 1–7
W	Mark 5:1–13
Th	Obadiah 15–21
F	Revelation 22:18–21
S	Luke 5:17–26

Prayer of the Week

O God, You make the minds of Your faithful to be of one will. Grant that we may love what You have commanded and desire what

You promise, that among the many changes of this world our hearts may be fixed where true joys are found; through Jesus Christ, Your Son, our Lord, who lives and reigns with You and the Holy Spirit, one God, now and forever. (L45)

or

Lord God, heavenly Father, through Your Son You promised us Your Holy Spirit, that He should convince the world of sin, of righteousness, and of judgment. Graciously enlighten our hearts, that we may confess our sins, through faith in Christ obtain everlasting righteousness, and in all our trials and temptations retain this consolation: that Christ is Lord over the devil and death and all things, and that He will graciously deliver us out of all our afflictions, and make us forever partakers of eternal salvation; through Your Son, Jesus Christ, our Lord, who lives and reigns with You and the Holy Spirit, one true God, now and forever. (VD)

Sixth Sunday of Easter
(*Rogate* One-Year Lectionary)

The Lection		*The Hymn*
A	Acts 17:16–31	556
	Psalm 66:8–20 (v. 8)	
	1 Peter 3:13–22	
	John 14:15–21	
B	Acts 10:34–48	556
	Psalm 98 (v. 2)	
	1 John 5:1–8	
	John 15:9–17	
C	Acts 16:9–15	556
	Psalm 67 (v. 3)	
	Revelation 21:9–14, 21–27	
	John 16:23–33	
	or John 5:1–9	
1Yr.	Numbers 21:4–9	766
	Psalm 107:1–9 (v. 19)	
	1 Timothy 2:1–6	
	or James 1:22–27	
	John 16:23–30 (31–33)	

The Liturgical Lessons for the Week

M	Ezekiel 39:24–29
T	Acts 19:1–7
W	Luke 10:21–24

Prayer of the Week

O God, the giver of all that is good, by Your holy inspiration grant that we may think those things that are right and by Your merciful guiding accomplish them; through Jesus Christ, Your Son, our Lord, who lives and reigns with You and the Holy Spirit, one God, now and forever. (L46)

or

Lord God, heavenly Father, through Your Son You have promised us that whatever we ask in His name You will give us. Mercifully keep us in Your Word, and grant us Your Holy Spirit, that He may govern us according to Your will; protect us from the power of the devil, from false doctrine and worship; and also defend our lives against all danger. Grant us Your blessing and peace, that we may in all things perceive Your merciful help, and both now and forever praise and glorify You as our gracious Father; through our Lord Jesus Christ, Your Son, who lives and reigns with You and the Holy Spirit, one true God, now and forever. (VD)

The Ascension of Our Lord

The Lection		*The Hymn*
ABC	Acts 1:1–11	491
	Psalm 47 (v. 5)	
	Ephesians 1:15–23	
	Luke 24:44–53	
1Yr.	2 Kings 2:5–15	491
	Psalm 110 (v. 1)	
	Acts 1:1–11	
	Mark 16:14–20	
	or Luke 24:44–53	

The Liturgical Lessons for the Week

F	Acts 21:7–14
S	John 16:25–33

Prayer of the Week

Almighty God, as Your only-begotten Son, our Lord Jesus Christ, ascended into the heavens, so may we also ascend in heart and mind and continually dwell there with Him, who lives and reigns with You and the Holy Spirit, one God, now and forever. (L47)

or

O Jesus Christ, almighty Son of God, You are no longer in humiliation here on earth, but are seated at the right hand of Your Father, Lord over all things. Mercifully send us Your Holy Spirit. Give Your Church pious pastors, preserve Your Word, control and restrain the devil and all who would oppress us. Uphold Your kingdom with Your might, until all Your enemies have been put under Your feet, that we may hold the victory over sin, death, and the devil; through You, who live and reign with God the Father and the Holy Spirit, one true God, now and forever. (VD)

Seventh Sunday of Easter
(*Exaudi* Sunday after the Ascension One-Year Lectionary)

The Lection		*The Hymn*
A	Acts 1:12–26	539
	Psalm 68:1–10 (v. 32)	
	1 Peter 4:12–19; 5:6–11	
	John 17:1–11	
B	Acts 1:12–26	539
	Psalm 1 (v. 6)	
	1 John 5:9–15	
	John 17:11b–19	
C	Acts 1:12–26	539
	Psalm 133 (v. 1)	
	Revelation 22:1–6 (7–11) 12–20	
	John 17:20–26	
1Yr.	Ezekiel 36:22–28	539
	Psalm 51:1–12 (v. 10)	
	1 Peter 4:7–11 (12–14)	
	John 15:26—16:4	

The Liturgical Lessons for the Week

M	Joel 3:16–21
T	Acts 3:1–10
W	Matthew 7:7–12
Th	Habakkuk 3:1–19
F	1 Thessalonians 5:25–28
S	John 12:44–50

Prayer of the Week

O King of glory, Lord of hosts, uplifted in triumph far above all heavens, leave us not without consolation but send us the Spirit of truth whom You promised from the Father; for You live and reign with Him and the Holy Spirit, one God, now and forever. (L48)

(Exaudi) Almighty, everlasting God, grant us always to have a devout will towards You, and the desire to serve Your majesty with a pure heart; through Jesus Christ, Your Son, our Lord, who lives and reigns with You and the Holy Spirit, one true God, now and forever. (*TLH*, p. 72)

or

Lord God, heavenly Father, we give thanks to You, that through Your Holy Spirit You have appointed us to bear witness of Your dear Son, our Lord Jesus Christ. And inasmuch as the world cannot endure such testimony and persecutes us in every way, grant us courage and comfort, that we may not be offended because of the cross, but continue steadfastly in Your testimony, and be always found among those who know You and Your Son, until we obtain eternal salvation through Your Son, Jesus Christ our Lord, who lives and reigns with You and the Holy Spirit, one true God, now and forever. (VD)

Pentecost
Pentecost Eve

The Lection		*The Hymn*
ABC	Exodus 19:1–9	500
	Psalm 113 (v. 3)	
	Romans 8:12–17 (22–27)	
	John 14:8–21	
1Yr.	Joel 3:1–5	500
	Psalm 85 (v. 11)	
	Romans 8:12–17	
	John 14:15–21	

Prayer of the Day

Almighty and ever-living God, You fulfilled Your promise by sending the gift of the Holy Spirit to unite disciples of all nations in the cross and resurrection of Your Son, Jesus Christ. By the preaching of the Gospel spread this gift to the ends of the earth; through the same Jesus Christ, our Lord, who lives and reigns with You and the Holy Spirit, one God, now and forever. (L49)

Pentecost
The Day of Pentecost

The Lection		*The Hymn*
A	Numbers 11:24–30	497
	Psalm 25:1–15 (v. 4)	
	Acts 2:1–21	
	John 7:37–39	
B	Ezekiel 37:1–14	497
	Psalm 139:1–12 (13–16) (v. 17)	
	Acts 2:1–21	
	John 15:26–27; 16:4b–15	
C	Genesis 11:1–9	497
	Psalm 143 (v. 10)	
	Acts 2:1–21	
	John 14:23–31	
1Yr.	Genesis 11:1–9	497
	Psalm 143 (v. 11)	
	Acts 2:1–21	
	John 14:23–31	

Prayer of the Day

O God, on this day You once taught the hearts of Your faithful people by sending them the light of Your Holy Spirit. Grant us in our day by the same Spirit to have a right understanding in all things and evermore to rejoice in His holy consolation; through Jesus Christ, Your Son, our Lord, who lives and reigns with You and the Holy Spirit, one God, now and forever. (L50)

or

Lord Jesus Christ, almighty Son of God, graciously send Your Holy Spirit into our hearts, through Your Word, that He may rule and govern us according to Your will, comfort us in every temptation and misfortune, and defend us by Your truth against every error, so that we may continue steadfast in the faith, increase in love and good works, and firmly trusting in Your grace, which You purchased for us by Your death, obtain eternal salvation; for You reign with the Father and the Holy Spirit, one true God, now and forever. (VD)

Pentecost
Pentecost Evening/Pentecost Monday

The Lection	*The Hymn*
ABC, 1Yr. Isaiah 57:15–21	650
Psalm 43 (v. 3)	
Acts 10:34a, 42–48	
John 3:16–21	

Prayer of the Day

O God, who gave Your Holy Spirit to the apostles, grant us that same Spirit that we may live in faith and abide in peace; through Jesus Christ, Your Son, our Lord, who lives and reigns with You and the Holy Spirit, one God, now and forever. (L51)

Pentecost
Pentecost Tuesday

The Lection	*The Hymn*
ABC Isaiah 32:14–20	768
Psalm 27 (v. 1)	
Acts 8:14–17	
John 10:1–10	
1Yr. Isaiah 32:14–20	768
Psalm 85 (v. 10)	
Acts 8:14–17	
John 10:1–10	

The Liturgical Lessons for the Week

W	Matthew 10:16–25
Th	Numbers 24:1–9
F	2 Corinthians 12:11–18
S	Matthew 8:1–13

Prayer of the Day

Almighty and ever-living God, You fulfilled Your promise by sending the gift of the Holy Spirit to unite disciples of all nations in the cross and resurrection of Your Son, Jesus Christ. By the preaching of the Gospel spread this gift to the ends of the earth; through the same Jesus Christ, our Lord, who lives and reigns with You and the Holy Spirit, one God, now and forever. (L49)

THE TIME OF THE CHURCH
Series A

The Holy Trinity

The Lection

A   Genesis 1:1—2:4a
        Psalm 8 (v. 9)
        Acts 2:14a, 22–36
        Matthew 28:16–20

The Hymn

498/499

The Liturgical Lessons for the Week

M   Genesis 18:1–8
T   2 Timothy 1:1–2
W   John 5:39–47
Th   Isaiah 48:17–19
F   1 John 3:1–10
S   John 3:1–21

Prayer of the Week

Almighty and everlasting God, You have given us grace to acknowledge the glory of the eternal Trinity by the confession of a true faith and to worship the Unity in the power of the Divine Majesty. Keep us steadfast in this faith and defend us from all adversities; for You, O Father, Son, and Holy Spirit, live and reign, one God, now and forever. (L52)

Sunday on May 24–28 (Proper 3)

The Lection

A   Isaiah 49:8–16a
        Psalm 115:(1–8) 9–18 (v. 1)
        Romans 1:8–17
        Matthew 6:24–34

The Hymn

732

The Liturgical Lessons for the Week

M   1 Corinthians 7:29–35
T   Revelation 7:9–17
W   James 4:15–17
Th   John 5:19–24
F   1 Timothy 1:3–14
S   Luke 12:22–31

Eternal God, You counsel us not to be anxious about earthly things. Keep alive in us a proper yearning for those heavenly treasures awaiting all who trust in Your mercy, that we may daily rejoice in Your salvation and serve You with constant devotion; through Jesus Christ, Your Son, our Lord, who lives and reigns with You and the Holy Spirit, one God, now and forever. (A61)

Sunday on May 29—June 4 (Proper 4)

The Lection		*The Hymn*
A	Deuteronomy 11:18–21, 26–28	768
	Psalm 4 (v. 8)	
	Romans 3:21–28	
	Matthew 7:15–29	

The Liturgical Lessons for the Week

M	Jeremiah 10:1–10
T	2 Timothy 2:14–19
W	John 5:25–29
Th	Isaiah 48:1–8
F	Romans 10:1–4
S	John 5:30–38

Prayer of the Week

Lord of all power and might, author and giver of all good things, instill in our hearts the love of Your name, impress on our minds the teachings of Your Word, and increase in our lives all that is holy and just; through Jesus Christ, Your Son, our Lord, who lives and reigns with You and the Holy Spirit, one God, now and forever. (A62)

Sunday on June 5–11 (Proper 5)

The Lection		*The Hymn*
A	Hosea 5:15—6:6	689
	Psalm 119:65–72 (v. 65)	
	Romans 4:13–25	
	Matthew 9:9–13	

The Liturgical Lessons for the Week

M	Genesis 17:1–8
T	James 2:8–13
W	Matthew 8:14–17
Th	Deuteronomy 5:22–33
F	2 Timothy 2:20–26
S	John 8:1–11

Almighty and most merciful God, You sent Your Son, Jesus Christ, to seek and to save the lost. Graciously open our ears and our hearts to hear His call and to follow Him by faith that we may feast with Him forever in His kingdom; through the same Jesus Christ, our Lord, who lives and reigns with You and the Holy Spirit, one God, now and forever. (A63)

Sunday on June 12–18 (Proper 6)

The Lection		*The Hymn*
A	Exodus 19:2–8	571 or 834
	Psalm 100 (v. 5)	
	Romans 5:6–15	
	Matthew 9:35—10:8 (9–20)	

The Liturgical Lessons for the Week

M	Numbers 23:18–24
T	1 Corinthians 3:1–9
W	Mark 1:16–20
Th	Jonah 1:1–3
F	Acts 3:17–26
S	John 7:40–53

Prayer of the Week

Almighty, eternal God, in the Word of Your apostles and prophets You have proclaimed to us Your saving will. Grant us faith to believe Your promises that we may receive eternal salvation; through Jesus Christ, our Lord, who lives and reigns with You and the Holy Spirit, one God, now and forever. (A64)

Sunday on June 19–25 (Proper 7)

The Lection		*The Hymn*
A	Jeremiah 20:7–13	659
	Psalm 91:1–10 (11–16) (v. 1)	
	Romans 6:12–23	
	Matthew 10:5a, 21–33	

The Liturgical Lessons for the Week

M	Joshua 2:1–7
T	Jude 17–23
W	John 7:1–9
Th	Hosea 11:1–11
F	2 Corinthians 13:1–10
S	Luke 10:10–16

O God, because Your abiding presence always goes with us, keep us aware of Your daily mercies that we may live secure and content in Your eternal love; through Jesus Christ, Your Son, our Lord, who lives and reigns with You and the Holy Spirit, one God, now and forever. (A65)

Sunday on June 26—July 2 (Proper 8)

The Lection		*The Hymn*
A	Jeremiah 28:5–9	685
	Psalm 119:153–160 (v. 154)	
	Romans 7:1–13	
	Matthew 10:34–42	

The Liturgical Lessons for the Week

M	Judges 2:1–5
T	Acts 4:13–22
W	Matthew 4:23–25
Th	2 Chronicles 33:9–13
F	Hebrews 13:1–6
S	John 7:32–36

Prayer of the Week

Almighty God, by the working of Your Holy Spirit, grant that we may gladly hear Your Word proclaimed among us and follow its directing; through Jesus Christ, Your Son, our Lord, who lives and reigns with You and the Holy Spirit, one God, now and forever. (A66)

Sunday on July 3–9 (Proper 9)

The Lection		*The Hymn*
A	Zechariah 9:9–12	699
	Psalm 145:1–14 (v. 19)	
	Romans 7:14–25a	
	Matthew 11:25–30	

The Liturgical Lessons for the Week

M	Isaiah 65:17–25
T	Acts 15:30–35
W	Matthew 12:9–14
Th	Micah 7:14–20
F	Acts 21:1–6
S	Matthew 12:15–21

Prayer of the Week

Gracious God, our heavenly Father, Your mercy attends us all our days. Be our strength and support amid the wearisome changes of this world, and at life's end grant us Your promised rest and the full joys of Your salvation; through Jesus Christ, Your Son, our Lord, who lives and reigns with You and the Holy Spirit, one God, now and forever. (A67)

Sunday on July 10–16 (Proper 10)

The Lection		*The Hymn*
A	Isaiah 55:10–13	577
	Psalm 65:(1–8) 9–13 (v. 5)	
	Romans 8:12–17	
	Matthew 13:1–9, 18–23	

The Liturgical Lessons for the Week

M	Judges 7:9–14
T	Romans 6:12–14
W	Luke 4:31–37
Th	Judges 7:15–23
F	Romans 6:15–19
S	Luke 4:38–39

Prayer of the Week

Blessed Lord, since You have caused all Holy Scriptures to be written for our learning, grant that we may so hear them, read, mark, learn, and inwardly digest them that we may embrace and ever hold fast the blessed hope of everlasting life; through Jesus Christ, Your Son, our Lord, who lives and reigns with You and the Holy Spirit, one God, now and forever. (A68)

Sunday on July 17–23 (Proper 11)

The Lection		*The Hymn*
A	Isaiah 44:6–8	772
	Psalm 119:57–64 (v. 89)	
	Romans 8:18–27	
	Matthew 13:24–30, 36–43	

The Liturgical Lessons for the Week

M	Exodus 23:1–9
T	Romans 6:20–23
W	Luke 11:14–26
Th	Job 5:8–16

F   2 Corinthians 1:3–7
S   John 8:12–20

Prayer of the Week

O God, so rule and govern our hearts and minds by Your Holy Spirit that, ever mindful of Your final judgment, we may be stirred up to holiness of living here and dwell with You in perfect joy hereafter; through Jesus Christ, Your Son, our Lord, who lives and reigns with You and the Holy Spirit, one God, now and forever. (A69)

Sunday on July 24–30 (Proper 12)

The Lection		*The Hymn*
A	Deuteronomy 7:6–9	713
	Psalm 125 (v. 2)	
	Romans 8:28–39	
	Matthew 13:44–52	

The Liturgical Lessons for the Week

M   Numbers 23:7–12
T   Acts 4:23–31
W   Luke 10:39–47
Th   Genesis 28:18–22
F   Acts 20:1–6
S   John 5:1–9

Prayer of the Week

Almighty and everlasting God, give us an increase of faith, hope, and love, that, receiving what You have promised, we may love what You have commanded; through Jesus Christ, Your Son, our Lord, who lives and reigns with You and the Holy Spirit, one God, now and forever. (A70)

Sunday on July 31—August 6 (Proper 13)

The Lection		*The Hymn*
A	Isaiah 55:1–5	642
	Psalm 136:1–9 (23–26) (v. 26)	
	Romans 9:1–5 (6–13)	
	Matthew 14:13–21	

The Liturgical Lessons for the Week

M   Isaiah 48:9–16
T   Galatians 3:1–9
W   Luke 11:27–33
Th   1 Samuel 24:1–7

F   1 Timothy 4:1–10
S   Luke 11:33–36

Prayer of the Week

Heavenly Father, though we do not deserve Your goodness, still You provide for all our needs of body and soul. Grant us Your Holy Spirit that we may acknowledge Your gifts, give thanks for all Your benefits, and serve You in willing obedience; through Jesus Christ, Your Son, our Lord, who lives and reigns with You and the Holy Spirit, one God, now and forever. (A71)

Sunday on August 7–13 (Proper 14)

The Lection   *The Hymn*

A   Job 38:4–18   717
        Psalm 18:1–6 (7–16) (v. 46)
        Romans 10:5–17
        Matthew 14:22–33

The Liturgical Lessons for the Week

M   Deuteronomy 32:1–9
T   Galatians 3:15–22
W   Matthew 8:23–27
Th   Numbers 13:25–33
F   James 1:2–15
S   Matthew 9:27–34

Prayer of the Week

Almighty and most merciful God, preserve us from all harm and danger that we, being ready in both body and soul, may cheerfully accomplish what You want done; through Jesus Christ, Your Son, our Lord, who lives and reigns with You and the Holy Spirit, one God, now and forever. (A72)

Sunday on August 14–20 (Proper 15)

The Lection   *The Hymn*

A   Isaiah 56:1, 6–8   653 or 615
        Psalm 67 (v. 5)
        Romans 11:1–2a, 13–15, 28–32
        Matthew 15:21–28

The Liturgical Lessons for the Week

M   Joshua 4:1–7
T   Acts 5:1–11
W   Luke 5:12–16

Th Joshua 4:8–14
F   Acts 7:1–8
S   Luke 9:12–17

Prayer of the Week

Almighty and everlasting Father, You give Your children many blessings even though we are undeserving. In every trial and temptation grant us steadfast confidence in Your loving-kindness and mercy; through Jesus Christ, Your Son, our Lord, who lives and reigns with You and the Holy Spirit, one God, now and forever. (A73)

Sunday on August 21–27 (Proper 16)

The Lection		*The Hymn*
A	Isaiah 51:1–6	645
	Psalm 138 (v. 8a)	
	Romans 11:33—12:8	
	Matthew 16:13–20	

The Liturgical Lessons for the Week

M   1 Samuel 7:12–17
T   Hebrews 9:1–10
W   Mark 3:1–6
Th 2 Samuel 2:1–4
F   James 4:7–17
S   Mark 4:1–9

Prayer of the Week

Almighty God, whom to know is everlasting life, grant us to know Your Son, Jesus, to be the way, the truth, and the life that we may boldly confess Him to be the Christ and steadfastly walk in the way that leads to life eternal; through the same Jesus Christ, our Lord, who lives and reigns with You and the Holy Spirit, one God, now and forever. (A74)

Sunday on August 28—September 3 (Proper 17)

The Lection		*The Hymn*
A	Jeremiah 15:15–21	531
	Psalm 26 (v. 8)	
	Romans 12:9–21	
	Matthew 16:21–28	

The Liturgical Lessons for the Week

M   1 Samuel 6:19–21
T   Jude 8–13

W	Mark 11:27–33
Th	Ecclesiastes 12:1–7
F	James 3:1–5
S	Matthew 15:10–20

Prayer of the Week

Almighty God, Your Son willingly endured the agony and shame of the cross for our redemption. Grant us courage to take up our cross daily and follow Him wherever He leads; through the same Jesus Christ, our Lord, who lives and reigns with You and the Holy Spirit, one God, now and forever. (A75)

Sunday on September 4–10 (Proper 18)

The Lection		*The Hymn*
A	Ezekiel 33:7–9	820
	Psalm 32:1–7 (v. 1)	
	Romans 13:1–10	
	Matthew 18:1–20	

The Liturgical Lessons for the Week

M	Exodus 20:18–26
T	Hebrews 6:1–8
W	Matthew 17:22–27
Th	Numbers 6:1–8
F	2 Thessalonians 2:1–12
S	Luke 16:14–18

Prayer of the Week

O God, from whom all good proceeds, grant to us, Your humble servants, Your holy inspiration, that we may set our minds on the things that are right and, by Your merciful guiding, accomplish them; through Jesus Christ, Your Son, our Lord, who lives and reigns with You and the Holy Spirit, one God, now and forever. (A76)

Sunday on September 11–17 (Proper 19)

The Lection		*The Hymn*
A	Genesis 50:15–21	501
	Psalm 103:1–12 (v. 13)	
	Romans 14:1–12	
	Matthew 18:21–35	

The Liturgical Lessons for the Week

M	Genesis 8:15–19
T	Acts 9:36–43

W	Luke 5:27–32
Th	2 Samuel 22:1–7
F	Acts 8:9–13
S	Matthew 12:1–8

Prayer of the Week

O God, our refuge and strength, the author of all godliness, hear the devout prayers of Your Church, especially in times of persecution, and grant that what we ask in faith we may obtain; through Jesus Christ, our Lord, who lives and reigns with You and the Holy Spirit, one God, now and forever. (A77)

Sunday on September 18–24 (Proper 20)

The Lection		*The Hymn*
A	Isaiah 55:6–9	555
	Psalm 27:1–9 (v. 4a)	
	Philippians 1:12–14, 19–30	
	Matthew 20:1–16	

The Liturgical Lessons for the Week

M	Malachi 4:4–6
T	Romans 9:27–33
W	Luke 13:10–17
Th	Zechariah 6:9–15
F	3 John 1–8
S	Mark 11:15–19

Prayer of the Week

Lord God, heavenly Father, since we cannot stand before You relying on anything we have done, help us trust in Your abiding grace and live according to Your Word; through Jesus Christ, Your Son, our Lord, who lives and reigns with You and the Holy Spirit, one God, now and forever. (A78)

Sunday on September 25—October 1 (Proper 21)

The Lection		*The Hymn*
A	Ezekiel 18:1–4, 25–32	655
	Psalm 25:1–10 (v. 4)	
	Philippians 2:1–4 (5–13) 14–18	
	Matthew 21:23–27 (28–32)	

The Liturgical Lessons for the Week

| M | Ezra 1:1–4 |
| T | Hebrews 5:11–14 |

W	Luke 6:32–38
Th	Esther 4:10–17
F	1 Thessalonians 4:1–12
S	Mark 7:9–13

Prayer of the Week

Almighty God, You exalted Your Son to the place of all honor and authority. Enlighten our minds by Your Holy Spirit that, confessing Jesus as Lord, we may be led into all truth; through the same Jesus Christ, our Lord, who lives and reigns with You and the Holy Spirit, one God, now and forever. (A79)

Sunday on October 2–8 (Proper 22)

The Lection		*The Hymn*
A	Isaiah 5:1–7	544
	Psalm 80:7–19 (v. 7)	
	Philippians 3:4b–14	
	Matthew 21:33–46	

The Liturgical Lessons for the Week

M	Nehemiah 4:1–6
T	Acts 14:19–28
W	Luke 12:49–53
Th	Ezra 10:1–5
F	2 Peter 3:14–18
S	Matthew 19:10–15

Prayer of the Week

Gracious God, You gave Your Son into the hands of sinful men who killed Him. Forgive us when we reject Your unfailing love, and grant us the fullness of Your salvation; through Jesus Christ, Your Son, our Lord, who lives and reigns with You and the Holy Spirit, one God, now and forever. (A80)

Sunday on October 9–15 (Proper 23)

The Lection		*The Hymn*
A	Isaiah 25:6–9	510
	Psalm 23 (v. 5a)	
	Philippians 4:4–13	
	Matthew 22:1–14	

The Liturgical Lessons for the Week

M	Leviticus 7:11–18
T	Colossians 4:1–6

W   Luke 21:1–4
Th   1 Chronicles 16:7–36
F   Philemon 21–25
S   Mark 4:10–20

Prayer of the Week

Almighty God, You invite us to trust in You for our salvation. Deal with us not in the severity of Your judgment but by the greatness of Your mercy; through Jesus Christ, Your Son, our Lord, who lives and reigns with You and the Holy Spirit, one God, now and forever. (A81)

Sunday on October 16–22 (Proper 24)

The Lection	*The Hymn*
A Isaiah 45:1–7	940
Psalm 96:1–9 (10–13) (v. 9a)	
1 Thessalonians 1:1–10	
Matthew 22:15–22	

The Liturgical Lessons for the Week

M   Zechariah 7:1–14
T   1 Timothy 5:1–8
W   Luke 14:1–6
Th   2 Chronicles 1:7–13
F   James 5:13–20
S   Matthew 21:12–17

Prayer of the Week

O God, the protector of all who trust in You, have mercy on us that with You as our ruler and guide we may so pass through things temporal that we lose not the things eternal; through Jesus Christ, Your Son, our Lord, who lives and reigns with You and the Holy Spirit, one God, now and forever. (A82)

Sunday on October 23–29 (Proper 25)

The Lection	*The Hymn*
A Leviticus 19:1–2, 15–18	411 or 579
Psalm 1 (v. 1a)	
1 Thessalonians 2:1–13	
Matthew 22:34–46	

The Liturgical Lessons for the Week

M   Zechariah 8:1–8
T   Acts 26:24–32

W	Luke 23:32–38
Th	Lamentations 3:55–66
F	Colossians 2:16–23
S	Matthew 17:14–21

Prayer of the Week

O God, You have commanded us to love You above all things and our neighbors as ourselves. Grant us the Spirit to think and do what is pleasing in Your sight, that our faith in You may never waver and our love for one another may not falter; through Jesus Christ, Your Son, our Lord, who lives and reigns with You and the Holy Spirit, one God, now and forever. (A83)

Sunday on October 30—November 5 (Proper 26)

The Lection

A	Micah 3:5–12
	Psalm 43 (v. 3)
	1 Thessalonians 4:1–12
	Matthew 23:1–12

The Hymn

585

The Liturgical Lessons for the Week

M	Ezra 8:24–30
T	1 Peter 1:10–16
W	Matthew 16:5–12
Th	Ecclesiastes 2:1–9
F	1 Timothy 5:9–16
S	Mark 4:21–25

Prayer of the Week

Merciful and gracious Lord, You cause Your Word to be proclaimed in every generation. Stir up our hearts and minds by Your Holy Spirit that we may receive this proclamation with humility and finally be exalted at the coming of Your Son, our Savior, Jesus Christ, who lives and reigns with You and the Holy Spirit, one God, now and forever. (A84)

Sunday on November 6–12 (Proper 27)

The Lection

A	Amos 5:18–24
	Psalm 70 (v. 4)
	1 Thessalonians 4:13–18
	Matthew 25:1–13

The Hymn

516

M   Numbers 14:1–12
T   2 Peter 1:3–11
W   Luke 21:20–24
Th   Zephaniah 3:8–10
F   Philippians 1:12–18
S   Luke 18:35–43

Prayer of the Week

Lord God, heavenly Father, send forth Your Son to lead home His bride, the Church, that with all the company of the redeemed we may finally enter into His eternal wedding feast; through the same Jesus Christ, our Lord, who lives and reigns with You and the Holy Spirit, one God, now and forever. (A85)

Sunday on November 13–19 (Proper 28)

The Lection		*The Hymn*
A	Zephaniah 1:7–16	508
	Psalm 90:1–12 (v. 17)	
	1 Thessalonians 5:1–11	
	Matthew 25:14–30	

The Liturgical Lessons for the Week

M   Amos 9:9–15
T   Hebrews 12:25–29
W   Mark 13:14–23
Th   Micah 4:6–10
F   Acts 28:23–31
S   Luke 14:15–24

Prayer of the Week

Almighty and ever-living God, You have given exceedingly great and precious promises to those who trust in You. Dispel from us the works of darkness and grant us to live in the light of Your Son, Jesus Christ, that our faith may never be found wanting; through the same Jesus Christ, our Lord, who lives and reigns with You and the Holy Spirit, one God, now and forever. (A86)

The Last Sunday of the Church Year
—Sunday on November 20–26 (Proper 29)

The Lection		*The Hymn*
A	Ezekiel 34:11–16, 20–24	532
	Psalm 95:1–7a (v. 7a)	

1 Corinthians 15:20–28
Matthew 25:31–46

Prayer of the Week

Eternal God, merciful Father, You have appointed Your Son as judge of the living and the dead. Enable us to wait for the day of His return with our eyes fixed on the kingdom prepared for Your own from the foundation of the world; through Jesus Christ, our Lord, who lives and reigns with You and the Holy Spirit, one God, now and forever. (A87)

THE TIME OF THE CHURCH

Series B

The Holy Trinity

Prayer of the Week

Almighty and everlasting God, You have given us grace to acknowledge the glory of the eternal Trinity by the confession of a true faith and to worship the Unity in the power of the Divine Majesty. Keep us steadfast in this faith and defend us from all adversities; for

You, O Father, Son, and Holy Spirit, live and reign, one God, now and forever. (L52)

Sunday on May 24–28 (Proper 3)

The Lection   *The Hymn*

B   Hosea 2:14–20   819
     Psalm 103:1–13 (v. 22)
     Acts 2:14a, 36–47
     Mark 2:(13–17) 18–22

The Liturgical Lessons for the Week

M   1 Corinthians 7:29–35
T   Revelation 7:9–17
W   James 4:15–17
Th   John 5:19–24
F   1 Timothy 1:3–14
S   Luke 12:22–31

Prayer of the Week

Merciful Father, You have given Your only Son as the sacrifice for sinners. Grant us grace to receive the fruits of His redeeming work with thanksgiving and daily to follow in His way; through Jesus Christ, our Lord, who lives and reigns with You and the Holy Spirit, one God, now and forever. (B61)

Sunday on May 29—June 4 (Proper 4)

The Lection   *The Hymn*

B   Deuteronomy 5:12–15   906
     Psalm 81:1–10 (v. 13)
     2 Corinthians 4:5–12
     Mark 2:23–28 (3:1–6)

The Liturgical Lessons for the Week

M   Jeremiah 10:1–10
T   2 Timothy 2:14–19
W   John 5:25–29
Th   Isaiah 48:1–8
F   Romans 10:1–4
S   John 5:30–38

Prayer of the Week

Eternal God, Your Son Jesus Christ is our true Sabbath rest. Help us to keep each day holy by receiving His Word of comfort that we may find our rest in Him, who lives and reigns with You and the Holy Spirit, one God, now and forever. (B62)

Sunday on June 5–11 (Proper 5)

The Lection		*The Hymn*
B	Genesis 3:8–15	668
	Psalm 130 (v. 7)	
	2 Corinthians 4:13—5:1	
	Mark 3:20–35	

The Liturgical Lessons for the Week

M	Genesis 17:1–8
T	James 2:8–13
W	Matthew 8:14–17
Th	Deuteronomy 5:22–33
F	2 Timothy 2:20–26
S	John 8:1–11

Prayer of the Week

Almighty and eternal God, Your Son Jesus triumphed over the prince of demons and freed us from bondage to sin. Help us to stand firm against every assault of Satan, and enable us always to do Your will; through Jesus Christ, our Lord, who lives and reigns with You and the Holy Spirit, one God, now and forever. (B63)

Sunday on June 12–18 (Proper 6)

The Lection		*The Hymn*
B	Ezekiel 17:22–24	500 or 834
	Psalm 1 (v. 6)	
	2 Corinthians 5:1–10 (11–17)	
	Mark 4:26–34	

The Liturgical Lessons for the Week

M	Numbers 23:18–24
T	1 Corinthians 3:1–9
W	Mark 1:16–20
Th	Jonah 1:1–3
F	Acts 3:17–26
S	John 7:40–53

Prayer of the Week

Blessed Lord, since You have caused all Holy Scriptures to be written for our learning, grant that we may so hear them, read, mark, learn, and inwardly digest them that we may embrace and ever hold fast the blessed hope of everlasting life; through Jesus Christ, Your Son, our Lord, who lives and reigns with You and the Holy Spirit, one God, now and forever. (B64)

Sunday on June 19–25 (Proper 7)

The Lection		*The Hymn*
B	Job 38:1–11	726
	Psalm 124 (v. 8)	
	2 Corinthians 6:1–13	
	Mark 4:35–41	

The Liturgical Lessons for the Week

M	Joshua 2:1–7
T	Jude 17–23
W	John 7:1–9
Th	Hosea 11:1–11
F	2 Corinthians 13:1–10
S	Luke 10:10–16

Prayer of the Week

Almighty God, in Your mercy guide the course of this world so that Your Church may joyfully serve You in godly peace and quietness; through Jesus Christ, Your Son, our Lord, who lives and reigns with You and the Holy Spirit, one God, now and forever. (B65)

Sunday on June 26—July 2 (Proper 8)

The Lection		*The Hymn*
B	Lamentations 3:22–33	755
	Psalm 30 (v. 10)	
	2 Corinthians 8:1–9, 13–15	
	Mark 5:21–43	

The Liturgical Lessons for the Week

M	Judges 2:1–5
T	Acts 4:13–22
W	Matthew 4:23–25
Th	2 Chronicles 33:9–13
F	Hebrews 13:1–6
S	John 7:32–36

Prayer of the Week

Heavenly Father, during His earthly ministry Your Son Jesus healed the sick and raised the dead. By the healing medicine of the Word and Sacraments pour into our hearts such love toward You that we may live eternally; through the same Jesus Christ, our Lord, who lives and reigns with You and the Holy Spirit, one God, now and forever. (B66)

Sunday on July 3–9 (Proper 9)

The Lection		*The Hymn*
B	Ezekiel 2:1–5	839
	Psalm 123 (v. 1)	
	2 Corinthians 12:1–10	
	Mark 6:1–13	

The Liturgical Lessons for the Week

M	Isaiah 65:17–25
T	Acts 15:30–35
W	Matthew 12:9–14
Th	Micah 7:14–20
F	Acts 21:1–6
S	Matthew 12:15–21

Prayer of the Week

O God, Your almighty power is made known chiefly in showing mercy. Grant us the fullness of Your grace that we may be called to repentance and made partakers of Your heavenly treasures; through Your Son, Jesus Christ, our Lord, who lives and reigns with You and the Holy Spirit, one God, now and forever. (B67)

Sunday on July 10–16 (Proper 10)

The Lection		*The Hymn*
B	Amos 7:7–15	743
	Psalm 85:(1–7) 8–13 (v. 7)	
	Ephesians 1:3–14	
	Mark 6:14–29	

The Liturgical Lessons for the Week

M	Judges 7:9–14
T	Romans 6:12–14
W	Luke 4;31–37
Th	Judges 7:15–23
F	Romans 6:15–19
S	Luke 4:38–39

Prayer of the Week

O Lord, You granted Your prophets strength to resist the temptations of the devil and courage to proclaim repentance. Give us pure hearts and minds to follow Your Son faithfully even into suffering and death; through the same Jesus Christ, our Lord, who lives and reigns with You and the Holy Spirit, one God, now and forever. (B68)

Sunday on July 17–23 (Proper 11)

The Lection		*The Hymn*
B	Jeremiah 23:1–6	644
	Psalm 23 (v. 6)	
	Ephesians 2:11–22	
	Mark 6:30–44	

The Liturgical Lessons for the Week

M	Exodus 23:1–9
T	Romans 6:20–23
W	Luke 11:14–26
Th	Job 5:8–16
F	2 Corinthians 1:3–7
S	John 8:12–20

Prayer of the Week

Heavenly Father, though we do not deserve Your goodness, still You provide for all our needs of body and soul. Grant us Your Holy Spirit that we may acknowledge Your gifts, give thanks for all Your benefits, and serve You in willing obedience; through Jesus Christ, Your Son, our Lord, who lives and reigns with You and the Holy Spirit, one God, now and forever. (B69)

Sunday on July 24–30 (Proper 12)

The Lection		*The Hymn*
B	Genesis 9.8–17	754
	Psalm 136:1–9 (v. 26)	
	Ephesians 3:14–21	
	Mark 6:45–56	

The Liturgical Lessons for the Week

M	Numbers 23:7–12
T	Acts 4:23–31
W	Luke 10:39–47
Th	Genesis 28:18–22
F	Acts 20:1–6
S	John 5:1–9

Almighty and most merciful God, the protector of all who trust in You, strengthen our faith and give us courage to believe that in Your love You will rescue us from all adversities; through Jesus Christ, Your Son, our Lord, who lives and reigns with You and the Holy Spirit, one God, now and forever. (B70)

Sunday on July 31—August 6 (Proper 13)

The Lection		*The Hymn*
B	Exodus 16:2–15	918
	Psalm 145:10–21 (v. 15)	
	Ephesians 4:1–16	
	John 6:22–35	

The Liturgical Lessons for the Week

M	Isaiah 48:9–16
T	Galatians 3:1–9
W	Luke 11:27–33
Th	1 Samuel 24:1–7
F	1 Timothy 4:1–10
S	Luke 11:33–36

Prayer of the Week

Merciful Father, You gave Your Son Jesus as the heavenly bread of life. Grant us faith to feast on Him in Your Word and Sacraments that we may be nourished unto life everlasting; through the same Jesus Christ, our Lord, who lives and reigns with You and the Holy Spirit, one God, now and forever. (B71)

Sunday on August 7–13 (Proper 14)

The Lection		*The Hymn*
B	1 Kings 19:1–8	534
	Psalm 34:1–8 (v. 3)	
	Ephesians 4:17—5:2	
	John 6:35–51	

The Liturgical Lessons for the Week

M	Deuteronomy 32:1–9
T	Galatians 3:15–22
W	Matthew 8:23–27
Th	Numbers 13:25–33
F	James 1:2–15
S	Matthew 9:27–34

Prayer of the Week

Gracious Father, Your blessed Son came down from heaven to be the true bread that gives life to the world. Grant that Christ, the bread of life, may live in us and we in Him, who lives and reigns with You and the Holy Spirit, one God, now and forever. (B72)

Sunday on August 14–20 (Proper 15)

The Lection		*The Hymn*
B	Proverbs 9:1–10	696
	or Joshua 24:1–2a, 14–18	
	Psalm 34:12–22 (v. 11)	
	Ephesians 5:6–21	
	John 6:51–69	

The Liturgical Lessons for the Week

M	Joshua 4:1–7
T	Acts 5:1–11
W	Luke 5:12–16
Th	Joshua 4:8–14
F	Acts 7:1–8
S	Luke 9:12–17

Prayer of the Week

Almighty God, whom to know is everlasting life, grant us to know Your Son, Jesus, to be the way, the truth, and the life, that we may steadfastly follow His steps in the way that leads to life eternal; through Jesus Christ, our Lord, who lives and reigns with You and the Holy Spirit, one God, now and forever. (B73)

Sunday on August 21–27 (Proper 16)

The Lection		*The Hymn*
B	Isaiah 29:11–19	865
	Psalm 14 (v. 7a)	
	Ephesians 5:22–33	
	Mark 7:1–13	

The Liturgical Lessons for the Week

M	1 Samuel 7:12–17
T	Hebrews 9:1–10
W	Mark 3:1–6
Th	2 Samuel 2:1–4
F	James 4:7–17
S	Mark 4:1–9

Prayer of the Week

Almighty and merciful God, defend Your Church from all false teaching and error that Your faithful people may confess You to be the only true God and rejoice in Your good gifts of life and salvation; through Jesus Christ, Your Son, our Lord, who lives and reigns with You and the Holy Spirit, one God, now and forever. (B74)

Sunday on August 28—September 3 (Proper 17)

The Lection		*The Hymn*
B	Deuteronomy 4:1–2, 6–9	566
	Psalm 119:129–136 (v. 132)	
	Ephesians 6:10–20	
	Mark 7:14–23	

The Liturgical Lessons for the Week

M	1 Samuel 6:19–21
T	Jude 8–13
W	Mark 11:27–33
Th	Ecclesiastes 12:1–7
F	James 3:1–5
S	Matthew 15:10–20

Prayer of the Week

O God, the source of all that is just and good, nourish in us every virtue and bring to completion every good intent that we may grow in grace and bring forth the fruit of good works; through Jesus Christ, Your Son, our Lord, who lives and reigns with You and the Holy Spirit, one God, now and forever. (B75)

Sunday on September 4–10 (Proper 18)

The Lection		*The Hymn*
B	Isaiah 35:4–7a	797
	Psalm 146 (v. 2)	
	James 2:1–10, 14–18	
	Mark 7:(24–30) 31–37	

The Liturgical Lessons for the Week

M	Exodus 20:18–26
T	Hebrews 6:1–8
W	Matthew 17:22–27
Th	Numbers 6:1–8
F	2 Thessalonians 2:1–12
S	Luke 16:14–18

O Lord, let Your merciful ears be open to the prayers of Your humble servants and grant that what they ask may be in accord with Your gracious will; through Jesus Christ, Your Son, our Lord, who lives and reigns with You and the Holy Spirit, one God, now and forever. (B76)

Sunday on September 11–17 (Proper 19)

The Lection		*The Hymn*
B	Isaiah 50:4–10	849
	Psalm 116:1–9 (v. 5)	
	James 3:1–12	
	Mark 9:14–29	

The Liturgical Lessons for the Week

M	Genesis 8:15–19
T	Acts 9:36–43
W	Luke 5:27–32
Th	2 Samuel 22:1–7
F	Acts 8:9–13
S	Matthew 12:1–8

Prayer of the Week

Lord Jesus Christ, our support and defense in every need, continue to preserve Your Church in safety, govern her by Your goodness, and bless her with Your peace; for You live and reign with the Father and the Holy Spirit, one God, now and forever. (B77)

Sunday on September 18–24 (Proper 20)

The Lection		*The Hymn*
B	Jeremiah 11:18–20	851
	Psalm 54 (v. 4)	
	James 3:13—4:10	
	Mark 9:30–37	

The Liturgical Lessons for the Week

M	Malachi 4:4–6
T	Romans 9:27–33
W	Luke 13:10–17
Th	Zechariah 6:9–15
F	3 John 1–8
S	Mark 11:15–19

O God, whose strength is made perfect in weakness, grant us humility and childlike faith that we may please You in both will and deed; through Jesus Christ, Your Son, our Lord, who lives and reigns with You and the Holy Spirit, one God, now and forever. (B78)

Sunday on September 25—October 1 (Proper 21)

The Lection		*The Hymn*
B	Numbers 11:4–6, 10–16, 24–29	505
	Psalm 104:27–35 (v. 24)	
	James 5:(1–12) 13–20	
	Mark 9:38–50	

The Liturgical Lessons for the Week

M	Ezra 1:1–4
T	Hebrews 5:11–14
W	Luke 6:32–38
Th	Esther 4:10–17
F	1 Thessalonians 4:1–12
S	Mark 7:9–13

Prayer of the Week

Everlasting Father, source of every blessing, mercifully direct and govern us by Your Holy Spirit that we may complete the works You have prepared for us to do; through Jesus Christ, Your Son, our Lord, who lives and reigns with You and the Holy Spirit, one God, now and forever. (B79)

Sunday on October 2–8 (Proper 22)

The Lection		*The Hymn*
B	Genesis 2:18–25	863
	Psalm 128 (v. 1)	
	Hebrews 2:1–13 (14–18)	
	Mark 10:2–16	

The Liturgical Lessons for the Week

M	Nehemiah 4:1–6
T	Acts 14:19–28
W	Luke 12:49–53
Th	Ezra 10:1–5
F	2 Peter 3:14–18
S	Matthew 19:10–15

Merciful Father, Your patience and loving-kindness toward us have no end. Grant that by Your Holy Spirit we may always think and do those things that are pleasing in Your sight; through Jesus Christ, Your Son, our Lord, who lives and reigns with You and the Holy Spirit, one God, now and forever. (B80)

Sunday on October 9–15 (Proper 23)

The Lection		*The Hymn*
B	Amos 5:6–7, 10–15	694
	Psalm 90:12–17 (v. 1)	
	Hebrews 3:12–19	
	Mark 10:17–22	

The Liturgical Lessons for the Week

M	Leviticus 7:11–18
T	Colossians 4:1–6
W	Luke 21:1–4
Th	1 Chronicles 16:7–36
F	Philemon 21–25
S	Mark 4:10–20

Prayer of the Week

Lord Jesus Christ, whose grace always precedes and follows us, help us to forsake all trust in earthly gain and to find in You our heavenly treasure; for You live and reign with the Father and the Holy Spirit, one God, now and forever. (B81)

Sunday on October 16–22 (Proper 24)

The Lection		*The Hymn*
B	Ecclesiastes 5:10–20	690
	Psalm 119:9–16 (v. 14)	
	Hebrews 4:1–13 (14–16)	
	Mark 10:23–31	

The Liturgical Lessons for the Week

M	Zechariah 7:1–14
T	1 Timothy 5:1–8
W	Luke 14:1–6
Th	2 Chronicles 1:7–13
F	James 5:13–20
S	Matthew 21:12–17

O God, Your divine wisdom sets in order all things in heaven and on earth. Put away from us all things hurtful and give us those things that are beneficial for us; through Jesus Christ, Your Son, our Lord, who lives and reigns with You and the Holy Spirit, one God, now and forever. (B82)

Sunday on October 23–29 (Proper 25)

The Lection		*The Hymn*
B	Jeremiah 31:7–9	713
	Psalm 126 (v. 5)	
	Hebrews 7:23–28	
	Mark 10:46–52	

The Liturgical Lessons for the Week

M	Zechariah 8:1–8
T	Acts 26:24–32
W	Luke 23:32–38
Th	Lamentations 3:55–66
F	Colossians 2:16–23
S	Matthew 17:14–21

Prayer of the Week

O God, the helper of all who call on You, have mercy on us and give us eyes of faith to see Your Son that we may follow Him on the way that leads to eternal life; through the same Jesus Christ, Your Son, our Lord, who lives and reigns with You and the Holy Spirit, one God, now and forever. (B83)

Sunday on October 30—November 5 (Proper 26)

The Lection		*The Hymn*
B	Deuteronomy 6:1–9	852
	Psalm 119:1–8 (v. 5)	
	Hebrews 9:11–14 (15–22)	
	Mark 12:28–37	

The Liturgical Lessons for the Week

M	Ezra 8:24–30
T	1 Peter 1:10–16
W	Matthew 16:5–12
Th	Ecclesiastes 2:1–9
F	1 Timothy 5:9–16
S	Mark 4:21–25

Lord Jesus Christ, our great High Priest, cleanse us by the power of Your redeeming blood that in purity and peace we may worship and adore Your holy name; for You live and reign with the Father and the Holy Spirit, one God, now and forever. (B84)

Sunday on November 6–12 (Proper 27)

The Lection		*The Hymn*
B	1 Kings 17:8–16	738
	Psalm 146 (v. 9a)	
	Hebrews 9:24–28	
	Mark 12:38–44	

The Liturgical Lessons for the Week

M	Numbers 14:1–12
T	2 Peter 1:3–11
W	Luke 21:20–24
Th	Zephaniah 3:8–10
F	Philippians 1:12–18
S	Luke 18:35–43

Prayer of the Week

Almighty and ever-living God, You have given exceedingly great and precious promises to those who trust in You. Grant us so firmly to believe in Your Son Jesus that our faith may never be found wanting; through the same Jesus Christ, our Lord, who lives and reigns with You and the Holy Spirit, one God, now and forever. (B85)

Sunday on November 13–19 (Proper 28)

The Lection		*The Hymn*
B	Daniel 12:1–3	508
	Psalm 16 (v. 11b, c)	
	Hebrews 10:11–25	
	Mark 13:1–13	

The Liturgical Lessons for the Week

M	Amos 9:9–15
T	Hebrews 12:25–29
W	Mark 13:14–23
Th	Micah 4:6–10
F	Acts 28:23–31
S	Luke 14:15–24

Prayer of the Week

O Lord, by Your bountiful goodness release us from the bonds of our sins, which by reason of our weakness we have brought upon ourselves, that we may stand firm until the day of our Lord Jesus Christ, who lives and reigns with You and the Holy Spirit, one God, now and forever. (B86)

The Last Sunday of the Church Year
—Sunday on November 20–26 (Proper 29)

The Lection		*The Hymn*
B	Isaiah 51:4–6	336
	Psalm 93 (v. 2)	
	Jude 20–25	
	Mark 13:24–37	
or		
	Daniel 7:9–10, 13–14	336
	Psalm 93 (v. 2)	
	Revelation 1:4b–8	
	John 18:33–37	

The Liturgical Lessons for the Week

M	Zechariah 8:9–13
T	Revelation 21:5–8
W	Matthew 24:15–25
Th	Zechariah 8:14–23
F	Revelation 22:1–5
S	Matthew 24:29–35

Prayer of the Week

Lord Jesus Christ, so govern our hearts and minds by Your Holy Spirit that, ever mindful of Your glorious return, we may persevere in both faith and holiness of living; for You live and reign with the Father and the Holy Spirit, one God, now and forever. (B87)

THE TIME OF THE CHURCH

Series C

The Holy Trinity

The Lection		*The Hymn*
C	Proverbs 8:1–4, 22–31	498/499
	Psalm 8 (v. 9)	
	Acts 2:14a, 22–36	
	John 8:48–59	

The Liturgical Lessons for the Week

M	Genesis 18:1–8
T	2 Timothy 1:1–2
W	John 5:39–47
Th	Isaiah 48:17–19
F	1 John 3:1–10
S	John 3:1–21

Prayer of the Week

Almighty and everlasting God, You have given us grace to acknowledge the glory of the eternal Trinity by the confession of a true faith and to worship the Unity in the power of the Divine Majesty. Keep us steadfast in this faith and defend us from all adversities; for You, O Father, Son, and Holy Spirit, live and reign, one God, now and forever. (L52)

Sunday on May 24–28 (Proper 3)

The Lection		*The Hymn*
C	Genesis 50:15–21	696
	Psalm 112:1–9 (v. 1)	
	Acts 2:14a, 36–47	
	Luke 6:(20–26) 27–42	

The Liturgical Lessons for the Week

M	1 Corinthians 7:29–35
T	Revelation 7:9–17
W	James 4:15–17
Th	John 5:19–24
F	1 Timothy 1:3–14
S	Luke 12:22–31

Almighty God, in Your mercy so guide the course of this world that we may forgive as we have been forgiven and joyfully serve You in godly peace and quietness; through Jesus Christ, Your Son, our Lord, who lives and reigns with You and the Holy Spirit, one God, now and forever. (C61)

Sunday on May 29—June 4 (Proper 4)

The Lection		*The Hymn*
C	1 Kings 8:22–24, 27–29, 41–43	755
	Psalm 96:1–9 (v. 2)	
	Galatians 1:1–12	
	Luke 7:1–10	

The Liturgical Lessons for the Week

M	Jeremiah 10:1–10
T	2 Timothy 2:14–19
W	John 5:25–29
Th	Isaiah 48:1–8
F	Romans 10:1–4
S	John 5:30–38

Prayer of the Week

O God, by Your almighty Word You set in order all things in heaven and on earth. Put away from us all things hurtful, and give us those things that are beneficial for us; through Jesus Christ, Your Son, our Lord, who lives and reigns with You and the Holy Spirit, one God, now and forever. (C62)

Sunday on June 5–11 (Proper 5)

The Lection		*The Hymn*
C	1 Kings 17:17–24	615
	Psalm 30 (v. 5b)	
	Galatians 1:11–24	
	Luke 7:11–17	

The Liturgical Lessons for the Week

M	Genesis 17:1–8
T	James 2:8–13
W	Matthew 8:14–17
Th	Deuteronomy 5:22–33
F	2 Timothy 2:20–26
S	John 8:1–11

Prayer of the Week

O Lord, Father of all mercy and God of all comfort, You always go before and follow after us. Grant that we may rejoice in Your gracious presence and continually be given to all good works; through Jesus Christ, Your Son, our Lord, who lives and reigns with You and the Holy Spirit, one God, now and forever. (C63)

Sunday on June 12–18 (Proper 6)

The Lection		*The Hymn*
C	2 Samuel 11:26—12:10, 13–14	915 or 834
	Psalm 32:1–7 (v. 5)	
	Galatians 2:15–21; 3:10–14	
	Luke 7:36—8:3	

The Liturgical Lessons for the Week

M	Numbers 23:18–24
T	1 Corinthians 3:1–9
W	Mark 1:16–20
Th	Jonah 1:1–3
F	Acts 3:17–26
S	John 7:40–53

Prayer of the Week

Almighty and everlasting God, increase in us Your gifts of faith, hope, and love that we may receive the forgiveness You have promised and love what You have commanded; through Jesus Christ, Your Son, our Lord, who lives and reigns with You and the Holy Spirit, one God, now and forever. (C64)

Sunday on June 19–25 (Proper 7)

The Lection		*The Hymn*
C	Isaiah 65:1–9	825
	Psalm 3 (v. 8)	
	Galatians 3:23—4:7	
	Luke 8:26–39	

The Liturgical Lessons for the Week

M	Joshua 2:1–7
T	Jude 17–23
W	John 7:1–9
Th	Hosea 11:1–11
F	2 Corinthians 13:1–10
S	Luke 10:10–16

Prayer of the Week

O God, You have prepared for those who love You such good things as surpass our understanding. Cast out all sins and evil desires from us, and pour into our hearts Your Holy Spirit to guide us into all blessedness; through Jesus Christ, Your Son, our Lord, who lives and reigns with You and the Holy Spirit, one God, now and forever. (C65)

Sunday on June 26—July 2 (Proper 8)

The Lection		*The Hymn*
C	1 Kings 19:9b–21	688
	Psalm 16 (v. 11)	
	Galatians 5:1, 13–25	
	Luke 9:51–62	

The Liturgical Lessons for the Week

M	Judges 2:1–5
T	Acts 4:13–22
W	Matthew 4:23–25
Th	2 Chronicles 33:9–13
F	Hebrews 13:1–6
S	John 7:32–36

Prayer of the Week

Lord of all power and might, author and giver of all good things, graft into our hearts the love of Your name and nourish us with all goodness that we may love and serve our neighbor; through Jesus Christ, Your Son, our Lord, who lives and reigns with You and the Holy Spirit, one God, now and forever. (C66)

Sunday on July 3–9 (Proper 9)

The Lection		*The Hymn*
C	Isaiah 66:10–14	533
	Psalm 66:1–7 (vv. 8–9)	
	Galatians 6:1–10, 14–18	
	Luke 10:1–20	

The Liturgical Lessons for the Week

M	Isaiah 65:17–25
T	Acts 15:30–35
W	Matthew 12:9–14
Th	Micah 7:14–20
F	Acts 21:1–6
S	Matthew 12:15–21

Almighty God, You have built Your Church on the foundation of the apostles and prophets with Christ Jesus Himself as the cornerstone. Continue to send Your messengers to preserve Your people in true peace that, by the preaching of Your Word, Your Church may be kept free from all harm and danger; through Jesus Christ, Your Son, our Lord, who lives and reigns with You and the Holy Spirit, one God, now and forever. (C67)

Sunday on July 10–16 (Proper 10)

The Lection		*The Hymn*
C	Leviticus (18:1–5) 19:9–18	845
	Psalm 41 (v. 1)	
	Colossians 1:1–14	
	Luke 10:25–37	

The Liturgical Lessons for the Week

M	Judges 7:9–14
T	Romans 6:12–14
W	Luke 4:31–37
Th	Judges 7:15–23
F	Romans 6:15–19
S	Luke 4:38–39

Prayer of the Week

Lord Jesus Christ, in Your deep compassion You rescue us from whatever may hurt us. Teach us to love You above all things and to love our neighbors as ourselves; for You live and reign with the Father and the Holy Spirit, one God, now and forever. (C68)

Sunday on July 17–23 (Proper 11)

The Lection		*The Hymn*
C	Genesis 18:1–10a (10b–14)	536
	Psalm 27:(1–6) 7–14 (v. 4)	
	Colossians 1:21–29	
	Luke 10:38–42	

The Liturgical Lessons for the Week

M	Exodus 23:1–9
T	Romans 6:20–23
W	Luke 11:14–26
Th	Job 5:8–16
F	2 Corinthians 1:3–7
S	John 8:12–20

Prayer of the Week

O Lord, grant us the Spirit to hear Your Word and know the one thing needful that by Your Word and Spirit we may live according to Your will; through Jesus Christ, Your Son, our Lord, who lives and reigns with You and the Holy Spirit, one God, now and forever. (C69)

Sunday on July 24–30 (Proper 12)

The Lection   *The Hymn*

C   Genesis 18:(17–19) 20–33   766
     Psalm 138 (v. 3)
     Colossians 2:6–15 (16–19)
     Luke 11:1–13

The Liturgical Lessons for the Week

M   Numbers 23:7–12
T   Acts 4:23–31
W   Luke 10:39–47
Th   Genesis 28:18–22
F   Acts 20:1–6
S   John 5:1–9

Prayer of the Week

O Lord, let Your merciful ears be attentive to the prayers of Your servants, and by Your Word and Spirit teach us how to pray that our petitions may be pleasing before You; through Jesus Christ, Your Son, our Lord, who lives and reigns with You and the Holy Spirit, one God, now and forever. (C70)

Sunday on July 31—August 6 (Proper 13)

The Lection   *The Hymn*

C   Ecclesiastes 1:2, 12–14; 2:18–26   782
     Psalm 100 (v. 3)
     Colossians 3:1–11
     Luke 12:13–21

The Liturgical Lessons for the Week

M   Isaiah 48:9–16
T   Galatians 3:1–9
W   Luke 11:27–33
Th   1 Samuel 24:1–7
F   1 Timothy 4:1–10
S   Luke 11:33–36

Prayer of the Week

O Lord, grant us wisdom to recognize the treasures You have stored up for us in heaven, that we may never despair but always rejoice and be thankful for the riches of Your grace; through Jesus Christ, Your Son, our Lord, who lives and reigns with You and the Holy Spirit, one God, now and forever. (C71)

Sunday on August 7–13 (Proper 14)

The Lection		*The Hymn*
C	Genesis 15:1–6	666
	Psalm 33:12–22 (v. 20)	
	Hebrews 11:1–16	
	Luke 12:22–34 (35–40)	

The Liturgical Lessons for the Week

M	Deuteronomy 32:1–9	
T	Galatians 3:15–22 W	Matthew 8:23–27
Th	Numbers 13:25–33	
F	James 1:2–15	
S	Matthew 9:27–34	

Prayer of the Week

Almighty and merciful God, it is by Your grace that we live as Your people who offer acceptable service. Grant that we may walk by faith, and not by sight, in the way that leads to eternal life; through Jesus Christ, Your Son, our Lord, who lives and reigns with You and the Holy Spirit, one God, now and forever. (C72)

Sunday on August 14–20 (Proper 15)

The Lection		*The Hymn*
C	Jeremiah 23:16–29	655
	Psalm 119:81–88 (v. 81)	
	Hebrews 11:17–31 (32–40); 12:1–3	
	Luke 12:49–53 (54–56)	

The Liturgical Lessons for the Week

M	Joshua 4:1–7
T	Acts 5:1–11
W	Luke 5:12–16
Th	Joshua 4:8–14
F	Acts 7:1–8
S	Luke 9:12–17

188

Prayer of the Week

Merciful Lord, cleanse and defend Your Church by the sacrifice of Christ. United with Him in Holy Baptism, give us grace to receive with thanksgiving the fruits of His redeeming work and daily follow in His way; through the same Jesus Christ, Your Son, our Lord, who lives and reigns with You and the Holy Spirit, one God, now and forever. (C73)

Sunday on August 21–27 (Proper 16)

The Lection

C   Isaiah 66:18–23
      Psalm 50:1–15 (v. 23)
      Hebrews 12:4–24 (25–29)
      Luke 13:22–30

The Hymn

510

The Liturgical Lessons for the Week

M   1 Samuel 7:12–17
T   Hebrews 9:1–10
W   Mark 3:1–6
Th   2 Samuel 2:1–4
F   James 4:7–17
S   Mark 4:1–9

Prayer of the Week

O Lord, You have called us to enter Your kingdom through the narrow door. Guide us by Your Word and Spirit, and lead us now and always into the feast of Your Son, Jesus Christ, who lives and reigns with You and the Holy Spirit, one God, now and forever. (C74)

Sunday on August 28—September 3 (Proper 17)

The Lection

C   Proverbs 25:2–10
      Psalm 131 (v. 2)
      Hebrews 13:1–17
      Luke 14:1–14

The Hymn

842

The Liturgical Lessons for the Week

M   1 Samuel 6:19–21
T   Jude 8–13
W   Mark 11:27–33
Th   Ecclesiastes 12:1–7
F   James 3:1–5
S   Matthew 15:10–20

Prayer of the Week

O Lord of grace and mercy, teach us by Your Holy Spirit to follow the example of Your Son in true humility, that we may withstand the temptations of the devil and with pure hearts and minds avoid ungodly pride; through the same Jesus Christ, our Lord, who lives and reigns with You and the Holy Spirit, one God, now and forever. (C75)

Sunday on September 4–10 (Proper 18)

The Lection

C   Deuteronomy 30:15–20
      Psalm 1 (v. 6)
      Philemon 1–21
      Luke 14:25–35

The Hymn

853

The Liturgical Lessons for the Week

M   Exodus 20:18–26
T   Hebrews 6:1–8
W   Matthew 17:22–27
Th   Numbers 6:1–8
F   2 Thessalonians 2:1–12
S   Luke 16:14–18

Prayer of the Week

O merciful Lord, You did not spare Your only Son but delivered Him up for us all. Grant us courage and strength to take up the cross and follow Him, who lives and reigns with You and the Holy Spirit, one God, now and forever. (C76)

Sunday on September 11–17 (Proper 19)

The Lection

C   Ezekiel 34:11–24
      Psalm 119:169–176 (v. 176)
      1 Timothy 1:(5–11) 12–17
      Luke 15:1–10

The Hymn

609/974

The Liturgical Lessons for the Week

M   Genesis 8:15–19
T   Acts 9:36–43
W   Luke 5:27–32
Th   2 Samuel 22:1–7
F   Acts 8:9–13
S   Matthew 12:1–8

Prayer of the Week

Lord Jesus, You are the Good Shepherd, without whom nothing is secure. Rescue and preserve us that we may not be lost forever but follow You, rejoicing in the way that leads to eternal life; for You live and reign with the Father and the Holy Spirit, one God, now and forever. (C77)

Sunday on September 18–24 (Proper 20)

The Lection		*The Hymn*
C	Amos 8:4–7	557
	Psalm 113 (v. 3)	
	1 Timothy 2:1–15	
	Luke 16:1–15	

The Liturgical Lessons for the Week

M	Malachi 4:4–6
T	Romans 9:27–33
W	Luke 13:10–17
Th	Zechariah 6:9–15
F	3 John 1–8
S	Mark 11:15–19

Prayer of the Week

O Lord, keep Your Church in Your perpetual mercy; and because without You we cannot but fall, preserve us from all things hurtful, and lead us to all things profitable to our salvation; through Jesus Christ, Your Son, our Lord, who lives and reigns with You and the Holy Spirit, one God, now and forever. (C78)

Sunday on September 25—October 1 (Proper 21)

The Lection		*The Hymn*
C	Amos 6:1–7	708
	Psalm 146 (v. 2)	
	1 Timothy 3:1–13	
	or 1 Timothy 6:6–19	
	Luke 16:19–31	

The Liturgical Lessons for the Week

M	Ezra 1:1–4
T	Hebrews 5:11–14
W	Luke 6:32–38
Th	Esther 4:10–17
F	1 Thessalonians 4:1–12
S	Mark 7:9–13

O God, You are the strength of all who trust in You, and without Your aid we can do no good thing. Grant us the help of Your grace that we may please You in both will and deed; through Jesus Christ, Your Son, our Lord, who lives and reigns with You and the Holy Spirit, one God, now and forever. (C79)

Sunday on October 2–8 (Proper 22)

The Lection		*The Hymn*
C	Habakkuk 1:1–4; 2:1–4	587
	Psalm 62 (v. 1)	
	2 Timothy 1:1–14	
	Luke 17:1–10	

The Liturgical Lessons for the Week

M	Nehemiah 4:1–6
T	Acts 14:19–28
W	Luke 12:49–53
Th	Ezra 10:1–5
F	2 Peter 3:14–18
S	Matthew 19:10–15

O God, our refuge and strength, the author of all godliness, by Your grace hear the prayers of Your Church. Grant that those things which we ask in faith we may receive through Your bountiful mercy; through Jesus Christ, Your Son, our Lord, who lives and reigns with You and the Holy Spirit, one God, now and forever. (C80)

Sunday on October 9–15 (Proper 23)

The Lection		*The Hymn*
C	Ruth 1:1–19a	846
	Psalm 111 (v. 10)	
	2 Timothy 2:1–13	
	Luke 17:11–19	

The Liturgical Lessons for the Week

M	Leviticus 7:11–18
T	Colossians 4:1–6
W	Luke 21:1–4
Th	1 Chronicles 16:7–36
F	Philemon 21–25
S	Mark 4:10–20

Prayer of the Week

Almighty God, You show mercy to Your people in all their troubles. Grant us always to recognize Your goodness, give thanks for Your compassion, and praise Your holy name; through Jesus Christ, Your Son, our Lord, who lives and reigns with You and the Holy Spirit, one God, now and forever. (C81)

Sunday on October 16–22 (Proper 24)

The Lection		*The Hymn*
C	Genesis 32:22–30	734
	Psalm 121 (vv. 1–2)	
	2 Timothy 3:14—4:5	
	Luke 18:1–8	

The Liturgical Lessons for the Week

M	Zechariah 7:1–14
T	1 Timothy 5:1–8
W	Luke 14:1–6
Th	2 Chronicles 1:7–13
F	James 5:13–20
S	Matthew 21:12–17

Prayer of the Week

O Lord, almighty and everlasting God, You have commanded us to pray and have promised to hear us. Mercifully grant that Your Holy Spirit may direct and govern our hearts in all things that we may persevere with steadfast faith in the confession of Your name; through Jesus Christ, Your Son, our Lord, who lives and reigns with You and the Holy Spirit, one God, now and forever. (C82)

Sunday on October 23–29 (Proper 25)

The Lection		*The Hymn*
C	Genesis 4:1–15	745
	Psalm 5 (v. 11a)	
	2 Timothy 4:6–8, 16–18	
	Luke 18:9–17	

The Liturgical Lessons for the Week

M	Zechariah 8:1–8
T	Acts 26:24–32
W	Luke 23:32–38
Th	Lamentations 3:55–66
F	Colossians 2:16–23
S	Matthew 17:14–21

Prayer of the Week

Almighty and everlasting God, You are always more ready to hear than we to pray and always ready to give more than we either desire or deserve. Pour down on us the abundance of Your mercy; forgive us those things of which our conscience is afraid; and give us those good things for which we are not worthy to ask except by the merits and mediation of Jesus Christ, Your Son, our Lord, who lives and reigns with You and the Holy Spirit, one God, now and forever. (C83)

Sunday on October 30—November 5 (Proper 26)

The Lection		*The Hymn*
C	Isaiah 1:10–18	728
	Psalm 130 (vv. 3–4)	
	2 Thessalonians 1:1–5 (6–10) 11–12	
	Luke 19:1–10	

The Liturgical Lessons for the Week

M	Ezra 8:24–30
T	1 Peter 1:10–16
W	Matthew 16:5–12
Th	Ecclesiastes 2:1–9
F	1 Timothy 5:9–16
S	Mark 4:21–25

Prayer of the Week

O Lord, stir up the hearts of Your faithful people to welcome and joyfully receive Your Son, our Savior, Jesus Christ, that He may find in us a fit dwelling place; who lives and reigns with You and the Holy Spirit, one God, now and forever. (C84)

Sunday on November 6–12 (Proper 27)

The Lection		*The Hymn*
C	Exodus 3:1–15	713
	Psalm 148 (v. 13)	
	2 Thessalonians 2:1–8, 13–17	
	Luke 20:27–40	

The Liturgical Lessons for the Week

M	Numbers 14:1–12
T	2 Peter 1:3–11
W	Luke 21:20–24
Th	Zephaniah 3:8–10
F	Philippians 1:12–18
S	Luke 18:35–43

Living God, Your almighty power is made known chiefly in showing mercy and pity. Grant us the fullness of Your grace to lay hold of Your promises and live forever in Your presence; through Jesus Christ, Your Son, our Lord, who lives and reigns with You and the Holy Spirit, one God, now and forever. (C85)

Sunday on November 13–19 (Proper 28)

The Lection		*The Hymn*
C	Malachi 4:1–6	508
	Psalm 98 (v. 9b)	
	2 Thessalonians 3:(1–5) 6–13	
	Luke 21:5–28 (29–36)	

The Liturgical Lessons for the Week

M	Amos 9:9–15
T	Hebrews 12:25–29
W	Mark 13:14–23
Th	Micah 4:6–10
F	Acts 28:23–31
S	Luke 14:15–24

Prayer of the Week

O Lord, almighty and ever-living God, You have given exceedingly great and precious promises to those who trust in You. Rule and govern our hearts and minds by Your Holy Spirit that we may live and abide forever in Your Son, who lives and reigns with You and the Holy Spirit, one God, now and forever. (C86)

The Last Sunday of the Church Year— Sunday on November 20–26 (Proper 29)

The Lection		*The Hymn*
C	Malachi 3:13–18	534
	Psalm 46 (v. 7)	
	Colossians 1:13–20	
	Luke 23:27–43	

The Liturgical Lessons for the Week

M	Zechariah 8:9–13
T	Revelation 21:5–8
W	Matthew 24:15–25
Th	Zechariah 8:14–23
F	Revelation 22:1–5
S	Matthew 24:29–35

Prayer of the Week

Lord Jesus Christ, You reign among us by the preaching of Your cross. Forgive Your people their offenses that we, being governed by Your bountiful goodness, may enter at last into Your eternal paradise; for You live and reign with the Father and the Holy Spirit, one God, now and forever. (C87)

THE TIME OF THE CHURCH

One-Year Lectionary

The Holy Trinity

The Lection	*The Hymn*
1Yr. Isaiah 6:1–7	498/499
Psalm 29 (v. 2)	
Romans 11:33–36	
John 3:1–15 (16–17)	

The Liturgical Lessons for the Week

M	Genesis 18:1–8
T	2 Timothy 1:1–2
W	Romans 11:25–36
Th	Isaiah 48:10–22
F	1 John 3:1–10
S	2 Corinthians 5:16–21

Prayer of the Week

Almighty and everlasting God, You have given us grace to acknowledge the glory of the eternal Trinity by the confession of a true faith and to worship the Unity in the power of the Divine Majesty. Keep us steadfast in this faith and defend us from all adversities; for You, O Father, Son, and Holy Spirit, live and reign, one God, now and forever. (L52)

or

O Lord God, heavenly Father: We poor sinners confess that in our flesh dwells no good thing, and that, left to ourselves, we die and perish in sin, since that which is born of flesh is flesh and cannot see the kingdom of God. But we pray that You would grant us Your grace and mercy, and for the sake of Your Son, Jesus Christ, send Your Holy Spirit into our hearts, that being regenerate we may firmly believe the forgiveness of sins according to Your promise in Baptism, and that we may daily increase in Christian love and in other good works, until we at last obtain eternal salvation; through Your beloved Son Jesus Christ, our Lord, who lives and reigns with You and the Holy Spirit, one true God, now and forever. (VD)

First Sunday after Trinity

The Lection

1Yr.   Genesis 15:1–6
      Psalm 33:12–22 (v. 20)
      1 John 4:16–21
      Luke 16:19–31

The Hymn

768

The Liturgical Lessons for the Week

M   Luke 17:1–10
T   2 Timothy 2:19–26
W   James 4:15–17
Th   1 Corinthians 7:29–35
F   John 6:47–58
S   Genesis 17:1–14

Prayer of the Week

O God, the strength of all who trust in You, mercifully accept our prayers; and because through the weakness of our mortal nature we can do no good thing, grant us Your grace to keep Your commandments that we may please You in both will and deed; through Jesus Christ, our Lord, who lives and reigns with You and the Holy Spirit, one God, now and forever. (H61)

or

Lord God, heavenly Father, rule and govern our hearts by Your Holy Spirit, that we may not, like the rich man, hear Your Word in vain, and become so devoted to things temporal that we forget things eternal; but that we readily and according to our ability serve those who are in need, and not defile ourselves with carousing and pride; in trial and misfortune keep us from despair, and grant us to put our trust wholly in Your fatherly help and grace, so that in faith and Christian patience we may overcome all things; through Your Son, Jesus Christ our Lord, who lives and reigns with You and the Holy Spirit, one true God, now and forever. (VD)

Second Sunday after Trinity

The Lection

1Yr. Proverbs 9:1–10
      Psalm 34:12–22 (v. 11)
      Ephesians 2:13–22
      or 1 John 3:13–18
      Luke 14:15–24

The Liturgical Lessons for the Week

M   Jeremiah 10:1–10
T   2 Timothy 2:14–19
W   Matthew 21:33–46
Th   Isaiah 48:1–8
F   Ephesians 2:1–12
S   Revelation 19:1–10

The Hymn

510 or 622

Prayer of the Week

O Lord, since You never fail to help and govern those whom You nurture in Your steadfast fear and love, work in us a perpetual fear and love of Your holy name; through Jesus Christ, our Lord, who lives and reigns with You and the Holy Spirit, one God, now and forever. (H62)

or

Lord God, heavenly Father, we give thanks to You, that through Your Holy Word You have called us to Your great supper. Enliven our hearts by Your Holy Spirit, that we may not hear Your Word without fruit, but that we may prepare ourselves rightly for Your kingdom, and not allow ourselves to be hindered by any worldly care; through Your beloved Son Jesus Christ, our Lord, who lives and reigns with You and the Holy Spirit, one true God, now and forever. (VD)

Third Sunday after Trinity

The Lection

1Yr. Micah 7:18–20
      Psalm 103:1–13 (v. 8)
      1 Timothy 1:12–17
      or 1 Peter 5:6–11
      Luke 15:1–10
      or Luke 15:11–32

The Hymn

608

M	Genesis 17:1–8
T	James 2:8–13
W	Matthew 18:7–20
Th	Deuteronomy 5:22–33
F	1 Timothy 1:8–17
S	John 8:1–11

Prayer of the Week

O God, the protector of all who trust in You, without whom nothing is strong and nothing is holy, multiply Your mercy on us that, with You as our ruler and guide, we may so pass through things temporal that we lose not the things eternal; through Jesus Christ, our Lord, who lives and reigns with You and the Holy Spirit, one God, now and forever. (H63)

or

Lord God, heavenly Father, we all like sheep have gone astray, having allowed ourselves to be led away from the right path by Satan and our own sinful flesh. Graciously forgive us all our sins for the sake of Your Son, Jesus Christ; and enliven our hearts by Your Holy Spirit that we may abide in Your Word, and in true repentance and a steadfast faith continue in Your Church unto the end, and obtain eternal salvation; through our Lord Jesus Christ, Your Son, who lives and reigns with You and the Holy Spirit, one true God, now and forever. (VD)

Fourth Sunday after Trinity

The Lection		*The Hymn*
1Yr.	Genesis 50:15–21	696
	Psalm 138 (v. 8b)	
	Romans 12:14–21	
	or Romans 8:18–23	
	Luke 6:36–42	

The Liturgical Lessons for the Week

M	Numbers 23:18–24
T	Isaiah 43:8–13
W	Luke 17:1–10
Th	Jonah 1:3–4
F	Acts 3:17–26
S	Matthew 7:1–12

Prayer of the Week

O Lord, grant that the course of this world may be so peaceably ordered by Your governance that Your Church may joyfully serve You in all godly quietness; through Jesus Christ, our Lord, who lives and reigns with You and the Holy Spirit, one God, now and forever. (H64)

or

O Lord God, heavenly Father: You are merciful, and through Christ promised us that You will neither judge nor condemn us, but graciously forgive us all our sins, and abundantly provide for all our wants of body and soul. We pray that by Your Holy Spirit You would establish in our hearts a confident faith in Your mercy, and teach us also to be merciful to our neighbor, that we may not judge or condemn others, but willingly forgive all, and, judging only ourselves, lead blessed lives in Your fear; through Your dear Son, Jesus Christ, our Lord, who lives and reigns with You and the Holy Spirit, one true God, now and forever. (VD)

Fifth Sunday after Trinity

The Lection

1Yr.   1 Kings 19:11–21
      Psalm 16 (v. 11)
      1 Corinthians 1:18–25
      or 1 Peter 3:8–15
      Luke 5:1–11

The Hymn

688

The Liturgical Lessons for the Week

M   Joshua 2:1–7
T   Jude 17–23
W   John 7:1–13
Th   Hosea 11:1–11
F   2 Corinthians 13:1–10
S   Luke 10:10–16

Prayer of the Week

O God, You have prepared for those who love You good things that surpass all understanding. Pour into our hearts such love toward You that we, loving You above all things, may obtain Your promises, which exceed all that we can desire; through Jesus Christ, Your Son, our Lord, who lives and reigns with You and the Holy Spirit, one God, now and forever. (H65)

or

O Jesus Christ, Son of the living God, You have given us Your Holy Word and have bountifully provided for all our earthly needs. We confess that we are unworthy of all these mercies, and that we have rather deserved punishment. But we beseech You, forgive us our sins, and prosper and bless us in our various callings, that by Your strength we may be sustained and defended, now and forever, and so praise and glorify You eternally; for You live and reign with the Father and the Holy Spirit, one true God, now and forever. (VD)

Sixth Sunday after Trinity

The Lection		*The Hymn*
1Yr.	Exodus 20:1–17	562
	Psalm 19 (v. 8)	
	Romans 6:(1–2) 3–11	
	Matthew 5:(17–19) 20–26	

The Liturgical Lessons for the Week

M	Judges 2:1–5
T	Acts 4:13–22
W	Matthew 4:23–25
Th	2 Chronicles 33:9–13
F	Hebrews 13:1–6
S	John 7:32–36

Prayer of the Week

Lord of all power and might, author and giver of all good things, graft into our hearts the love of Your name, increase in us true religion, nourish us with all goodness, and of Your great mercy keep us in the same; through Jesus Christ, Your Son, our Lord, who lives and reigns with You and the Holy Spirit, one God, now and forever. (H66)

or

Lord God, heavenly Father, we confess that we are poor, wretched sinners, and that there is no good in us; our hearts, flesh, and blood being so corrupted by sin that we are never in this life without sinful lusts and desires. Dear Father, forgive us these sins, and let Your Holy Spirit so cleanse our hearts that we may desire and love Your

Word, abide by it, and thus by Your grace be forever saved; through our Lord Jesus Christ, Your Son, who lives and reigns with You and the Holy Spirit, one true God, now and forever. (VD)

Seventh Sunday after Trinity

The Lection
1Yr. Genesis 2:7–17
Psalm 33:1–11 (v. 6)
Romans 6:19–23
Mark 8:1–9

The Hymn
819

The Liturgical Lessons for the Week
M Isaiah 65:17–25
T Acts 15:30–35
W Matthew 12:9–21
Th Micah 7:14–20
F Acts 21:1
S Matthew 15:32–39

Prayer of the Week

O God, whose never-failing providence orders all things both in heaven and earth, we humbly implore You to put away from us all hurtful things and to give us those things that are profitable for us; through Jesus Christ, Your Son, our Lord, who lives and reigns with You and the Holy Spirit, one God, now and forever. (H67)

or

Lord God, heavenly Father, in the wilderness by Your Son You abundantly fed four thousand men, besides women and children, with seven loaves and a few small fish. Graciously abide among us with Your blessing, and keep us from covetousness and the cares of this life, that we may seek first Your kingdom and Your righteousness, and in all things needed for body and soul, experience Your ever-present help; through Your Son, our Lord Jesus Christ, who lives and reigns with You and the Holy Spirit, one true God, now and forever. (VD)

Eighth Sunday after Trinity

The Lection
1Yr. Jeremiah 23:16–29
Psalm 26 (v. 12)
Acts 20:27–38
or Romans 8:12–17
Matthew 7:15–23

The Hymn
745

The Liturgical Lessons for the Week

M Judges 7:9–14
T Romans 6:12–14
W Luke 4:31–39
Th Judges 7:15–23
F Romans 6:15–19
S Deuteronomy 13:1–11

Prayer of the Week

Grant to us, Lord, the Spirit to think and do always such things as are right, that we, who cannot do anything that is good without You, may be enabled by You to live according to Your will; through Jesus Christ, Your Son, our Lord, who lives and reigns with You and the Holy Spirit, one God, now and forever. (H68)

or

Lord God, heavenly Father, we most heartily thank You that You have caused us to come to the knowledge of Your Word. We pray: Graciously keep us steadfast in this knowledge unto death, that we may obtain eternal life; send us, now and ever, pious pastors who faithfully preach Your Word, without offense or false doctrine, and grant them long life. Defend us from all false teachings, and frustrate the counsels of all who pervert Your Word, who come to us in sheep's clothing, but inwardly are ravenous wolves, that Your true Church may evermore be established among us, and be defended and preserved from such false teachers; through our Lord Jesus Christ, Your Son, who lives and reigns with You and the Holy Spirit, one true God, now and forever. (VD)

Ninth Sunday after Trinity

The Lection   *The Hymn*

1Yr. 2 Samuel 22:26–34   730
Psalm 51:1–12 (v. 18)
1 Corinthians 10:6–13
Luke 16:1–9 (10–13)

The Liturgical Lessons for the Week

M Exodus 23:1–9
T Romans 6:20–23
W Luke 11:14–26
Th Job 5:8–16
F 2 Corinthians 1:3–7
S John 8:12–20

Let Your merciful ears, O Lord, be open to the prayers of Your humble servants; and that they may obtain their petitions, make them to ask such things as shall please You; through Jesus Christ, Your Son, our Lord, who lives and reigns with You and the Holy Spirit, one God, now and forever. (H69)

or

Lord God, heavenly Father, You have bountifully given us Your blessing and our daily bread. Preserve us from covetousness, and so enliven our hearts that we willingly share Your blessed gifts with our needy brethren; that we may be found faithful stewards of Your gifts, and abide in Your grace when we shall be removed from our stewardship, and shall come before Your judgment, through our Lord Jesus Christ, who lives and reigns with You and the Holy Spirit, one true God, now and forever. (VD)

Tenth Sunday after Trinity

The Lection	*The Hymn*
1Yr. Jeremiah 8:4–12	644
or Jeremiah 7:1–11	
Psalm 92 (v. 4)	
Romans 9:30–10:4	
or 1 Corinthians 12:1–11	
Luke 19:41–48	

The Liturgical Lessons for the Week

M	Numbers 23:7–12
T	Acts 4:23–31
W	Luke 10:39–47
Th	Genesis 28:18–22
F	Acts 20:1–6
S	John 5:1–9

Prayer of the Week

O God, You declare Your almighty power above all in showing mercy and pity. Mercifully grant us such a measure of Your grace we may obtain Your gracious promises and be made partakers of Your heavenly treasures; through Jesus Christ, Your Son, our Lord, who lives and reigns with You and the Holy Spirit, one God, now and forever. (H70)

or

Almighty and everlasting God, by Your Holy Spirit You have revealed to us the Gospel of Your Son, Jesus Christ. Enliven our hearts that we may sincerely receive Your Word, and not make light of it, or hear it without fruit, but that we may fear You and daily grow in faith in Your mercy, and finally obtain eternal salvation; through Your Son, Jesus Christ, our Lord, who lives and reigns with You and the Holy Spirit, one true God, now and forever. (VD)

Eleventh Sunday after Trinity

The Lection   *The Hymn*

1Yr.   Genesis 4:1–15   559
       Psalm 50:7–23 (v. 14)
       Ephesians 2:1–10
         or 1 Corinthians 15:1–10
       Luke 18:9–14

The Liturgical Lessons for the Week

M   Isaiah 48:9–16
T   Galatians 3:1–9
W   Luke 11:27–36
Th   1 Samuel 24:1–7
F   1 Timothy 4:1–10
S   Titus 3:1–11

Prayer of the Week

Almighty and everlasting God, always more ready to hear than we to pray and to give more than we either desire or deserve, pour down upon us the abundance of Your mercy, forgiving those things of which our conscience is afraid and giving us those good things that we are not worthy to ask, except through the merits and mediation of Christ, our Lord, who lives and reigns with You and the Holy Spirit, one God, now and forever. (H71)

or

Lord God, heavenly Father, guide and direct us by Your Holy Spirit, that we may not forget our sins and be filled with pride, but continue in daily repentance and renewal, seeking comfort only in the blessed knowledge that You will be merciful to us, forgive us our sins, and grant us eternal life; through Your beloved Son, Jesus Christ, our Lord, who lives and reigns with You and the Holy Spirit, one true God, now and forever. (VD)

Twelfth Sunday after Trinity

Prayer of the Week

Almighty and merciful God, by Your gift alone Your faithful people render true and laudable service. Help us steadfastly to live in this life according to Your promises and finally attain Your heavenly glory; through Jesus Christ, Your Son, our Lord, who lives and reigns with You and the Holy Spirit, one God, now and forever. (H72)

or

Almighty and everlasting God, who created all things, we thank You that You have given us sound bodies, and have graciously preserved our tongues and other members from the power of the adversary. Grant us Your grace, that we may rightly use our ears and tongues; help us to hear Your Word diligently and devoutly, and with our tongues so to praise and glorify Your grace, that no one is offended by our words, but that all may be edified by them; through Your beloved Son, Jesus Christ, our Lord, who lives and reigns with You and the Holy Spirit, one true God, now and forever. (VD)

Thirteenth Sunday after Trinity

M   Joshua 4:1–7
T   Acts 5:1–11
W   Luke 5:12–16
Th   Joshua 4:8–14
F   Acts 7:1–8
S   Luke 9:12–17

Prayer of the Week

Almighty and everlasting God, give us an increase of faith, hope, and charity; and that we may obtain what You have promised, make us love what You have commanded; through Jesus Christ, Your Son, our Lord, who lives and reigns with You and the Holy Spirit, one God, now and forever. (H73)

or

Lord God, heavenly Father, we most heartily thank You that You have granted us to live in this accepted time, when we may hear Your holy Gospel, know Your fatherly will, and behold Your Son, Jesus Christ! We pray, most merciful Father: Let the light of Your Holy Word remain with us, and so govern our hearts by Your Holy Spirit, that we may never forsake Your Word, but remain steadfast in it, and finally obtain eternal salvation; through Your beloved Son, Jesus Christ, our Lord, who lives and reigns with You and the Holy Spirit, one true God, now and forever. (VD)

Fourteenth Sunday after Trinity

The Lection	*The Hymn*
1Yr. Proverbs 4:10–23	849
Psalm 119:9–16 (v. 12)	
Galatians 5:16–24	
Luke 17:11–19	

The Liturgical Lessons for the Week

M   1 Samuel 7:12–17
T   Hebrews 9:1–10
W   Mark 3:1–6
Th   2 Samuel 2:1–4
F   James 4:7–17
S   Mark 4:1–9

Prayer of the Week

O Lord, keep Your Church with Your perpetual mercy; and because of our frailty we cannot but fall, keep us ever by Your help from all things hurtful and lead us to all things profitable to our salvation; through Jesus Christ, Your Son, our Lord, who lives and reigns with You and the Holy Spirit, one God, now and forever. (H74)

or

Lord God, heavenly Father, by Your blessed Word and Your holy Baptism You have mercifully cleansed all who believe from the fearful leprosy of sin, and You daily grant us Your gracious help in all our need. Enlighten our hearts by Your Holy Spirit, that we may never forget these Your blessings, but ever live in Your fear, and, trusting fully in Your grace, with thankful hearts continually praise and glorify You; through Your Son, our Lord Jesus Christ, who lives and reigns with You and the Holy Spirit, one true God, now and forever. (VD)

Fifteenth Sunday after Trinity

The Lection
1Yr. 1 Kings 17:8–16
      Psalm 146 (v. 9a)
      Galatians 5:25–6:10
      Matthew 6:24–34

The Hymn
760

The Liturgical Lessons for the Week

M   1 Samuel 6:19–21
T   Jude 8–13
W   Mark 11:27–33
Th   Ecclesiastes 12:1–7
F   James 3:1–5
S   Matthew 15:10–20

Prayer of the Week

O Lord, we implore You, let Your continual pity cleanse and defend Your Church; and because she cannot continue in safety without Your aid, preserve her evermore by Your help and goodness; through Jesus Christ, Your Son, our Lord, who lives and reigns with You and the Holy Spirit, one God, now and forever. (H75)

or

Lord God, heavenly Father, we thank You for all Your benefits: that You have given us life and graciously sustained us to this day. We pray, do not take Your blessing from us; preserve us from covetousness, that we may serve You only, love and abide in You, and not defile ourselves by idolatrous love of wealth, but hope and trust only in Your grace; through Jesus Christ our Lord, who lives and reigns with You and the Holy Spirit, one true God, now and forever. (VD)

Sixteenth Sunday after Trinity

The Lection		*The Hymn*
1Yr.	1 Kings 17:17–24	758
	Psalm 30 (v. 5b)	
	Ephesians 3:13–21	
	Luke 7:11–17	

The Liturgical Lessons for the Week

M	Exodus 20:18–26
T	Hebrews 6:1–8
W	Matthew 17:22–27
Th	Numbers 6:1–8
F	2 Thessalonians 2:1–12
S	Luke 16:14–18

Prayer of the Week

O Lord, we pray that Your grace may always go before and follow after us, that we may continually be given to all good works; through Jesus Christ, Your Son, our Lord, who lives and reigns with You and the Holy Spirit, one God, now and forever. (H76)

or

Lord God, heavenly Father, You sent Your Son to be made flesh, that by His death He might atone for our sins and deliver us from eternal death. We pray, confirm in our hearts the hope that our Lord Jesus Christ, who with but a word raised the widow's son, in like manner will raise us on the last day and grant us eternal life; through Your beloved Son, Jesus Christ, our Lord, who lives and reigns with You and the Holy Spirit, one true God, now and forever. (VD)

Seventeenth Sunday after Trinity

Prayer of the Week

Lord, we implore You, grant Your people grace to withstand the temptations of the devil and with pure hearts and minds to follow You, the only God; through Jesus Christ, Your Son, our Lord, who lives and reigns with You and the Holy Spirit, one God, now and forever. (H77)

or

Lord God, heavenly Father: Guide and direct us by Your Holy Spirit that we may not exalt ourselves, but humbly fear You, with our whole hearts hear and keep Your Word, and keep the day of rest holy, that we also may be sanctified by Your Word; help us, first, to place our hope and confidence in Your Son, Jesus Christ, who alone is our righteousness and Redeemer, and, then, so to amend and better our lives in accordance with Your Word, that we may avoid all offenses and finally obtain eternal salvation; through Your grace in Christ, who lives and reigns with You and the Holy Spirit, one true God, now and forever. (VD)

Eighteenth Sunday after Trinity

M   Malachi 4:4–6
T   Romans 9:27–33
W   Luke 13:10–17
Th   Zechariah 6:9–15
F   3 John 1–8
S   Mark 11:15–19

Prayer of the Week

O God, because without You we are not able to please You, mercifully grant that Your Holy Spirit may in all things direct and rule our hearts; through Jesus Christ, Your Son, our Lord, who lives and reigns with You and the Holy Spirit, one God, now and forever. (H78)

or

Lord God, heavenly Father: We are poor, miserable sinners; we know Your will, but cannot fulfill it because of the weakness of our flesh and blood, and because our enemy, the devil, will not leave us in peace. Therefore we pray, pour Your Holy Spirit in our hearts, that in steadfast faith we may cling to Your Son Jesus Christ, find comfort in His Passion and death, believe the forgiveness of sins through Him, and in willing obedience to Your will lead holy lives on earth, until by Your grace, through a blessed death, we depart from this world of sorrow, and obtain eternal life; through Your Son, Jesus Christ our Lord, who lives and reigns with You and the Holy Spirit, one true God, now and forever. (VD)

Nineteenth Sunday after Trinity

The Lection	*The Hymn*
1Yr. Genesis 28:10–17	708
Psalm 84 (v. 8)	
Ephesians 4:22–28	
Matthew 9:1–8	

The Liturgical Lessons for the Week

M   Ezra 1:1–4
T   Hebrews 5:11–14
W   Luke 6:32–38
Th   Esther 4:10–17
F   1 Thessalonians 4:1–12
S   Mark 7:9–13

Almighty and merciful God, of Your bountiful goodness keep from us all things that may hurt us that we, being ready in both body and soul, may cheerfully accomplish whatever You would have us do; through Jesus Christ, Your Son, our Lord, who lives and reigns with You and the Holy Spirit, one God, now and forever. (H79)

or

O mighty and everlasting God, by Your Son, Jesus Christ, You mercifully helped the paralytic both in body and soul: We pray, for the sake of Your great mercy, be gracious also to us; forgive us all our sins, and so govern us by Your Holy Spirit, that we may not ourselves be the cause of sickness and other afflictions; keep us in Your fear, and strengthen us by Your grace that we may escape temporal and eternal wrath and punishment; through Your Son, Jesus Christ, our Lord, who lives and reigns with You and the Holy Spirit, one true God, now and forever. (VD)

Twentieth Sunday after Trinity

The Lection	*The Hymn*
1Yr. Isaiah 55:1–9	828
Psalm 27:1–9 (v. 8)	
Ephesians 5:15–21	
Matthew 22:1–14	
or Matthew 21:33–44	

The Liturgical Lessons for the Week

M	Nehemiah 4:1–6
T	Acts 14:19–28
W	Luke 12:49–53
Th	Ezra 10:1–5
F	2 Peter 3:14–18
S	Matthew 19:10–15

Prayer of the Week

O Lord, grant to Your faithful people pardon and peace that they may be cleansed from all their sins and serve You with a quiet mind; through Jesus Christ, Your Son, our Lord, who lives and reigns with You and the Holy Spirit, one God, now and forever. (H80)

or

Lord God, heavenly Father: We thank You, that of Your great mercy You have called us by Your Holy Word to the blessed marriage feast of Your Son, and through Him forgive us all our sins; but, being daily assaulted by temptation, offense, and danger, and being weak in ourselves and given to sin, we beseech You graciously to protect us by Your Holy Spirit, that we might not fall into sin; and if we fall and defile our wedding garment, with which Your Son has clothed us, graciously help us again and lead us to repentance, that we fall not forever; preserve in us a constant faith in Your grace; through our Lord Jesus Christ, who lives and reigns with You and the Holy Spirit, one true God, now and forever. (VD)

Twenty-first Sunday after Trinity

The Lection		*The Hymn*
1Yr.	Genesis 1:1—2:3	607
	Psalm 8 (v. 9)	
	Ephesians 6:10–17	
	John 4:46–54	

The Liturgical Lessons for the Week

M	Leviticus 7:11–18
T	Colossians 4:1–6
W	Luke 21:1–4
Th	1 Chronicles 16:7–36
F	Philemon 21–25
S	Mark 4:10–20

Prayer of the Week

O Lord, keep Your household, the Church, in continual godliness that through Your protection she may be free from all adversities and devoutly given to serve You in good works; through Jesus Christ, Your Son, our Lord, who lives and reigns with You and the Holy Spirit, one God, now and forever. (H81)

or

Almighty and everlasting God, by Your Son You have promised us the forgiveness of sins, righteousness, and everlasting life: By Your Holy Spirit so enliven our hearts that in daily prayer we may seek our help in Christ against all temptations, and, constantly believing His promise, obtain that for which we pray, and at last be saved; through Your Son, Jesus Christ, who lives and reigns with You and the Holy Spirit, one true God, now and forever. (VD)

Twenty-second Sunday after Trinity

The Lection	*The Hymn*
1Yr. Micah 6:6–8	611
Psalm 116:12–19 (v. 13)	
Philippians 1:3–11	
Matthew 18:21–35	

The Liturgical Lessons for the Week

M	Zechariah 7:1–14
T	1 Timothy 5:1–8
W	Luke 14:1–6
Th	2 Chronicles 1:7–13
F	James 5:13–20
S	Matthew 21:12–17

Prayer of the Week

O God, our refuge and strength, the author of all godliness, hear the devout prayers of Your Church, especially in times of persecution, and grant that what we ask in faith we may obtain; through Jesus Christ, Your Son, our Lord, who lives and reigns with You and the Holy Spirit, one God, now and forever. (H82)

or

O almighty, eternal God: We confess that we are poor sinners and cannot answer one time out of a thousand, when You contend with us; but with all our hearts we thank You, that You have taken all our guilt from us and laid it upon Your dear Son, Jesus Christ, and made Him to atone for it. We pray, graciously sustain us in faith, and so govern us by Your Holy Spirit, that we may live according to Your will, in neighborly love, service and helpfulness, and not give way to wrath or revenge, that we may not incur Your wrath, but always find in You a gracious Father; through Jesus Christ our Lord, who lives and reigns with You and the Holy Spirit, one true God, now and forever. (VD)

Twenty-third Sunday after Trinity

The Lection	*The Hymn*
1Yr. Proverbs 8:11–22	714
Psalm 111 (v. 10a)	
Philippians 3:17–21	
Matthew 22:15–22	

M   Zechariah 8:1–8
T   Acts 26:24–32
W   Luke 23:32–38
Th   Lamentations 3:55–66
F   Colossians 2:16–23
S   Matthew 17:14–21

Prayer of the Week

O Lord, absolve Your people from their offenses that from the bonds of our sins, which by reason of our frailty we have brought upon ourselves, we may be delivered by Your bountiful goodness; through Jesus Christ, Your Son, our Lord, who lives and reigns with You and the Holy Spirit, one God, now and forever. (H83)

or

Lord God, heavenly Father: We thank You that unto this time You have granted us peace and graciously spared us from war and foreign dominion. We pray, graciously let us continue to live in Your fear according to Your will, giving no cause for wars or other punishment; govern and direct our leaders, that they may not hinder the obedience due to You, but maintain righteousness, that we may enjoy happiness and blessing under their government; through our Lord Jesus Christ, who lives and reigns with You and the Holy Spirit, one true God, now and forever. (VD)

Twenty-fourth Sunday after Trinity

The Lection   *The Hymn*

1Yr.   Isaiah 51:9–16   755
       Psalm 126 (v. 1)
       Colossians 1:9–14
       Matthew 9:18–26

The Liturgical Lessons for the Week

M   Ezra 8:24–30
T   1 Peter 1:10–16
W   Matthew 16:5–12
Th   Ecclesiastes 2:1–9
F   1 Timothy 5:9–16
S   Mark 4:21–25

Stir up, O Lord, the wills of Your faithful people that they, plenteously bringing forth the fruit of good works, may by You be plenteously rewarded; through Jesus Christ, Your Son, our Lord, who lives and reigns with You and the Holy Spirit, one God, now and forever. (H84)

or

O almighty and everlasting God, by Your dear Son You have promised us forgiveness of our sins and deliverance from eternal death: We pray that by Your Holy Spirit You will daily increase our faith in Your grace through Christ, and establish in us the certain hope that we shall not die, but peacefully sleep, and be raised on the last day to eternal life and salvation; through our Lord Jesus Christ, Your Son, who lives and reigns with You and the Holy Spirit, one true God, now and forever. (VD)

Twenty-fifth Sunday after Trinity

The Lection

1Yr. Exodus 32:1–20
     or Job 14:1–6
     Psalm 14 (v. 7)
     or Psalm 102:1–13 (v. 12)
     1 Thessalonians 4:13–18
     Matthew 24:15–28
     or Luke 17:20–30

The Hymn

658

The Liturgical Lessons for the Week

M   Numbers 14:1–12
T   2 Peter 1:3–11
W   Luke 21:20–24
Th   Zephaniah 3:8–10
F   Philippians 1:12–18
S   Luke 18:35–43

Prayer of the Week

Almighty God, we implore You, show Your mercy to Your humble servants that we, who put no trust in our own merits, may not be dealt with after the severity of Your judgment but according to Your mercy; through Jesus Christ, Your Son, our Lord, who lives and reigns with You and the Holy Spirit, one God, now and forever. (H85)

Lord God, heavenly Father, we most heartily thank You that, by Your Word, You have brought us out of the darkness of error into the light of Your grace: Mercifully help us to walk in that light, guard us from all error and false doctrine, and grant that we may not become ungrateful and despise and persecute Your Word, but receive it with all our heart, govern our lives according to it, and put all our trust in Your grace, through the merit of Your dear Son, our Lord Jesus Christ, who lives and reigns with You and the Holy Spirit, one true God, now and forever. (VD)

Twenty-sixth Sunday after Trinity

The Lection		*The Hymn*
1Yr.	Daniel 7:9–14	508
	Psalm 50:1–15 (v. 15)	
	2 Peter 3:3–14	
	Matthew 25:31–46	

The Liturgical Lessons for the Week

M	Amos 9:9–15
T	Hebrews 12:25–29
W	Mark 13:14–23
Th	Micah 4:6–10
F	Acts 28:23–31
S	Luke 14:15–24

Prayer of the Week

O Lord, so rule and govern our hearts and minds by Your Holy Spirit that, ever mindful of the end of all things and the day of Your just judgment, we may be stirred up to holiness of living here and dwell with You forever hereafter; through Jesus Christ, Your Son, our Lord, who lives and reigns with You and the Holy Spirit, one God, now and forever. (H86)

or

O almighty, eternal and merciful God, by Your beloved Son, our Lord and Savior Jesus Christ, You established the kingdom of grace for us in Your Holy Church here on earth, that we might believe the forgiveness of our sins, since You are a God who has no pleasure in the death of the wicked, but that the wicked turn from his way and live: Graciously forgive us all our sins; through Your Son, Jesus Christ, who lives and reigns with You and the Holy Spirit, one true God, now and forever. (VD)

Last Sunday of the Church Year

Prayer of the Week

O Lord, absolve Your people from their offenses that, from the bonds of our sins which by reason of our frailty we have brought upon ourselves, we may be delivered by Your bountiful goodness; through Jesus Christ, Your Son, our Lord, who lives and reigns with You and the Holy Spirit, one God, now and forever. (H87)

or

Lord God, heavenly Father, send forth Your Son, we pray, to lead home His bride, the Church, that with all the company of the redeemed we may finally enter into His eternal wedding feast; through Jesus Christ, our Lord, who lives and reigns with You and the Holy Spirit, one God, now and forever. (H88)

or

Lord God, heavenly Father, make us watchful and heedful in awaiting the coming of Your Son, our Lord Jesus Christ, that when He shall stand at the door and knock, He may find us not sleeping in carelessness and sin, but awake and rejoicing in His appearance; through Your beloved Son, Jesus Christ, our Lord, who lives and reigns with You and the Holy Spirit, one true God, now and forever. (VD)

4
Scripture Readings

DAILY LECTIONARY

One of the most distinctive—and beneficial—characteristics of the Daily Lectionary is the way in which the days of the year are arranged for ease of use: first, according to the Church's Time of Easter, followed by readings arranged by the civil calendar date for the remainder of the yearly cycle. This makes it easy to know (and find) exactly where you should be on any given day of the year.

The Daily Lectionary begins with Ash Wednesday in preparation for Holy Week and Easter. This choice of starting point reflects the origins of the Church Year, which began and developed around the Time of Easter (the weeks before and after the annual celebration of Christ's Passion and resurrection). The days following Ash Wednesday are noted in relation to the Sundays in Lent and the Sundays of Easter, through the Feast of Pentecost and concluding with Holy Trinity.

The rest of the Daily Lectionary is arranged according to the civil calendar and the dates that we all use to order and schedule our lives in this world. This portion of the calendar begins with the earliest date that may follow the Feast of the Holy Trinity—that is, May 18, in those years when Easter occurs at its earliest possible time. The days progress consecutively through the months of the civil calendar (June, July, August, and so on through February) to the latest possible date that may precede Ash Wednesday—that is, March 9, in those years when Easter occurs at its latest possible time. In this way, you only need to find a particular civil calendar date to find the appropriate readings.

THE TIME OF EASTER

Lenten Season

Ash Wed. Gen. 1:1–19
Mark 1:1–13

Th Gen. 1:20–2:3
Mark 1:14–28

F Gen. 2:4–25
Mark 1:29–45

S Gen. 3:1–24
Mark 2:1–17

Lent 1 Gen. 4:1–26
Mark 2:18–28

M Gen. 6:1–7:5
Mark 3:1–19

T Gen. 7:11–8:12
Mark 3:20–35

W Gen. 8:13–9:17
Gen. 9:18–11:26
Mark 4:1–20

Th Gen. 11:27–12:20
Mark 4:21–41

F Gen. 13:1–18
Gen. 14:1–24
Mark 5:1–20

S Gen. 15:1–21
Mark 5:21–43

Lent 2 Gen. 16:1–9, 15–17:22
Mark 6:1–13

M Gen. 18:1–15
Gen. 18:16–20:18
Mark 6:14–34

T Gen. 21:1–21
Mark 6:35–56

W Gen. 22:1–19
Mark 7:1–23

Th Gen. 24:1–31
Mark 7:24–37

F Gen. 24:32–52, 61–6
Gen 25:1–26:15
Mark 8:1–21

S Gen. 27:1–29
Mark 8:22–38

Lent 3 Gen. 27:30–45; 28:10–22
Mark 9:1–13

M Gen. 29:1–30
Gen. 29:31–34:31
Mark 9:14–32

T Gen. 35:1–29
Mark 9:33–50

W Gen. 37:1–36

Mark 10:1–12

Th Gen. 39:1–23
Mark 10:13–31

F Gen. 40:1–23
Mark 10:32–52

S Gen. 41:1–27
Mark 11:1–19

Lent 4 Gen. 41:28–57
Mark 11:20–33

M Gen. 42:1–34, 38
Mark 12:1–12

T Gen. 43:1–28
Mark 12:13–27

W Gen. 44:1–18, 32–34
Mark 12:28–44

Th Gen. 45:1–20, 24–28
Mark 13:1–23

F Gen. 47:1–31
Gen. 48:1–49:28
Mark 13:24–37

S Gen. 49:29–50:7, 14–26
Mark 14:1–11

Lent 5 Ex. 1:1–22
Mark 14:12–31

M Ex. 2:1–22
Mark 14:32–52

T Ex. 2:23–3:22
Mark 14:53–72

W Ex. 4:1–18
Mark 15:1–15

Th Ex. 4:19–31
Mark 15:16–32

F Ex. 5:1–6:1
Mark 15:33–47

S Ex. 7:1–25
Mark 16:1–20

Holy Week

Palm Sun. Ex. 8:1–32
Psalm 118
Heb. 1:1–14

M Ex. 9:1–28
Lam. 1:1–22
Heb. 2:1–18

T Ex. 9:29–10:20
Lam. 2:1–22
Heb. 3:1–19

W Ex. 10:21–11:10
Lam. 3:1–66
Heb. 4:1–16

Holy Thurs. Ex. 12:1–28
Lam. 4:1–22
Heb. 5:1–14
Psalm 31

Good Fri. Ex. 12:29–32; 13:1–16
Lam. 5:1–22
Heb. 6:1–20
Psalm 22

Holy Sat. Ex. 13:17–14:9
Heb. 7:1–22

Easter Season

Easter Sun. Ex. 14:10–31
Heb. 7:23–8:13

M Ex. 15:1–18
Heb. 9:1–28

T Ex. 15:19–16:12
Heb. 10:1–18

W Ex. 16:13–35
Heb. 10:19–39

Th Ex. 17:1–16
Heb. 11:1–29

F Ex. 18:5–27
Heb. 12:1–24

S Ex. 19:1–25
Heb. 13:1–21

Easter 2 Ex. 20:1–24
Luke 4:1–15

M Ex. 22:20–23:13
Luke 4:16–30

T Ex. 23:14–33
Luke 4:31–44

W Ex. 24:1–18
Luke 5:1–16

Th Ex. 25:1–22
Ex. 25:23–30:38
Luke 5:17–39

F Ex. 31:1–18
Luke 6:1–19

S Ex. 32:1–14
Luke 6:20–38

Easter 3 Ex. 32:15–35
Luke 6:39–49

M Ex. 33:1–23
Luke 7:1–17

T Ex. 34:1–28
Luke 7:18–35

W Ex. 34:29–35:21
Ex. 35:22–38:20
Luke 7:36–50

Th Ex. 38:21–39:8, 22–23, 27–31
Luke 8:1–21

F Ex. 39:32–40:16
Luke 8:22–39

S Ex. 40:17–38
Lev. 1:1–7:38
Luke 8:40–56

Easter 4 Lev. 8:1–13,

	30–36	**Easter 7**	Num. 14:1–25		John 6:60–71
	Luke 9:1–17		Luke 18:18–34	25	Eccl. 2:1–26
M	Lev. 9:1–24	M	Num. 14:26–45		John 7:1–13
	Luke 9:18–36		*Num. 15:1–41*	26	Eccl. 3:1–22
T	Lev. 10:1–20		Luke 18:35–19:10		John 7:14–31
	Lev. 11:1–15:33	T	Num. 16:1–22	27	Eccl. 4:1–16
	Luke 9:37–62		Luke 19:11–28		John 7:32–53
W	Lev. 16:1–24	W	Num. 16:23–40	28	Eccl. 5:1–20
	Luke 10:1–22		Luke 19:29–48		John 8:1–20
Th	Lev. 17:1–16	Th	Num. 16:41–17:13	29	Eccl. 6:1–7:10
	Luke 10:23–42		*Num. 18:1–19:22*		John 8:21–38
F	Lev. 18:1–7, 20–19:8		Luke 20:1–18	30	Eccl. 7:11–29
	Luke 11:1–13	F	Num. 20:1–21		John 8:39–59
S	Lev. 19:9–18, 26–37		Luke 20:19–44	31	Eccl. 8:1–17
	Luke 11:14–36	S	Num. 20:22–21:9		John 9:1–23
			Luke 20:45–21:19		
Easter 5	Lev. 20:1–16, 22–27			**JUNE**	
	Luke 11:37–54	**Pentecost Day**	Num. 21:10–35	1	Eccl. 9:1–17
M	Lev. 21:1–24		Luke 21:20–38		John 9:24–41
	Luke 12:1–12	M	Num. 22:1–20	2	Eccl. 10:1–20
T	Lev. 23:1–22		Luke 22:1–23		John 10:1–21
	Luke 12:13–34	T	Num. 22:21–23:3	3	Eccl. 11:1–10
W	Lev. 23:23–44		Luke 22:24–46		John 10:22–42
	Luke 12:35–53	W	Num. 23:4–28	4	Eccl. 12:1–14
Th	Lev. 24:1–23		Luke 22:47–71		John 11:1–16
	Lev. 25:1–55	Th	Num. 24:1–25	5	Prov. 1:8–33
	Luke 12:54–13:17		Luke 23:1–25		John 11:17–37
F	Lev. 26:1–20	F	Num. 27:12–23	6	Prov. 3:5–24
	Luke 13:18–35		Luke 23:26–56		John 11:38–57
S	Lev. 26:21–33, 39–44	S	Num. 32:1–6, 16–27	7	Prov. 4:1–27
	Num. 1:1–2:34		Luke 24:1–27		John 12:1–19
	Luke 14:1–24			8	Prov. 5:1–23
		THE TIME OF THE CHURCH			*Prov. 6:1–7:27*
Easter 6	Num. 3:1–16, 39–48	**Holy Trinity**	Num. 35:9–30		John 12:20–36a
	Num. 4:1–8:4		*Acts 1:1–7:60*	9	Prov. 8:1–21
	Luke 14:25–15:10		Luke 24:28–53		John 12:36b–50
M	Num. 8:5–26			10	Prov. 8:22–36
	Luke 15:11–32	**MAY**			John 13:1–20
T	Num. 9:1–23	18	Song 1:1–2:7	11	Prov. 9:1–18
	Luke 16:1–18		John 5:1–18		John 13:21–38
W	Num. 10:11–36	19	Song 2:8–3:11	12	Prov. 10:1–23
	Luke 16:19–31		John 5:19–29		*Prov. 11:1–12:28*
Ascension	Num. 11:1–23, 31–35	20	Song 4:1–5:1		John 14:1–17
	Luke 17:1–19		John 5:30–47	13	Prov. 13:1–25
F	Num. 11:24–29; 12:1–16	21	Song 5:2–6:3		John 14:18–31
	Luke 17:20–37		John 6:1–21	14	Prov. 14:1–27
S	Num. 13:1–3, 17–33	22	Song 6:4–7:5		John 15:1–11
	Luke 18:1–17		John 6:22–40	15	Prov. 15:1–29
		23	Song 7:6–8:14		John 15:12–27
			John 6:41–59	16	Prov. 16:1–24
		24	Eccl. 1:1–18		John 16:1–16
			Esther 1:1–10:3	17	Prov. 17:1–28
					Prov. 18:1–20:4
					John 16:17–33
				18	Prov. 20:5–25
					Prov. 21:1–31
					John 17:1–26

224

6:1–7:50 | 12

2 Cor. 1:23–2:17

25 | 1 Kings 7:51–8:21

2 Cor. 3:1–18

26 | 1 Kings 8:22–30, 46–63

2 Cor. 4:1–18

27 | 1 Kings 9:1–9; 10:1–13

2 Cor. 5:1–21

28 | 1 Kings 11:1–26

2 Cor. 6:1–18

29 | 1 Kings 11:42–12:19

2 Cor. 7:1–16

30 | 1 Kings 12:20–13:5, 33–34

1 Kings 14:1–16:28

2 Cor. 8:1–24

31 | 1 Kings 16:29–17:24

2 Cor. 9:1–15

2 Cor. 10:1–13:14

SEPTEMBER

1 | 1 Kings 18:1–19

Eph. 1:1–23

2 | 1 Kings 18:20–40

Eph. 2:1–22

3 | 1 Kings 19:1–21

1 Kings 20:1–22:53

Eph. 3:1–21

4 | 2 Kings 2:1–18

Eph. 4:1–24

5 | 2 Kings 2:19–25; 4:1–7

Eph. 4:25–5:14

6 | 2 Kings 4:8–22, 32–37

Eph. 5:15–33

7 | 2 Kings 4:38–5:8

Eph. 6:1–24

8 | 2 Kings 5:9–27

Phil. 1:1–20

9 | 2 Kings 6:1–23

2 Kings 6:24–8:29

Phil. 1:21–2:11

10 | 2 Kings 9:1–13; 10:18–29

2 Kings 13:1–18

Phil. 2:12–30

11 | 2 Chron. 29:1–24

Phil. 3:1–21

---

2 Chron. 31:1–21

Phil. 4:1–23

13 | 2 Chron. 32:1–22

Hos. 1:1–14:9

Col. 1:1–23

14 | 2 Chron. 33:1–25

Jonah 1:1–4:11

Col. 1:24–2:7

15 | 2 Chron. 34:1–4, 8–11, 14–33

Nah. 1:1–3:19

Col. 2:8–23

16 | 2 Chron. 35:1–7, 16–25

Zeph. 1:1–3:20

Col. 3:1–25

17 | 2 Chron. 36:1–23

Col. 4:1–18

Philemon 1–25

18 | Neh. 1:1–2:10

Hag. 1:1–2:23

1 Tim. 1:1–20

19 | Neh. 2:11–20; 4:1–6

1 Tim. 2:1–15

20 | Neh. 4:7–23

1 Tim. 3:1–16

21 | Neh. 5:1–16; 6:1–9, 15–16

1 Tim. 4:1–16

22 | Neh. 7:1–4; 8:1–18

Ezra 1:1–10:19

1 Tim. 5:1–16

23 | Neh. 9:1–21

1 Tim. 5:17–6:2

24 | Neh. 9:22–38

Neh. 10:1–13:31

1 Tim. 6:3–21

25 | Mal. 1:1–14

Matt. 3:1–17

26 | Mal. 2:1–3:5

Matt. 4:1–11

27 | Mal. 3:6–4:6

Matt. 4:12–25

28 | Deut. 1:1–18

Matt. 5:1–20

29 | Deut. 1:19–36

Matt. 5:21–48

30 | Deut. 1:37–2:15

Matt. 6:1–15

OCTOBER

1 | Deut. 2:16–37

Matt. 6:16–34

2 | Deut. 3:1–29

Matt. 7:1–12

3 | Deut. 4:1–20

Matt. 7:13–29

4 | Deut. 4:21–40

Matt. 8:1–17

5 | Deut. 5:1–21

Matt. 8:18–34

6 | Deut. 5:22–6:9

Matt. 9:1–17

7 | Deut. 6:10–25

Matt. 9:18–38

8 | Deut. 7:1–19

Matt. 10:1–23

9 | Deut. 8:1–20

Matt. 10:24–42

10 | Deut. 9:1–22

Matt. 11:1–19

11 | Deut. 9:23–10:22

Matt. 11:20–30

12 | Deut. 11:1–25

Matt. 12:1–21

13 | Deut. 11:26–12:12

Matt. 12:22–37

14 | Deut. 12:13–32

Matt. 12:38–50

15 | Deut. 13:1–18

Matt. 13:1–23

16 | Deut. 14:1–2, 22–23; 14:28–15:15

Matt. 13:24–43

17 | Deut. 15:19–16:22

Matt. 13:44–58

18 | Deut. 17:1–20

Matt. 14:1–21

19 | Deut. 18:1–22

Matt. 14:22–36

20 | Deut. 19:1–20

Matt. 15:1–20

21 | Deut. 20:1–20

Matt. 15:21–39

22 | Deut. 21:1–23

Deut. 22:1–24:9

Matt. 16:1–12

23 | Deut. 24:10–25:10

Matt. 16:13–28

24 | Deut. 25:17–26:19

Matt. 17:1–13

25 | Deut. 27:1–26

Matt. 17:14–27
26 Deut. 28:1–22
Matt. 18:1–20
27 Deut. 29:1–29
Matt. 18:21–35
28 Deut. 30:1–20
Matt. 19:1–15
29 Deut. 31:1–29
Matt. 19:16–30
30 Deut. 31:30–32:27
Matt. 20:1–16
31 Deut. 32:28–52
Deut. 33:1–29
Matt. 20:17–34

NOVEMBER

1 Deut. 34:1–12
Matt. 21:1–22
2 Jer. 1:1–19
Matt. 21:23–46
3 Jer. 3:6–4:2
Matt. 22:1–22
4 Jer. 5:1–19
Matt. 22:23–46
5 Jer. 7:1–29
Matt. 23:1–12
6 Jer. 8:18–9:12
Matt. 23:13–39
7 Jer. 11:1–23
Jer. 12:1–19:15
Matt. 24:1–28
8 Jer. 20:1–18
Matt. 24:29–51
9 Jer. 22:1–23
Matt. 25:1–13
10 Jer. 23:1–20
Matt. 25:14–30
11 Jer. 23:21–40
Matt. 25:31–46
12 Jer. 25:1–18
Matt. 26:1–19
13 Jer. 26:1–19
Matt. 26:20–35
Rev. 13:1–18
14 Jer. 29:1–19
Matt. 26:36–56
Rev. 14:1–20
15 Jer. 30:1–24
Matt. 26:57–75
Rev. 15:1–8
16 Jer. 31:1–17, 23–34
Matt. 27:1–10
Rev. 16:1–21
17 Jer. 33:1–22
Jer. 34:1–36:32; 45:1–51:64

Matt. 27:11–32
18 Jer. 37:1–21
Matt. 27:33–56
Rev. 17:1–18
19 Jer. 38:1–28
Jer. 39:1–44:30
Matt. 27:57–66
20 Dan. 1:1–21
Matt. 28:1–20
21 Dan. 2:1–23
Rev. 18:1–24
22 Dan. 2:24–49
Rev. 19:1–21
23 Dan. 3:1–30
Rev. 20:1–15
24 Dan. 4:1–37
Rev. 21:1–8
25 Dan. 5:1–30
Dan. 7:1–8:27
Rev. 21:9–27;
26 Dan. 6:1–28;
Dan. 9:1–27
Rev. 22:1–21

THE TIME OF CHRISTMAS

Advent Season

NOVEMBER

27 Is. 1:1–28
1 Peter 1:1–12
28 Is. 2:1–22
Is. 3:1–4:6
1 Peter 1:13–25
29 Is. 5:1–25
Amos 1:1–9:15
1 Peter 2:1–12
30 Is. 6:1–7:9
1 Peter 2:13–25

DECEMBER

1 Is. 7:10–8:8
1 Peter 3:1–22
2 Is. 8:9–9:7
1 Peter 4:1–19
3 Is. 9:8–10:11
1 Peter 5:1–14
4 Is. 10:12–27a, 33–34
2 Peter 1:1–21
5 Is. 11:1–12:6
2 Peter 2:1–22
6 Is. 14:1–23
2 Peter 3:1–18
7 Is. 24:1–13
1 John 1:1–2:14
8 Is. 24:14–25:12
Obad. 1–21

9 1 John 2:15–29
Is. 26:1–19
1 John 3:1–24
10 Is. 26:20–27:13
1 John 4:1–21
11 Is. 28:14–29
1 John 5:1–21
2 John 1–13
3 John 1–15
12 Is. 29:1–14
Jude 1–25
13 Is. 29:15–30:14
Rev. 1:1–20
14 Is. 30:15–26
Rev. 2:1–29
15 Is. 30:27–31:9
Rev. 3:1–22
16 Is. 32:1–20
Rev. 4:1–11
17 Is. 33:1–24
Rev. 5:1–14
18 Is. 34:1–2, 8–35:10
Micah 1:1–7:20
Rev. 6:1–17
19 Is. 40:1–17
Rev. 7:1–17
20 Is. 40:18–41:10
Rev. 8:1–13
21 Is. 42:1–25
Rev. 9:1–12
22 Is. 43:1–24
Rev. 9:13–10:11
23 Is. 43:25–44:20
Rev. 11:1–19

Christmas Season

DECEMBER

24 Is. 44:21–45:13, 20–25
Dan. 10:1–12:13
Is. 48:1–22
Rev. 12:1–17
25 Is. 49:1–18
Matt. 1:1–17
26 Is. 49:22–26; 50:4–51:8, 12–16
Matt. 1:18–25
27 Is. 51:17–52:12
Matt. 2:1–12
28 Is. 52:13–54:10
Matt. 2:13–23
29 Is. 55:1–13
Luke 1:1–25
30 Is. 58:1–59:3, 14–21

	Luke 1:26–38
31	Is. 60:1–22
	Luke 1:39–56

JANUARY

1	Is. 61:1–11
	Luke 1:57–80
2	Is. 62:1–12
	Luke 2:1–20
3	Is. 63:1–14
	Luke 2:21–40
4	Is. 63:15–65:2
	Luke 2:41–52
5	Is. 65:8–25
	Luke 3:1–20

Epiphany Season

JANUARY

6	Is. 66:1–20
	Luke 3:21–38
7	Ezek. 1:1–14, 22–28
	Hab. 1:1–3:19
	Rom. 1:1–17
8	Ezek. 2:1–3:11
	Rom. 1:18–32
9	Ezek. 3:12–27
	Ezek. 4:1–11:25
	Rom. 2:1–16
10	Ezek. 18:1–4, 19–32
	Ezek. 19:1–24:27
	Rom. 2:17–29
11	Ezek. 33:1–20
	Rom. 3:1–18
12	Ezek. 34:1–24
	Rom. 3:19–31
13	Ezek. 36:13–28
	Rom. 4:1–25
14	Ezek. 36:33–37:14
	Rom. 5:1–21
15	Ezek. 37:15–28
	Rom. 6:1–23
16	Ezek. 38:1–23
	Rom. 7:1–20
17	Ezek. 39:1–10, 17–29
	Rom. 7:21–8:17
18	Ezek. 40:1–4; 43:1–12
	Ezek. 40:5—42:20; 43:13–27
	Rom. 8:18–39
19	Ezek. 44:1–16, 23–29
	Rom. 9:1–18
20	Ezek. 47:1–14, 21–23
	Rom. 9:19–33
21	Joel 1:1–20
	Rom. 10:1–21
22	Joel 2:1–17
	Rom. 11:1–24
23	Joel 2:18–32
	Rom. 11:25—12:13
24	Joel 3:1–21
	Rom. 12:14—13:14
25	Zech. 1:1–21
	Rom. 14:1–23
26	Zech. 2:1—3:10
	Rom. 15:1–13
27	Zech. 4:1—5:11
	Rom. 15:14–33
28	Zech. 6:1—7:14
	Rom. 16:17–27
29	Zech. 8:1–23
	2 Tim. 1:1–18
30	Zech. 9:1–17
	2 Tim. 2:1–26
31	Zech. 10:1—11:3
	2 Tim. 3:1–17

FEBRUARY

1	Zech. 11:4–17
	2 Tim. 4:1–18
2	Zech. 12:1—13:9
	Titus 1:1—2:6
3	Zech. 14:1–21
	Titus 2:7—3:15
4	Job 1:1–22
	John 1:1–18
5	Job 2:1—3:10
	John 1:19–34
6	Job 3:11–26
	John 1:35–51
7	Job 4:1–21
	John 2:1–12
8	Job 5:1–27
	John 2:13–25
9	Job 6:1–13
	John 3:1–21
10	Job 6:14–30
	John 3:22—4:6

If Ash Wednesday, turn to Ash Wednesday, page 222.

11	Job 7:1–21
	John 4:7–26
12	Job 8:1–22
	John 4:27–45
13	Job 9:1–35
	John 4:46–54
14	Job 10:1–22
	John 5:1–18
15	Job 11:1–20
	John 5:19–29
16	Job 12:1–6, 12–25
	John 5:30–47
17	Job 13:1–12
	John 6:1–21
18	Job 13:13–28
	John 6:22–40
19	Job 14:1–22
	John 6:41–59
20	Job 15:1–23, 30–35
	John 6:60–71
21	Job 16:1–22
	John 7:1–13
22	Job 17:1–16
	John 7:14–31
23	Job 18:1–21
	John 7:32–53
24	Job 19:1–12, 21–27
	John 8:1–20
25	Job 20:1–23, 29
	John 8:21–38
26	Job 21:1–21
	Job 21:22–30:15
	John 8:39–59
27	Job 30:16–31
	John 9:1–23
28	Job 31:1–12, 33–40
	John 9:24–41
29	Job 32:1–22
	John 10:1–21

MARCH

1	Job 33:1–18
	John 10:22–42
2	Job 33:19–34:9
	John 11:1–16
3	Job 34:10–33
	John 11:17–37
4	Job 36:1–21
	John 11:38–57
5	Job 37:1–24
	John 12:1–19
6	Job 38:1–18
	Job 38:19–39:30
	John 12:20–36a
7	Job 40:1–24
	John 12:36b–50
8	Job 41:1–20, 31–34
	John 13:1–20
9	Job 42:1–17
	John 13:21–38

The Psalms for Weekdays
The Proverbs for Sundays

Great Chapters of the Bible

Genesis 1–3 (Origins)

Genesis 22 (Testing)

Exodus 19–20 (Commandments)

Matthew 1–2 (Incarnation)

1 Corinthians 13–15 (Newness)

Matthew 5–7 (Beatitudes)

John 14 (Comfort)

Luke 23–24 (Crucifixion/Resurrection)

Mark 15–16 (Crucifixion/Resurrection)

Acts 7 (Stephen's Defense)

Isaiah 38 (Hezekiah's Prayer)

2 Chronicles 6 (Solomon's Prayer)

Esther 4 (Courage)

Acts 1–2 (Ascension/Pentecost)

John 19–20 (Crucifixion/Resurrection)

Revelation 20–22 (Final Victory)

Isaiah 52–53 (Messiah)

John 17 (Priestly Prayer)

Matthew 27–28 (Crucifixion/Resurrection)

Hebrews 11, 12 (Faithfulness)

Romans 3–6, 8 (Justification)

Exodus 15:1–18 (Moses' Song)

Habakkuk 3 (Habakkuk's Prayer)

5
Book of Concord
Readings

Book of Concord Reading Guide

Week 39. Solid Declaration (pp. 510–15)

M   14–20
T   I 1–6
W   7–15
Th 16–25
F   26–32

Week 40. Solid Declaration (pp. 515–23)

M   33–42
T   43–49
W   50–62
Th II 1–7
F   8–14

Week 41. Solid Declaration (pp. 523–30)

M   15–19
T   20–28
W   29–40
Th 41–47
F   48–56

Week 42. Solid Declaration (pp. 530–38)

M   57–64
T   65–73
W   74–83
Th 84–90
F   III 1–7

Week 43. Solid Declaration (pp. 538–43)

M   8–17
T   18–25
W   26–30
Th 31–35
F   36–43

Week 44. Solid Declaration (pp. 543–50)

M   44–56
T   57–67
W   IV 1–8
Th 9–18
F   19–32

Week 45. Solid Declaration (pp. 550–59)

M   33–40
T   V 1–9
W   10–19
Th 20–27
F   VI 1–8

Week 46. Solid Declaration (pp. 559–66)

M   9–16
T   17–26
W   VII 1–8
Th 9–19
F   20–27

Week 47. Solid Declaration (pp. 566–75)

M   28–41
T   42–51
W   52–62
Th 63–72
F   73–84

Week 48. Solid Declaration (pp. 575–84)

M   85–97
T   98–106
W   107–19
Th 120–VIII 6
F   7–19

Week 49. Solid Declaration (pp. 584–93)

M   20–30
T   31–43
W   44–53
Th 54–63
F   64–75

Week 50. Solid Declaration (pp. 593–602)

M   76–86
T   87–IX 3
W   X 1–13
Th 14–25
F   26–XI 3

Week 51. Solid Declaration (pp. 602–11)

M   4–14
T   15–27
W   28–36
Th 37–47
F   48–64

Week 52. Solid Declaration (pp. 611–19)

M   65–77
T   78–86
W   87–XII 4
Th 5–27
F   28–40

6
Feasts, Festivals, and Commemorations

The feasts and festivals are listed in roman type. The observations listed in **boldface** are principal feasts of Christ and, when they occur on a Sunday, normally replace the regularly scheduled pericopes for corporate worship for that Sunday of the Church Year. The commemorations are shown in *italics*. The collects provide opportunity to commemorate the date without replacing the regularly scheduled pericopes on those days.

January

Circumcision and Name of Jesus (January 1)

The Lection

ABC, 1Yr. Numbers 6:22–27
        Psalm 8 (v. 9)
        Galatians 3:23–29
        Luke 2:21

The Hymn

900 or 896

Prayer of the Day

Lord God, You made Your beloved Son, our Savior, subject to the Law and caused Him to shed His blood on our behalf. Grant us the true circumcision of the Spirit that our hearts may be made pure from all sins; through Jesus Christ, our Lord, who lives and reigns with You and the Holy Spirit, one God, now and forever. (F07)

or

O merciful and eternal God, heavenly Father, You caused Your Son to endure circumcision and to be made subject to the law that we might be redeemed from the curse of the law. Grant us grace to become partakers of this redemption and thus obtain eternal salvation; through Your beloved Son, Jesus Christ, our Lord, who lives and reigns with You and the Holy Spirit, one true God, now and forever. (VD)

J. K. Wilhelm Loehe, Pastor (January 2)

Prayer of the Day

Most glorious Trinity, in Your mercy we commit to You this day our bodies and souls, all our ways and goings, all our deeds and purposes. We pray You, so open our hearts and mouths that we may praise Your name, which above all names alone is holy. And since You have created for us the praise of Your holy name, grant that our lives may be for Your honor and that we may serve You in love and fear; for You, O Father, Son, and Holy Spirit, live and reign, one God, now and forever. (1134)

Basil the Great of Caesarea, Gregory of Nazianzus, and
Gregory of Nyssa, Pastors and Confessors (January 10)

Prayer of the Day

Almighty God, You revealed to Your Church Your eternal being of glorious majesty and perfect love as one God in a Trinity of persons. May Your Church, with bishops like Basil of Caesarea, Gregory of Nazianzus, and Gregory of Nyssa, receive grace to continue steadfast in the confession of the true faith and constant in our worship of You, Father, Son, and Holy Spirit, who live and reign, one God, now and forever. (1135)

The Confession of St. Peter (January 18)

The Lection	*The Hymn*
ABC, 1Yr. Acts 4:8–13	512
Psalm 118:19–29 (v. 26)	
2 Peter 1:1–15	
Mark 8:27–35 (36—9:1)	

Prayer of the Day

Heavenly Father, You revealed to the apostle Peter the blessed truth that Your Son Jesus is the Christ. Strengthen us by the proclamation of this truth that we, too, may joyfully confess that there is salvation in no one else; through the same Jesus Christ, our Lord, who lives and reigns with You and the Holy Spirit, one God, now and forever. (F08)

Sarah (January 20)

Prayer of the Day

Lord and Father of all, You looked with favor upon Sarai in her advanced years, putting on her a new name, *Sarah*, and with it the promise of multitudinous blessings from her aged womb. Give us a youthful hope in the joy of our own new name, being baptized into the promised Messiah, that we, too, might be fruitful in Your kingdom, abounding in the works of Your Spirit; through Jesus Christ, our Lord, who lives and reigns with You and the Holy Spirit, one God, now and forever. (1137)

St. Timothy, Pastor and Confessor (January 24)

The Lection	*The Hymn*
ABC, 1Yr. Acts 16:1–5	682
Psalm 71:15–24 (v. 6)	
1 Timothy 6:11–16	
Matthew 24:42–47	

Prayer of the Day

Lord Jesus Christ, You have always given to Your Church on earth faithful shepherds such as Timothy to guide and feed Your flock. Make all pastors diligent to preach Your Holy Word and administer Your Means of Grace, and grant Your people wisdom to follow in the way that leads to life eternal; for You live and reign with the Father and the Holy Spirit, one God, now and forever. (F09)

The Conversion of St. Paul (January 25)

The Lection	*The Hymn*
ABC, 1Yr. Acts 9:1–22	611 or 834
Psalm 67 (v. 5)	
Galatians 1:11–24	
Matthew 19:27–30	

Prayer of the Day

Almighty God, You turned the heart of him who persecuted the Church and by his preaching caused the light of the Gospel to shine throughout the world. Grant us ever to rejoice in the saving light of Your Gospel and, following the example of the apostle Paul, to spread it to the ends of the earth; through Jesus Christ, Your Son, our Lord, who lives and reigns with You and the Holy Spirit, one God, now and forever. (F10)

St. Titus, Pastor and Confessor (January 26)

The Lection	*The Hymn*
ABC, 1Yr. Acts 20:28–35	586
Psalm 71:1–14 (v. 17)	
Titus 1:1–9	
Luke 10:1–9	

Prayer of the Day

Almighty God, You called Titus to the work of pastor and teacher. Make all shepherds of Your flock diligent in preaching Your

Holy Word so that the whole world may know the immeasurable riches of our Savior, Jesus Christ, who lives and reigns with You and the Holy Spirit, one God, now and forever. (F11)

John Chrysostom, Preacher (January 27)

Prayer of the Day

O God, You gave to Your servant John Chrysostom grace to proclaim the Gospel with eloquence and power. As bishop of the great congregations of Antioch and Constantinople, he fearlessly bore reproach for the honor of Your name. Mercifully grant to all bishops and pastors such excellence in preaching and fidelity in ministering Your Word that Your people shall be partakers of the divine nature; through Jesus Christ, our Lord, who lives and reigns with You and the Holy Spirit, one God, now and forever. (1138)

February

The Purification of Mary and the Presentation of Our Lord (February 2)

The Lection

ABC, 1Yr.   1 Samuel 1:21–28
           Psalm 84 (v. 4)
           Hebrews 2:14–18
           Luke 2:22–32 (33–40)

The Hymn

519

Prayer of the Day

Almighty and ever-living God, as Your only-begotten Son was this day presented in the temple in the substance of our flesh, grant that we may be presented to You with pure and clean hearts; through Jesus Christ, our Lord, who lives and reigns with You and the Holy Spirit, one God, now and forever. (F12)

Jacob (Israel), Patriarch (February 5)

Prayer of the Day

Lord Jesus, scepter that rises out of Jacob, Lamb of God who takes away the sin of the world, rule our hearts through Your suffering cross and forgive us our sins, that we may become partakers of

Your divine life; for You live and reign with the Father and the Holy Spirit, one God, now and forever. (1140)

Silas, Fellow Worker of St. Peter and St. Paul (February 10)

Prayer of the Day

Almighty and everlasting God, Your servant Silas preached the Gospel alongside the apostles Peter and Paul to the peoples of Asia Minor, Greece, and Macedonia. We give You thanks for raising up in this and every land evangelists and heralds of Your kingdom, that the Church may continue to proclaim the unsearchable riches of our Savior, Jesus Christ, who lives and reigns with You and the Holy Spirit, one God, now and forever. (1141)

Aquila, Priscilla, Apollos (February 13)

Prayer of the Day

Triune God, whose very name is holy, teach us to be faithful hearers and learners of Your Word, fervent in the Spirit as Apollos was, that we may teach it correctly against those who have been led astray into falsehood and error and that we might follow the example of Aquila and Priscilla for the good of the Church You established here and entrusted into our humble care; for You, O Father, Son, and Holy Spirit, live and reign, one God, now and forever. (1144)

Valentine, Martyr (February 14)

Prayer of the Day

Almighty and everlasting God, You kindled the flame of Your love in the heart of Your holy martyr Valentine. Grant to us, Your humble servants, a like faith and the power of love, that we who rejoice in Christ's triumph may embody His love in our lives; through Jesus Christ, our Lord, who lives and reigns with You and the Holy Spirit, one God, now and forever. (1145)

Philemon and Onesimus (February 15)

Prayer of the Day

Lord God, heavenly Father, You sent Onesimus back to Philemon as a brother in Christ, freeing him from his slavery to sin through the preaching of the apostle Paul. Cleanse the depths of sin within our souls and bid resentment cease for past offenses, that, by Your mercy, we may be reconciled to our brothers and sisters and our lives will reflect Your peace; through Jesus Christ, our Lord. (1146)

Philipp Melanchthon (birth), Confessor (February 16)

Prayer of the Day

Almighty God, we praise You for the service of Philipp Melanchthon to the one, holy, catholic, and apostolic Church in the renewal of its life in fidelity to Your Word and promise. Raise up in these gray and latter days faithful teachers and pastors, inspired by Your Spirit, whose voices will give strength to Your Church and proclaim the ongoing reality of Your kingdom; through Your Son, Jesus Christ, our Lord. (1147)

Martin Luther, Doctor and Confessor (February 18)

Prayer of the Day

O God, our refuge and our strength, You raised up Your servant Martin Luther to reform and renew Your Church in the light of Your living Word, Jesus Christ, our Lord. Defend and purify the Church in our own day, and grant that we may boldly proclaim Christ's faithfulness unto death and His vindicating resurrection, which You made known to Your servant Martin through Jesus Christ, our Savior, who lives and reigns with You and the Holy Spirit, one God, now and forever. (1148)

Polycarp of Smyrna, Pastor and Martyr (February 23)

Prayer of the Day

O God, the maker of heaven and earth, You gave boldness to confess Jesus Christ as King and Savior and steadfastness to die for the faith to Your venerable servant, the holy and gentle Polycarp. Grant us grace to follow his example in sharing the cup of Christ's suffering so that we may also share in His glorious resurrection; through Jesus Christ, our Lord, who lives and reigns with You and the Holy Spirit, one God, now and forever. (1150)

St. Matthias, Apostle (February 24)

Prayer of the Day

Almighty God, You chose Your servant Matthias to be numbered among the Twelve. Grant that Your Church, ever preserved from false teachers, may be taught and guided by faithful and true pastors; through Jesus Christ, our Lord, who lives and reigns with You and the Holy Spirit, one God, now and forever. (F13)

March

Perpetua and Felicitas, Martyrs (March 7)

Prayer of the Day

O God and Ruler over all our foes of body and soul, You strengthened Your servants Perpetua and Felicitas, giving them a confident and clear confession in the face of roaring beasts. Grant that we who remember their faithful martyrdom may share in their blessed assurance of victory over all earthly and spiritual enemies and hold fast to the promise of everlasting life secured for us through Jesus Christ, our Lord, who lives and reigns with You and the Holy Spirit, one God, now and forever. (1154)

Patrick, Missionary to Ireland (March 17)

Prayer of the Day

Almighty God, You chose Your servant Patrick to be a missionary to the Irish people who were wandering in darkness and error. You bound unto them the trinitarian name through Baptism and faith that they might dwell in the light of Christ. Bind unto us this same strong name of the Trinity as we remember our Baptism and walk in His light, that we may come to dwell at last in the eternal light of the presence of Your Son, Jesus Christ, our Lord, who lives and reigns with You and the Holy Spirit, one God, now and forever. (1157)

St. Joseph, Guardian of Jesus (March 19)

The Lection

ABC, 1Yr.   2 Samuel 7:4–16
     Psalm 127 (v. 1a)
     Romans 4:13–18
     Matthew 2:13–15, 19–23

The Hymn

863

Prayer of the Day

Almighty God, from the house of Your servant David You raised up Joseph to be the guardian of Your incarnate Son and the husband of His mother, Mary. Grant us grace to follow the example of this faithful workman in heeding Your counsel and obeying Your commands; through Jesus Christ, our Lord, who lives and reigns with You and the Holy Spirit, one God, now and forever. (F14)

The Annunciation of Our Lord (March 25)

The Lection

ABC, 1Yr.   Isaiah 7:10–14
     Psalm 45:7–17 (v. 6)
     Hebrews 10:4–10
     Luke 1:26–38

The Hymn

356

Prayer of the Day

O Lord, as we have known the incarnation of Your Son, Jesus Christ, by the message of the angel to the virgin Mary, so by the message of His cross and passion bring us to the glory of His resurrection; through the same Jesus Christ, our Lord, who lives and reigns with You and the Holy Spirit, one God, now and forever. (F15)

or

O almighty God, of Your great mercy You caused Your Son to be conceived by the Holy Spirit, and to become incarnate of the blessed Virgin Mary according to the angel's annunciation: Grant us by Your grace, that our sinful conception may be purified by His holy conception; through Your beloved Son, Jesus Christ, our Lord, who lives and reigns with You and the Holy Spirit, one true God, now and forever. (VD)

Joseph, Patriarch (March 31)

Prayer of the Day

Lord God, heavenly Father, in the kingdom of Egypt the needy and suffering people were told to go to Joseph and do all that he shall say to them. May the needy and suffering people in the kingdom of Your Church now be provided for by those who follow in the example of Joseph as they love their neighbors as themselves; through Jesus Christ, our Lord, who lives and reigns with You and the Holy Spirit, one God, now and forever. (1158)

April

Lucas Cranach and Albrecht Dürer, Artists (April 6)

Prayer of the Day

O God, by Your Holy Spirit You give wisdom to some, knowledge to others, and to some the gift of beauty. We praise You that through Your servants Lucas Cranach and Albrecht Dürer, and through their gift of artistic representation, they preach to us of Your mighty acts of redemption and the great piety of the saints who have served You in humility and faith. May Your Church never be without such gifts; through Jesus Christ, our Lord, who lives and reigns with You and the Holy Spirit, one God, now and forever. (1159)

Johannes Bugenhagen, Pastor (April 20)

Prayer of the Day

Almighty and everlasting God, Your Son called the twelve to be His apostles and sent out the seventy-two to preach and to heal. You continue to send out faithful pastors to feed the people of God with the holy food of the Gospel and the Sacraments. We give You thanks for providing Martin Luther with a faithful pastor and confessor in Johannes Bugenhagen and for his care of Luther's widow and children. May we all be blessed to have such pastors to take care of our needs in body and soul; through Jesus Christ, our Lord, who lives and reigns with You and the Holy Spirit, one God, now and forever. (1160)

Anselm of Canterbury, Theologian (April 21)

Prayer of the Day

Almighty God, You raised up Your servant Anselm as a devout and learned scholar to teach the Church of his day to believe and confess in Your eternal nature, Your perfect justice, and Your saving mercy. Continue to provide Your Church in every age with saints who embody Your saving faith as they give us a reason for the hope that is in us; through Jesus Christ, our Lord, who lives and reigns with You and the Holy Spirit, one God, now and forever. (1161)

Johann Walter, Kantor (April 24)

Prayer of the Day

God of majesty, whom saints and angels delight to worship in heaven, we give You thanks that You provided music for Your Church through Johann Walter, kantor in the church of the Reformation. Through music You give us joy on earth as we participate in the songs of heaven. Bring us to the fulfillment of that song that will be ours when we stand with all Your saints before Your unveiled glory; through Jesus Christ, our Lord, who lives and reigns with You and the Holy Spirit, one God, now and forever. (1162)

St. Mark, Evangelist (April 25)

The Lection	*The Hymn*
ABC, 1Yr. Isaiah 52:7–10	836
Psalm 146 (v. 5)	
2 Timothy 4:5–18	
Mark 16:14–20	

Prayer of the Day

Almighty God, You have enriched Your Church with the proclamation of the Gospel through the evangelist Mark. Grant that we may firmly believe these glad tidings and daily walk according to Your Word; through Jesus Christ, our Lord, who lives and reigns with You and the Holy Spirit, one God, now and forever. (F16)

248

May

St. Philip and St. James, Apostles (May 1)

The Lection
ABC, 1Yr.   Isaiah 30:18–21
      Psalm 36:5–12 (v. 8)
      Ephesians 2:19–22
      John 14:1–14

The Hymn
861

Prayer of the Day

Almighty God, Your Son revealed Himself to Philip and James and gave them the knowledge of everlasting life. Grant us perfectly to know Your Son, Jesus Christ, to be the way, the truth, and the life, and steadfastly to walk in the way that leads to eternal life; through the same Jesus Christ, our Lord, who lives and reigns with You and the Holy Spirit, one God, now and forever. (F17)

Athanasius of Alexandria, Pastor and Confessor (May 2)

Prayer of the Day

O God of truth and mercy, You upheld Your servant Athanasius to confess with boldness the catholic faith against all hostility and resistance. Uphold Your Church that trusts solely in the grace of Your eternal Word, who took upon Himself our humanity that we might share His divinity; who lives and reigns with You and the Holy Spirit, one God, now and forever. (1163)

Friedrich Wyneken, Pastor and Missionary (May 4)

Prayer of the Day

Lord Jesus Christ, You want all to be saved and to come to the knowledge of the truth. We give You thanks for sending Friedrich Wyneken as missionary and pastor in Indiana, Ohio, and Michigan to evangelize the Native Americans in these states; to be a founder of Concordia Theological Seminary in Fort Wayne; and to serve as second president of The Lutheran Church—Missouri Synod. Protect and encourage all missionaries who confess the true faith among the nations by proclaiming Christ crucified; for You live and reign with the Father and the Holy Spirit, one God, now and forever. (1164)

Frederick the Wise, Christian Ruler (May 5)

Prayer of the Day

Heavenly Father, You provided wisdom and skill to Frederick the Wise as elector of Saxony during the early years of the Reformation, using his rule and authority to protect Martin Luther and preserve the preaching of the Gospel. Graciously regard all Your servants who make, administer, and judge the laws of this nation, and look with favor upon all the rulers of the earth. Grant them wisdom and understanding that they might provide sanctuary for Your Church to continue to proclaim the true faith; for You live and reign with the Son and the Holy Spirit, one God, now and forever. (1165)

C. F. W. Walther, Theologian (May 7)

Prayer of the Day

Almighty God, through Your servant C. F. W. Walther You brought Lutheran pilgrims from Germany to confess the true faith. May the priesthood of Your saints now receive the Gospel of a crucified and risen Savior in faith as they offer back to You in love sacrifices of praise and thanksgiving, for You live and reign with the Son and the Holy Spirit, one God, now and forever. (1166)

Job (May 9)

Prayer of the Day

Lord God, heavenly Father, You showed forth as blameless, true, God-fearing, just, and sanctified Your suffering prophet, the righteous Job. Through his valiant endurance and long-suffering patience, You taught us how to live in a broken world under Your great mercy as You set us free from our sins and rescued us from the punishments we deserve, through the all-sufficient sacrifice of Your only-begotten Son, who with You and the Holy Spirit, lives and reigns, one God, now and forever. (1167)

Cyril and Methodius, Missionaries to the Slavs (May 11)

Prayer of the Day

Almighty and everlasting God, by the power of the Holy Spirit You moved Your servant Cyril and his brother, Methodius, to bring the light of the Gospel to the Slavs, a people broken by hostility and division. By the love of Christ, overcome all bitterness and strife among us, and form us into one united family who live under the mercies of the Prince of Peace; who lives and reigns with You and the Holy Spirit, one God, now and forever. (1168)

Emperor Constantine, Christian Ruler, and Helena, Mother of Constantine (May 21)

Prayer of the Day

Almighty God, through Your servant Constantine, Your Church flourished, and by his mother, Helena, the Church of the Holy Sepulchre in Jerusalem became a holy place for many pilgrims. Grant to us this same zeal for Your Church and charity toward Your people, that we may be fruitful in good works and steadfast in faith. Keep us ever grateful for Your abundant provision, with our eyes fixed, as Helena's were, on the highest and greatest treasure of all, the cross of Christ; through Jesus Christ, our Lord, who lives and reigns with You and the Holy Spirit, one God, now and forever. (1031)

Esther (May 24)

Prayer of the Day

O God, You graced Your servant Queen Esther not only with beauty and elegance but also with faith and wisdom. Grant that we, too, might use the qualities that You have generously bestowed on us for the glory of Your mighty name and for the good of Your people, that through Your work in us, we may be advocates of the oppressed and defenders of the weak, preserving our faith in the great High Priest who intercedes on our behalf, Jesus Christ, who lives and reigns with you and the Holy Spirit, one God, now and forever. (1032)

Bede the Venerable, Theologian (May 25)

Prayer of the Day

Heavenly Father, when he was still a child You called Your servant Bede to devote his life to serve You in the venerable disciplines of religion and scholarship. As he labored in the Spirit to bring the riches of Your truth to his generation, grant that we may also strive to make You known in all the world in our various vocations; through

Jesus Christ, our Lord, who lives and reigns with You and the Holy Spirit, one God, for ever and ever. (1033)

The Visitation (May 31—Three-Year Lectionary)

<table>
<tr><td colspan="2">The Lection</td><td>The Hymn</td></tr>
<tr><td>ABC</td><td>Isaiah 11:1–5</td><td>385</td></tr>
<tr><td></td><td>Psalm 138 (v. 8a)</td><td></td></tr>
<tr><td></td><td>Romans 12:9–16</td><td></td></tr>
<tr><td></td><td>Luke 1:39–45 (46–56)</td><td></td></tr>
</table>

Prayer of the Day

Almighty God, You chose the virgin Mary to be the mother of Your Son and made known through her Your gracious regard for the poor and lowly and despised. Grant that we may receive Your Word in humility and faith, and so be made one with Jesus Christ, Your Son, our Lord, who lives and reigns with You and the Holy Spirit, one God, now and forever. (F18)

June

Justin, Martyr (June 1)

Prayer of the Day

Almighty and everlasting God, You found Your martyr Justin wandering from teacher to teacher, searching for the true God. Grant that all who seek for a deeper knowledge of the sublime wisdom of Your eternal Word may be found by You, who sent Your Son to seek and to save the lost; through Jesus Christ, our Lord, who lives and reigns with You and the Holy Spirit, one God, now and forever. (1034)

Boniface of Mainz, Missionary to the Germans (June 5)

Prayer of the Day

Almighty God, You called Boniface to be a witness and martyr in Germany, and by his labor and suffering, You raised up a people for Your own possession. Pour out Your Holy Spirit upon Your Church in every land, that by the service and sacrifice of many, Your holy name may be glorified and Your kingdom enlarged; through Jesus

Christ, our Lord, who lives and reigns with You and the Holy Spirit, one God, now and forever. (1035)

St. Barnabas, Apostle (June 11)

The Lection   *The Hymn*
ABC, 1Yr.   Isaiah 42:5–12   837
         Psalm 112 (v. 1)
         Acts 11:19–30; 13:1–3
         Mark 6:7–13

Prayer of the Day

Almighty God, Your faithful servant Barnabas sought not his own renown but gave generously of his life and substance for the encouragement of the apostles and their ministry. Grant that we may follow his example in lives given to charity and the proclamation of the Gospel; through Your Son, Jesus Christ, our Lord, who lives and reigns with You and the Holy Spirit, one God, now and forever. (F19)

The Ecumenical Council of Nicaea, AD 325 (June 12)

Prayer of the Day

Lord God, heavenly Father, at the first ecumenical Council of Nicaea, Your Church boldly confessed that it believed in one Lord Jesus Christ as being of one substance with the Father. Grant us courage to confess this saving faith with Your Church through all the ages; through Jesus Christ, our Lord. (1037)

Elisha (June 14)

Prayer of the Day

Lord God, heavenly Father, through the prophet Elisha, You continued the prophetic pattern of teaching Your people the true faith and demonstrating through miracles Your presence in the creation to heal it of its brokenness. Grant that Your Church may see in Your Son, our Lord Jesus Christ, the final end-times prophet whose teaching and miracles continue in Your Church through the healing medicine of the Gospel and the Sacraments; through Jesus Christ, our Lord. (1038)

The Nativity of St. John the Baptist (June 24)

The Lection

ABC, 1Yr.   Isaiah 40:1–5
        Psalm 85:(1–6) 7–13 (v. 9)
        Acts 13:13–26
        Luke 1:57–80

The Hymn

346

Prayer of the Day

Almighty God, through John the Baptist, the forerunner of Christ, You once proclaimed salvation. Now grant that we may know this salvation and serve You in holiness and righteousness all the days of our life; through our Lord Jesus Christ, Your Son, who lives and reigns with You and the Holy Spirit, one God, now and forever. (F20)

Presentation of the Augsburg Confession (June 25)

Prayer of the Day

Lord God, heavenly Father, You preserved the teaching of the apostolic Church through the confession of the true faith at Augsburg. Continue to cast the bright beams of Your light upon Your Church that we, being instructed by the doctrine of the blessed apostles, may walk in the light of Your truth and finally attain to the light of everlasting life; through Jesus Christ, our Lord, who lives and reigns with You and the Holy Spirit, one God, now and forever. (1041)

Jeremiah (June 26)

Prayer of the Day

Lord God, heavenly Father, through the prophet Jeremiah, You continued the prophetic pattern of teaching Your people the true faith and demonstrating through miracles Your presence in the creation to heal it of its brokenness. Grant that Your Church may see in Your Son, our Lord Jesus Christ, the final end-times prophet whose teaching and miracles continue in Your Church through the healing medicine of the Gospel and the Sacraments; through Jesus Christ, our Lord. (1042)

Cyril of Alexandria, Pastor and Confessor (June 27)

Prayer of the Day

Heavenly Father, Your servant Cyril steadfastly proclaimed Your Son, Jesus Christ, to be one person, fully God and fully man. By Your infinite mercy, keep us constant in faith and worship of Your Son, who lives and reigns with You and the Holy Spirit, one God, now and forever. (1043)

Irenaeus of Lyons, Pastor (June 28)

Prayer of the Day

Almighty God, You upheld Your servant Irenaeus with strength to confess the truth against every blast of vain doctrine. By Your mercy, keep us steadfast in the true faith, that in constancy we may walk in peace on the way that leads to eternal life through Jesus Christ, our Lord, who lives and reigns with You and the Holy Spirit, one God, now and forever. (1044)

St. Peter and St. Paul, Apostles (June 29)

The Lection		*The Hymn*
ABC, 1Yr.	Acts 15:1–12 (13–21)	647
	Psalm 46 (v. 11)	
	Galatians 2:1–10	
	Matthew 16:13–19	

Prayer of the Day

Merciful and eternal God, Your holy apostles Peter and Paul received grace and strength to lay down their lives for the sake of Your Son. Strengthen us by Your Holy Spirit that we may confess Your truth and at all times be ready to lay down our lives for Him who laid down His life for us, even Jesus Christ, our Lord, who lives and reigns with You and the Holy Spirit, one God, now and forever. (F21)

July

The Visitation (July 2—One-Year Lectionary)

The Lection		*The Hymn*
1Yr.	Isaiah 11:1–5	385
	Psalm 138 (v. 8a)	

Romans 12:9–16
Luke 1:39–45 (46–56)

Prayer of the Day

Almighty God, You chose the virgin Mary to be the mother of Your Son and made known through her Your gracious regard for the poor and lowly and despised. Grant that we may receive Your Word in humility and faith, and so be made one with Jesus Christ, Your Son, our Lord, who lives and reigns with You and the Holy Spirit, one God, now and forever. (F18)

Isaiah (July 6)

Prayer of the Day

Lord God, heavenly Father, through the prophet Isaiah, You continued the prophetic pattern of teaching Your people the true faith and demonstrating through miracles Your presence in the creation to heal it of its brokenness. Grant that Your Church may see in Your Son, our Lord Jesus Christ, the final end-times prophet whose teaching and miracles continue in Your Church through the healing medicine of the Gospel and the Sacraments; through Jesus Christ, our Lord. (1049)

Ruth (July 16)

Prayer of the Day

Faithful God, You promised to preserve Your people and save Your inheritance, using unlikely and unexpected vessels in extending the genealogy that would bring about the birth of Your blessed Son. Give us the loyalty of Ruth and her trust in the one true God, that we, too, might honor You through our submission and respect and be counted among Your chosen people, by the grace of Jesus Christ, our Lord, and the Holy Spirit, who reign together with You, now and forever. (1058)

Elijah (July 20)

Prayer of the Day

Lord God, heavenly Father, through the prophet Elijah, You continued the prophetic pattern of teaching Your people the true faith and demonstrating through miracles Your presence in creation to heal it of its brokenness. Grant that Your Church may see in Your Son, our Lord Jesus Christ, the final end-times prophet whose teaching and miracles continue in Your Church through the healing medicine of the Gospel and the Sacraments; through Jesus Christ, our Lord. (1061)

Ezekiel (July 21)

Prayer of the Day

Lord God, heavenly Father, through the prophet Ezekiel, You continued the prophetic pattern of teaching Your people the true faith and demonstrating through miracles Your presence in creation to heal it of its brokenness. Grant that Your Church may see in Your Son, our Lord Jesus Christ, the final end-times prophet whose teaching and miracles continue in Your Church through the healing medicine of the Gospel and the Sacraments; through Jesus Christ, our Lord. (1062)

St. Mary Magdalene (July 22)

The Lection		*The Hymn*
ABC, 1Yr.	Proverbs 31:10–31	465
	Psalm 73:23–28 (v. 1)	
	Acts 13:26–31	
	John 20:1–2, 10–18	

Prayer of the Day

Almighty God, Your Son, Jesus Christ, restored Mary Magdalene to health and called her to be the first witness of His resurrection. Heal us from all our infirmities, and call us to know You in the power of Your Son's unending life; through the same Jesus Christ, our Lord, who lives and reigns with You and the Holy Spirit, one God, now and forever. (F22)

St. James the Elder, Apostle (July 25)

The Lection		*The Hymn*
ABC, 1Yr.	Acts 11:27—12:5	420
	Psalm 56 (v. 4)	
	Romans 8:28–39	
	Mark 10:35–45	

O gracious God, Your servant and apostle James was the first among the Twelve to suffer martyrdom for the name of Jesus Christ. Pour out upon the leaders of Your Church that spirit of self-denying service that they may forsake all false and passing allurements and follow Christ alone, who lives and reigns with You and the Holy Spirit, one God, now and forever. (F23)

Johann Sebastian Bach, Kantor (July 28)

Prayer of the Day

Almighty God, beautiful in majesty and majestic in holiness, You have taught us in Holy Scripture to sing Your praises and have given to Your servant Johann Sebastian Bach grace to show forth Your glory in his music. Continue to grant this gift of inspiration to all Your servants who write and make music for Your people, that with joy we on earth may glimpse Your beauty and at length know the inexhaustible richness of Your new creation in Jesus Christ, our Lord, who lives and reigns with You and the Holy Spirit, one God, now and forever. (1066)

Mary, Martha, and Lazarus of Bethany (July 29)

Prayer of the Day

Heavenly Father, Your beloved Son befriended frail humans like us to make us Your own. Teach us to be like Jesus' dear friends from Bethany, that we might serve Him faithfully like Martha, learn from Him earnestly like Mary, and ultimately be raised by Him like Lazarus. Through their Lord and ours, Jesus Christ, who lives and reigns with You and the Holy Spirit, one God, now and forever. (1067)

Robert Barnes, Confessor and Martyr (July 30)

Prayer of the Day

Almighty God, heavenly Father, You gave courage to Your servant Robert Barnes to give up his life for confessing the true faith during the Reformation. May we continue steadfast in our confession of the apostolic faith and to suffer all, even death, rather than fall away from it; through Jesus Christ, our Lord. (1068)

Joseph of Arimathea (July 31)

Prayer of the Day

Merciful God, Your servant Joseph of Arimathea prepared the body of our Lord and Savior for burial with reverence and godly fear and laid Him in his own tomb. As we follow the example of Joseph, grant to us, Your faithful people, that same grace and courage to love and serve Jesus with sincere devotion all the days of our lives; through Jesus Christ, our Lord, who lives and reigns with You and the Holy Spirit, one God, now and forever. (1069)

August

Joanna, Mary, and Salome, Myrrhbearers (August 3)

Prayer of the Day

Mighty God, Your crucified and buried Son did not remain in the tomb for long. Give us joy in the tasks set before us, that we might carry out faithful acts of service as did Joanna, Mary, and Salome, offering to You the sweet perfume of our grateful hearts, so that we, too, may see the glory of Your resurrection and proclaim the Good News with unrestrained eagerness and fervor worked in us through our Lord Jesus Christ, who rose and reigns with You and the Holy Spirit, one God, now and forever. (1071)

Lawrence, Deacon and Martyr (August 10)

Prayer of the Day

Almighty God, You called Lawrence to be a deacon in Your Church to serve Your saints with deeds of love, and You gave him the crown of martyrdom. Give us the same charity of heart that we may fulfill Your love by defending and supporting the poor, that by loving them we may love You with all our hearts; through Jesus Christ, our Lord, who lives and reigns with You and the Holy Spirit, one God, now and forever. (1075)

St. Mary, Mother of Our Lord (August 15)

The Lection	*The Hymn*
ABC, 1Yr. Isaiah 61:7–11	670
Psalm 45:10–17 (v. 6)	

Galatians 4:4–7
Luke 1:(39–45) 46–55

Prayer of the Day

Almighty God, You chose the virgin Mary to be the mother of Your only Son. Grant that we, who are redeemed by His blood, may share with her in the glory of Your eternal kingdom; through Jesus Christ, Your Son, our Lord, who lives and reigns with You and the Holy Spirit, one God, now and forever. (F24)

Isaac (August 16)

Prayer of the Day

Almighty God, heavenly Father, through the patriarch Isaac You preserved the seed of the Messiah and brought forth the new creation. Continue to preserve the Church as the Israel of God as she manifests the glory of Your holy name by continuing to worship Your Son, the child of Mary; through Jesus Christ, our Lord. (1076)

Johann Gerhard, Theologian (August 17)

Prayer of the Day

Most High God, we owe You great thanks that in the sacred mystery of the Supper You feed us with the body and blood of Your Son. May we approach this heavenly meal with true faith, firmly convinced that the body we eat is the one given into death for us and that the blood we drink is the blood shed for our sins; through Jesus Christ, our Lord. (1077)

Bernard of Clairvaux, Hymnwriter and Theologian (August 19)

Prayer of the Day

O God, enkindled with the fire of Your love, Your servant Bernard of Clairvaux became a burning and shining light in Your Church. By Your mercy, grant that we also may be aflame with the spirit of love and discipline and may ever walk in Your presence as children of light; through Jesus Christ, our Lord, who lives and reigns with You and the Holy Spirit, one God, now and forever. (1079)

Samuel (August 20)

Almighty God, in Your mercy You gave Samuel courage to call Israel to repentance and to renew their dedication to the Lord. Call us to repentance as Nathan called David to repentance, so by the blood of Jesus, the Son of David, we may receive the forgiveness of all our sins; through Jesus Christ, our Lord. (1080)

St. Bartholomew, Apostle (August 24)

The Lection		*The Hymn*
ABC, 1Yr.	Proverbs 3:1–8	583
	Psalm 121 (v. 8)	
	2 Corinthians 4:7–10	
	Luke 22:24–30	
	or John 1:43–51	

Prayer of the Day

Almighty God, Your Son, Jesus Christ, chose Bartholomew to be an apostle to preach the blessed Gospel. Grant that Your Church may love what he believed and preach what he taught; through Jesus Christ, our Lord, who lives and reigns with You and the Holy Spirit, one God, now and forever. (F25)

Monica, Mother of Augustine (August 27)

Prayer of the Day

O Lord, You strengthened Your patient servant Monica through spiritual discipline to persevere in offering her love, her prayers, and her tears for the conversion of her husband and of Augustine, their son. Deepen our devotion to bring others, even our own family, to acknowledge Jesus Christ as Savior and Lord, who with You and the Holy Spirit lives and reigns, one God, now and forever. (1081)

Augustine of Hippo, Pastor and Theologian (August 28)

Prayer of the Day

O Lord God, the light of the minds that know You, the life of the souls that love You, and the strength of the hearts that serve You, give us strength to follow the example of Your servant Augustine of Hippo, so that knowing You we may truly love You and loving You we may fully serve You—for to serve You is perfect freedom; through Jesus Christ our Lord, who lives and reigns with you and the Holy Spirit, one God, now and forever. (1082)

The Martyrdom of St. John the Baptist (August 29)

The Lection	*The Hymn*
ABC, 1Yr. Revelation 6:9–11	750
Psalm 71:1–8 (v. 23)	
Romans 6:1–5	
Mark 6:14–29	

Prayer of the Day

Almighty God, You gave Your servant John the Baptist to be the forerunner of Your Son, Jesus Christ, in both his preaching of repentance and his innocent death. Grant that we, who have died and risen with Christ in Holy Baptism, may daily repent of our sins, patiently suffer for the sake of the truth, and fearlessly bear witness to His victory over death; through the same Jesus Christ, our Lord, who lives and reigns with You and the Holy Spirit, one God, now and forever. (F26)

September

Joshua (September 1)

Prayer of the Day

Lord Jesus Christ, Your servant Joshua led the children of Israel through the waters of the Jordan River into a land flowing with milk and honey. As our Joshua, lead us, we pray, through the waters of our Baptism into the promised land of our eternal home, where You live and reign with the Father and the Holy Spirit, one God, now and forever. (1083)

Hannah (September 2)

Prayer of the Day

God the Father Almighty, maker of all things, You looked on the affliction of Your barren servant Hannah and did not forget her but answered her prayers with the gift of a son. So hear our supplications and petitions and fill our emptiness; granting us trust in Your provision, so that we, like Hannah, might render unto You all thankfulness and praise, and delight in the miraculous birth of Your Son, Jesus Christ, who lives and reigns with You and the Holy Spirit, one God, now and forever. (1084)

Gregory the Great, Pastor (September 3)

Prayer of the Day

Almighty and merciful God, You raised up Gregory of Rome to be a pastor to those who shepherd God's flock and inspired him to send missionaries to preach the Gospel to the English people. Preserve in Your Church the catholic and apostolic faith that Your people may continue to be fruitful in every good work and receive the crown of glory that never fades away; through Jesus Christ, our Lord, who lives and reigns with You and the Holy Spirit, one God, now and forever. (1085)

Moses (September 4)

Prayer of the Day

Lord God, heavenly Father, through the prophet Moses, You began the prophetic pattern of teaching Your people the true faith and demonstrating through miracles Your presence in creation to heal it of its brokenness. Grant that Your Church may see in Your Son, our Lord Jesus Christ, the final end-times prophet whose teaching and miracles continue in Your Church through the healing medicine of the Gospel and the Sacraments; through Jesus Christ, our Lord. (1086)

Zachariah and Elizabeth (September 5)

Prayer of the Day

O God, who alone knits all infants in the womb, You chose improbable servants—old and childless—to conceive and parent the forerunner of Christ and, in so doing, demonstrated again Your strength in weakness. Grant us, who are as unlikely and unworthy as Zechariah and Elizabeth, the opportunity to love and serve You according to Your good and gracious will; through Jesus Christ, our Lord, who lives and reigns with You and the Holy Spirit, now and forever. (1087)

Holy Cross Day (September 14)

The Lection   *The Hymn*

ABC, 1Yr.   Numbers 21:4–9   454 or 455
      Psalm 40:1–11 (v. 13)
      1 Corinthians 1:18–25
      John 12:20–33

Prayer of the Day

Merciful God, Your Son, Jesus Christ, was lifted high upon the cross that He might bear the sins of the world and draw all people to Himself. Grant that we who glory in His death for our redemption may faithfully heed His call to bear the cross and follow Him, who lives and reigns with You and the Holy Spirit, one God, now and forever. (F27)

Cyprian of Carthage, Pastor and Martyr (September 16)

Prayer of the Day

Almighty God, You gave Your servant Cyprian boldness to confess the name of our Savior, Jesus Christ, before the rulers of this world and courage to die for the faith he proclaimed. Give us strength always to be ready to give a reason for the hope that is in us and to suffer gladly for the sake of our Lord Jesus Christ, who lives and reigns with You and the Holy Spirit, one God, now and forever. (1091)

St. Matthew, Apostle and Evangelist (September 21)

The Lection   *The Hymn*

ABC, 1Yr.   Ezekiel 2:8—3:11   730
      Psalm 119:33–40 (v 35)
      Ephesians 4:7–16
      Matthew 9:9–13

Prayer of the Day

O Son of God, our blessed Savior Jesus Christ, You called Matthew the tax collector to be an apostle and evangelist. Through his faithful and inspired witness, grant that we also may follow You, leaving behind all covetous desires and love of riches; for You live and reign with the Father and the Holy Spirit, one God, now and forever. (F28)

Jonah (September 22)

Prayer of the Day

Lord God, heavenly Father, through the prophet Jonah, You continued the prophetic pattern of teaching Your people the true faith and demonstrating through miracles Your presence in creation to heal it of its brokenness. Grant that Your Church may see in Your Son, our Lord Jesus Christ, the final end-times prophet whose teaching and miracles continue in Your Church through the healing medicine of the Gospel and the Sacraments; through Jesus Christ, our Lord. (1092)

St. Michael and All Angels (September 29)

The Lection		*The Hymn*
ABC, 1Yr.	Daniel 10:10–14; 12:1–3	522
	Psalm 91 (v. 11)	
	Revelation 12:7–12	
	Matthew 18:1–11	
	or Luke 10:17–20	

Prayer of the Day

Everlasting God, You have ordained and constituted the service of angels and men in a wonderful order. Mercifully grant that, as Your holy angels always serve and worship You in heaven, so by Your appointment they may also help and defend us here on earth; through Your Son, Jesus Christ, our Lord, who lives and reigns with You and the Holy Spirit, one God, now and forever. (F29)

Jerome, Translator of Holy Scripture (September 30)

Prayer of the Day

O Lord, God of truth, Your Word is a lamp to our feet and a light on our path. You gave Your servant Jerome delight in his study of Holy Scripture. May those who continue to read, mark, and inwardly digest Your Word find in it the food of salvation and the fountain of life; through Jesus Christ, our Lord, who lives and reigns with You and the Holy Spirit, one God, now and forever. (1093)

October

Henry Melchior Muhlenberg, Pastor (October 7)

Prayer of the Day

Lord Jesus Christ, the Good Shepherd of Your people, we give You thanks for Your servant Henry Melchior Muhlenberg, who was faithful in the care and nurture of the flock entrusted to his care. So they may follow his example and the teaching of his holy life, give strength to pastors today who shepherd Your flock so that, by Your grace, Your people may grow into the fullness of life intended for them in paradise; for You live and reign with the Father and the Holy Spirit, one God, now and forever. (1096)

Abraham (October 9)

Prayer of the Day

Lord God, heavenly Father, You promised Abraham that he would be the father of many nations, You led him to the land of Canaan, and You sealed Your covenant with him by the shedding of blood. May we see in Jesus, the Seed of Abraham, the promise of the new covenant of Your Holy Church, sealed with Jesus' blood on the cross and given to us now in the cup of the new testament; through the same Jesus Christ, our Lord, who lives and reigns with You and the Holy Spirit, one God, now and forever. (1097)

Philip the Deacon (October 11)

Prayer of the Day

Almighty and everlasting God, we give thanks to You for Your servant Philip the Deacon. You called him to preach the Gospel to the peoples of Samaria and Ethiopia. Raise up in this and every land messengers of Your kingdom, that Your Church may proclaim the immeasurable riches of our Savior, Jesus Christ, who lives and reigns with You and the Holy Spirit, now and forever. (1098)

Ignatius of Antioch, Pastor and Martyr (October 17)

Prayer of the Day

Almighty God, we praise Your name for Ignatius of Antioch, pastor and martyr. He offered himself as grain to be ground by the teeth of wild beasts so that he might present to You the pure bread of sacrifice. Accept the willing tribute of all that we are and all that we have, and give us a portion in the pure and unspotted offering of Your Son, Jesus Christ, who lives and reigns with You and the Holy Spirit, one God, now and forever. (1100)

St. Luke, Evangelist (October 18)

The Lection	*The Hymn*
ABC, 1Yr.　Isaiah 35:5–8	810

Psalm 147:1–11 (v. 12)
2 Timothy 4:5–18
Luke 10:1–9

Prayer of the Day

Almighty God, our Father, Your blessed Son called Luke the physician to be an evangelist and physician of the soul. Grant that the healing medicine of the Gospel and the Sacraments may put to flight the diseases of our souls that with willing hearts we may ever love and serve You; through Jesus Christ, Your Son, our Lord, who lives and reigns with You and the Holy Spirit, one God, now and forever. (F30)

St. James of Jerusalem, Brother of Jesus and Martyr (October 23)

The Lection	*The Hymn*
ABC, 1Yr.　Acts 15:12–22a	797

Psalm 133 (v. 1)
James 1:1–12
Matthew 13:54–58

Prayer of the Day

Heavenly Father, shepherd of Your people, You raised up James the Just, brother of our Lord, to lead and guide Your Church. Grant that we may follow his example of prayer and reconciliation and be strengthened by the witness of his death; through Jesus Christ, Your Son, our Lord, who lives and reigns with You and the Holy Spirit, one God, now and forever. (F31)

Dorcas (Tabitha), Lydia, and Phoebe, Faithful Women (October 25)

Prayer of the Day

Almighty God, You stirred to compassion the hearts of Your dear servants Dorcas, Lydia, and Phoebe to uphold and sustain Your Church by their devoted and charitable deeds. Give us the same will to love You, open our eyes to see You in the least ones, and strengthen our hands to serve You in others, for the sake of Your Son, Jesus Christ, our Lord, who lives and reigns with You and the Holy Spirit, one God, now and forever. (1101)

Philipp Nicolai, Johann Heermann, and Paul Gerhardt, Hymnwriters (October 26)

Prayer of the Day

Almighty God, the apostle Paul taught us to praise You in psalms and hymns and spiritual songs. We thank You this day for those who have given to Your Church great hymns, especially Your servants Philipp Nicolai, Johann Heermann, and Paul Gerhardt. May Your Church never lack hymnwriters who through their words and music give You praise. Fill us with the desire to praise and thank You for Your great goodness; through Jesus Christ, our Lord, who lives and reigns with You and the Holy Spirit, one God, now and forever. (1102)

St. Simon and St. Jude, Apostles (October 28)

The Lection	*The Hymn*
ABC, 1Yr. Jeremiah 26:1–16	856
Psalm 43 (v. 5b)	
1 Peter 1:3–9	
John 15:(12–16) 17–21	

Prayer of the Day

Almighty God, You chose Your servants Simon and Jude to be numbered among the glorious company of the apostles. As they were faithful and zealous in their mission, so may we with ardent devotion make known the love and mercy of our Lord and Savior Jesus Christ, who lives and reigns with You and the Holy Spirit, one God, now and forever. (F32)

Reformation Day (October 31)

The Lection   *The Hymn*

ABC, 1Yr.   Revelation 14:6–7   656/657 or 555
     Psalm 46 (v. 7)
     Romans 3:19–28
     John 8:31–36
     or Matthew 11:12–19

Prayer of the Day

Almighty and gracious Lord, pour out Your Holy Spirit on Your
faithful people. Keep us steadfast in Your grace and truth, protect and
deliver us in times of temptation, defend us against all enemies, and
grant to Your Church Your saving peace; through Jesus Christ, Your
Son, our Lord, who lives and reigns with You and the Holy Spirit,
one God, now and forever. (F33)

November

All Saints' Day (November 1)

The Lection   *The Hymn*

ABC, 1Yr.   Revelation 7:(2–8) 9–17   677
     Psalm 149 (v. 4)
     1 John 3:1–3
     Matthew 5:1–12

Prayer of the Day

Almighty and everlasting God, You knit together Your faithful
people of all times and places into one holy communion, the mystical
body of Your Son, Jesus Christ. Grant us so to follow Your blessed
saints in all virtuous and godly living that, together with them, we
may come to the unspeakable joys You have prepared for those who
love You; through Jesus Christ, our Lord, who lives and reigns with
You and the Holy Spirit, one God, now and forever. (F34)

or

O almighty and everlasting God, through Your only-begotten
and beloved Son, Jesus Christ, You will sanctify all Your elect and
beloved: Give us grace to follow their faith, hope, and love, that we
together with all Your saints may obtain eternal life; through Your

Son, Jesus Christ, our Lord, who lives and reigns with You and the Holy Spirit, one true God, now and forever. (VD)

Johannes von Staupitz, Luther's Father Confessor (November 8)

Prayer of the Day

Almighty, everlasting God, for our many sins we justly deserve eternal condemnation. In Your mercy, You sent Your dear Son, our Lord Jesus Christ, who won for us forgiveness of sins and everlasting salvation. Grant us a true confession so that dead to sin we may hear the sweet words of Absolution from our confessor as Luther heard them from his pastor, Johannes von Staupitz, and be released from all our sin; through Jesus Christ, our Lord, who lives and reigns with You and the Holy Spirit, one God, now and forever. (1105)

Martin Chemnitz (birth), Pastor and Confessor (November 9)

Prayer of the Day

Lord God, heavenly Father, through the teaching of Martin Chemnitz, You prepare us for the coming of Your Son to lead home His Bride, the Church, that with all the company of the redeemed we may finally enter into His eternal wedding feast; through the same Jesus Christ, our Lord, who lives and reigns with You and the Holy Spirit, one God, now and forever. (1106)

Martin of Tours, Pastor (November 11)

Prayer of the Day

Lord God of hosts, Your servant Martin the soldier embodied the spirit of sacrifice. He became a bishop in Your Church to defend the catholic faith. Give us grace to follow in his steps so that when our Lord returns we may be clothed with the baptismal garment of righteousness and peace; through Jesus Christ, our Lord, who lives and reigns with You and the Holy Spirit, one God, now and forever. (1107)

Emperor Justinian, Christian Ruler and Confessor of Christ (November 14)

Prayer of the Day

Lord God, heavenly Father, through the governance of Christian leaders such as Emperor Justinian, Your name is freely confessed in our nation and throughout the world. Grant that we may continue to choose trustworthy leaders who serve You faithfully in our generation and make wise decisions that contribute to the general welfare of Your people; through Jesus Christ, our Lord. (1108)

Elizabeth of Hungary (November 19)

Prayer of the Day

Mighty King, whose inheritance is not of this world, inspire in us the humility and benevolent charity of Elizabeth of Hungary. She scorned her bejeweled crown with thoughts of the thorned one her Savior donned for her sake and ours, that we, too, might live a life of sacrifice, pleasing in Your sight and worthy of the name of Your Son, Christ Jesus, who with the Holy Spirit reigns with You forever in the everlasting kingdom. (1111)

Clement of Rome, Pastor (November 23)

Prayer of the Day

Almighty God, Your servant Clement of Rome called the Church in Corinth to repentance and faith to unite them in Christian love. Grant that Your Church may be anchored in Your truth by the presence of the Holy Spirit and kept blameless in Your service until the coming of our Lord Jesus Christ, who lives and reigns with You and the Holy Spirit, one God, now and forever. (1113)

Noah (November 29)

Prayer of the Day

Almighty and eternal God, according to Your strict judgment You condemned the unbelieving world through the flood, yet according to Your great mercy You preserved believing Noah and his family, eight souls in all. Grant that we may be kept safe and secure in the holy ark of the Christian Church, so that with all believers in Your promise, we would be declared worthy of eternal life; through Jesus Christ, our Lord. (1117)

St. Andrew, Apostle (November 30)

The Lection		*The Hymn*
ABC, 1Yr.	Ezekiel 3:16–21	586
	Psalm 139:1–12 (v. 17)	
	Romans 10:8b–18	
	John 1:35–42a	

Prayer of the Day

Almighty God, by Your grace the apostle Andrew obeyed the call of Your Son to be a disciple. Grant us also to follow the same Lord Jesus Christ in heart and life, who lives and reigns with You and the Holy Spirit, one God, now and forever. (F01)

December

John of Damascus, Theologian and Hymnwriter (December 4)

Prayer of the Day

O Lord, through Your servant John of Damascus, You proclaimed with power the mysteries of the true faith. Confirm our faith so that we may confess Jesus to be true God and true Man, singing the praises of the risen Lord, and so that by the power of the resurrection we may also attain the joys of eternal life; through Jesus Christ, our Lord, who lives and reigns with You and the Holy Spirit, one God, now and forever. (1119)

Nicholas of Myra, Pastor (December 6)

Prayer of the Day

Almighty God, You bestowed upon Your servant Nicholas of Myra the perpetual gift of charity. Grant Your Church the grace to deal in generosity and love with children and with all who are poor and distressed and to plead the cause of those who have no helper, especially those tossed by tempests of doubt or grief. We ask this for the sake of Him who gave His life for us, Your Son, our Savior, Jesus Christ, our Lord, who lives and reigns with You and the Holy Spirit, one God, now and forever. (1121)

Ambrose of Milan, Pastor and Hymnwriter (December 7)

Prayer of the Day

O God, You gave Your servant Ambrose grace to proclaim the Gospel with eloquence and power. As bishop of the great congregation of Milan, he fearlessly bore reproach for the honor of Your name. Mercifully grant to all bishops and pastors such excellence in preaching and fidelity in ministering Your Word that Your people shall be partakers of the divine nature; through Jesus Christ, our Lord, who lives and reigns with You and the Holy Spirit, one God, now and forever. (1122)

Lucia, Martyr (December 13)

Prayer of the Day

O Almighty God, by whose grace and power Your holy martyr Lucia triumphed over suffering and remained ever faithful unto death, grant us, who now remember her with thanksgiving, to be so true in our witness to You in this world that we may receive with her new eyes without tears and the crown of light and life; through Jesus Christ, our Lord, who lives and reigns with You and the Holy Spirit, one God, now and forever. (1126)

Daniel the Prophet and the Three Young Men (December 17)

Prayer of the Day Lord God, heavenly Father, You rescued Daniel from the lions' den and the three young men from the fiery furnace through the miraculous intervention of an angel. Save us now through the presence of Jesus, the Lion of Judah, who has conquered all our enemies through His blood and taken away all our sins as the Lamb of God, who now reigns from His heavenly throne with You and the Holy Spirit, one God, now and forever. (1130)

Adam and Eve (December 19)

Prayer of the Day

Lord God, heavenly Father, You created Adam in your image and gave him Eve as his helpmate, and after their fall into sin, You promised them a Savior who would crush the devil's might. By Your mercy, number us among those who have come out of the great tribulation with the seal of the living God on our foreheads and whose robes have been made white in the blood of the Lamb; through Jesus Christ, our Lord. (1131)

Katharina von Bora Luther (December 20)

Prayer of the Day

O God, our refuge and our strength, You raised up Your servant Katharina to support her husband in the task to reform and renew your Church in the light of Your Word. Defend and purify the Church today and grant that, through faith, we may boldly support and encourage our pastors and teachers of the faith as they and proclaim and administer the riches of Your grace made known in Jesus Christ, our Lord, who lives and reigns with You and the Holy Spirit, one God, now and forever. (1132)

St. Thomas, Apostle (December 21)

The Lection		*The Hymn*
ABC, 1Yr.	Judges 6:36–40	720
	Psalm 136:1–4 (v. 26)	
	Ephesians 4:7, 11–16	
	John 20:24–29	

Prayer of the Day

Almighty and ever-living God, You strengthened Your apostle Thomas with firm and certain faith in the resurrection of Your Son. Grant us such faith in Jesus Christ, our Lord and our God, that we may never be found wanting in Your sight; through the same Jesus Christ, who lives and reigns with You and the Holy Spirit, one God, now and forever. (F02)

St. Stephen, Martyr (December 26)

The Lection		*The Hymn*
ABC, 1Yr.	2 Chronicles 24:17–22	661
	Psalm 119:137–44 (v. 142)	
	Acts 6:8—7:2a, 51–60	
	Matthew 23:34–39	

Prayer of the Day

Heavenly Father, in the midst of our sufferings for the sake of Christ grant us grace to follow the example of the first martyr, Stephen, that we also may look to the One who suffered and was crucified on our behalf and pray for those who do us wrong; through Jesus Christ, our Lord, who lives and reigns with You and the Holy Spirit, one God, now and forever. (F03)

St. John, Apostle and Evangelist (December 27)

The Lection   *The Hymn*

ABC, 1Yr.   Revelation 1:1–6   523
  Psalm 11 (v. 4a)
  1 John 1:1—2:2
  John 21:20–25

Prayer of the Day

Merciful Lord, cast the bright beams of Your light upon Your Church that we, being instructed in the doctrine of Your blessed apostle and evangelist John, may come to the light of everlasting life; for You live and reign with the Father and the Holy Spirit, one God, now and forever. (F04)

The Holy Innocents, Martyrs (December 28)

The Lection   *The Hymn*

ABC, 1Yr.   Jeremiah 31:15–17   969 or 764
  Psalm 54 (v. 4)
  Revelation 14:1–5
  Matthew 2:13–18

Prayer of the Day

Almighty God, the martyred innocents of Bethlehem showed forth Your praise not by speaking but by dying. Put to death in us all that is in conflict with Your will that our lives may bear witness to the faith we profess with our lips; through Jesus Christ, our Lord, who lives and reigns with You and the Holy Spirit, one God, now and forever. (F05)

David (December 29)

Prayer of the Day

God of majesty, whom saints and angels delight to worship in heaven, we give You thanks for David who, through the Psalter, gave Your people hymns to sing with joy in our worship on earth so that we may glimpse Your beauty. Bring us to the fulfillment of that hope of perfection that will be ours as we stand before Your unveiled glory;

through Jesus Christ, our Lord, who lives and reigns with You and the Holy Spirit, one God, now and forever. (1133)

New Year's Eve (December 31)

Prayer of the Day

Eternal God, we commit to Your mercy and forgiveness the year now ending and commend to Your blessing and love the times yet to come. In the new year, abide among us with Your Holy Spirit that we may always trust in the saving name of our Lord Jesus Christ, who lives and reigns with You and the Holy Spirit, one God, now and forever. (F06)

or

Almighty and everlasting God, from whom comes down every good and perfect gift, we give You thanks for all Your benefits, temporal and spiritual, bestowed upon us in the year past, and we beseech You of Your goodness, grant us a favorable and joyful year, defend us from all dangers and adversities, and send upon us the fullness of Your blessing; through Jesus Christ, Your Son, our Lord, who lives and reigns with You and the Holy Spirit, one true God, now and forever. (*TLH*, p. 57)

Occasions

Anniversary of a Congregation

The Lection   *The Hymn*
ABC, 1Yr.   1 Kings 8:22–30   912
    Psalm 84 (v. 4)
    Revelation 21:1–5
    Luke 19:1–10

Prayer of the Day

Almighty God, You have promised to be with Your Church forever. We praise You for Your presence in this place of worship and ask Your ongoing blessing upon those who gather here. Dwell continually among us with Your Holy Word and Sacraments, strengthen our fellowship in the bonds of love and peace, and increase our faithful witness to Your salvation; through Jesus Christ, Your Son, our Lord, who lives and reigns with You and the Holy Spirit, one God, now and forever. (F35)

Mission Observance

The Lection   *The Hymn*
ABC, 1Yr.   Isaiah 62:1–7   823/824
    Psalm 96 (v. 2)
    Romans 10:11–17
    Luke 24:44–53

Prayer of the Day

Almighty God, in Your kindness You cause the light of the Gospel to shine among us. By the working of Your Holy Spirit, help us to share the good news of Your salvation that all who hear it may rejoice in the gift of Your unending love; through Jesus Christ, Your Son, who lives and reigns with You and the Holy Spirit, one God, now and forever. (F36)

or

O Lord God almighty, mercifully grant that we, who know You by faith, may with our whole heart believe in Jesus Christ, our only Savior, serve Him, and steadfastly confess and glorify Him, making known His saving Word among all nations; through the same, Your

Son, our Lord, who lives and reigns with You and the Holy Spirit, one true God, now and forever. (*TLH*, p. 94)

or

Almighty God, since You have called Your Church to witness that in Christ You reconciled us to Yourself, grant that by Your Holy Spirit we may proclaim the good news of Your salvation, that all who hear it may receive the gift of salvation; through Jesus Christ, Your Son, our Lord, who lives and reigns with You and the Holy Spirit, one true God, now and forever.

Christian Education

The Lection		*The Hymn*
ABC, 1Yr.	Deuteronomy 6:4–15	861 or 864
	Psalm 119:129–36 (v. 105)	
	Acts 2:37–41	
	Luke 18:15–17	

Prayer of the Day

Lord Jesus Christ, You have entrusted to Your people the task of teaching all nations. Enlighten with the wisdom of Your Holy Spirit those who teach and those who learn that the joyous truth of the Gospel may be known in every generation; for You live and reign with the Father and the Holy Spirit, one God, now and forever. (F37)

Harvest Observance

The Lection		*The Hymn*
ABC, 1Yr.	Deuteronomy 26:1–11	894
	Psalm 65 (v. 1)	
	2 Corinthians 9:6–15	
	Luke 12:13–21	

Prayer of the Day

Almighty God, You crown the fields with Your blessing and permit us to gather in the fruits of the earth. As stewards of Your creation, may we receive Your gifts in humble thankfulness and share Your bounty with those in need; through Jesus Christ, our Lord, who lives and reigns with You and the Holy Spirit, one God, now and forever. (F38)

or